NEZHNIE

Weaver & Innovative Artist

BY LINDA REES

Image Line Publications, St. Louis

Published in the United States by
        Image Line Publications, St. Louis, Missouri

First Edition

ISBN 0-9755775-0-6
Library of Congress Control Number: 2004094552

Photography credits: Unless a photographer is attributed, photographs of artwork
are by Sheldon Helfman.

For information address

IMAGE LINE PUBLICATIONS
1908A Senate St.
St. Louis, Missouri 63118

Book design and composition by Julie McWilliams

Printed in the United States by
Independent Publishing Corporation
St. Louis, Missouri 63011

contents

Preface...v

Acknowledgements...xi

Citations..xiii

An Artist Who Listened to Herself 1

A Partnership of Artists 13

In the Studio 21

Early Works, the 1960s.......................................35

Commissions for Public Buildings.......................49

Mid-Career/Portraits..71

Striving for Balance and Perspective 97

The Holocaust Tapestries....................................111

A Melding of Media 129

Epilogue 141

Appendices...147

Index 163

Preface

The idea to write a book about Muriel Nezhnie Helfman surfaced in my conscious thought as an imperative. I had never met Muriel and had only seen one exhibit of her work ten years prior to this decision. However, it seemed very important that some formal documentation of her career be recorded. I had no idea what her philosophy or training was, no idea if I would agree with her tenets. I simply was curious to discover what had driven her to produce a cohesive body of work of the magnitude of the "Images of the Holocaust," my one connection to her career. What governed my conviction was my own need to better understand the motivations compelling artists to work in the tapestry medium.

My introduction to handwoven fabrics came as a child. A longtime friend of my parents lived in northern Mexico, and over the years he sent us several serapes. They were not the exquisitely patterned traditional Saltillo style, but the bold, contemporary, striped type used to decorate Mexican restaurants. The color combinations fascinated me. I spent hours wondering how people could place red next to pink or, worse yet, next to yellow. It was an era when girls were obsessed about colors "clashing." Still, I had to admit that I loved the overall results. When I was twelve, I saw a film at school about weaving. I told myself that some day I would learn to weave. During my last year of college, I discovered that weaving was taught in the art department and I signed up. As I walked into the studio with its maze of looms, I knew I had taken control of my life. That was in 1965; I have been weaving ever since.

Although I initially explored many techniques, the weft-faced tapestry style appealed to me most. By the mid 1970s, I concentrated exclusively on weaving tapestries. Clearly, not every weaver is suited to this slow form of production, nor do most artists view it as a particularly easy tool for creative expression. The structural characteristics of how an image takes shape limit design flexibility. However, both the process and visual effect can be quite satisfying. In general, faster and more experimental approaches to creating fiber art dominated the 1970s.

At the end of the decade, I saw two exhibits of Polish tapestries that had a profound effect on me. I had never seen such expressive work. Many Polish weavers had been influential in the more innovative trends of the past years, but these weavings were pictorial and, although not as dense as traditional tapestry, still within its parameters. I vowed to achieve that kind of fresh artistic treatment, but within a firm structural format. I had the impression that other tapestry artists had the same reaction. It was as if we all went back to our studios to learn whatever it would take to create fluid imagery while maintaining the desired surface quality defined as tapestry weave.

Despite the fact that tapestry weavers had to struggle to get any recognition from an art community that was intent on breaking away from tradition, the number of tapestry weavers grew dramatically in the early 1980s. Although I continued to be interested in developing my personal vision, many weavers considered producing tapestries for commissions to be the route to elevating their status and financial outlook. Indeed, tapestry had proven to be a reliable format for large commissions because of the durability of its structure.

Creating speculative work for exhibition, which could occupy a loom for many months, seemed a far less viable option. As a result, few tapestry weavers put much emphasis on entering competitions or exhibiting their work. Consequently, few artists had the opportunity to see the works of their colleagues, either in magazine reviews or at exhibitions. This probably explains why there was only a marginal sense of community among tapestry weavers at that time.

By 1986, a feeling of isolation from the rest of the field inspired me to write about tapestry. There were a few very good instructional books on the subject, but almost no dialogue about conceptual issues. I envisioned writing a thoughtful little book, like the one Theo Morman published about her inlay technique, *Weaving as an Art Form: A Personal Statement*. I wanted to talk about the consequences of working in a profoundly slow medium, and about what the benefits, and limitations, might be of having to create the structure at the same time as the image. Unfortunately, while I had a lot to say, I could not find the framework in which to present my observations. Also, my life was in transition and the momentum faded away.

By the end of the decade, the climate had changed. That same sense of isolation that I was feeling was surely reverberating around the country because tapestry weavers did begin to coalesce. Diminishing opportunities for commission work coincided with an increasing occurrence of exhibits focusing exclusively on tapestry. The American Tapestry Alliance (ATA) emerged and was followed in the early 1990s by another organization, the International Tapestry Network (ITNET). Both groups published periodicals and organized conferences, including exhibitions that further elevated the visibility of tapestry. Smaller regional tapestry groups formed, which also sponsored exhibitions. Participation in exhibitions increased the prestige of the artists, at least within the field, thus giving more incentive to produce art pieces.

It is interesting to note that Nezhnie was a decade ahead of the majority of weavers producing tapestries in the 1980s. She did her major commission work during the 1970s and began her daring venture into personal expression as the 1980s approached. It was exposure through the initial exhibits sponsored by ATA that her artwork gained recognition, along with that of many other North American artists newer to the field.

During the 1990s, the tapestry community was visible and thriving. As the 20th century closed, a chance event inspired me again to write a book. A friend wanted my opinion about a magazine article. The author's assessment of major influences on contemporary American tapestry artists did not align with mine. That, in itself, is not particularly unique, but I was immediately aware that neither position had much documentation to back it up. I began a dialogue with weavers and found that a myriad of events were responsible for shaping our directions. For one thing, I discovered that very few of the tapestry artists I knew had even seen the work of the Polish weavers whose work had influenced me definitively. That caused me to question my own assumptions. My frustration about the void in objective philosophical or analytical information being written about the subject resurfaced.

Over the years, the major weaving journals tried to keep abreast of work being created in the medium by publishing special issues featuring tapestry. Unfortunately, while quite successful at highlighting the skill and styles of contemporary artists, commentary was relatively superficial. Otherwise, only a few brief but excellent essays in exhibition catalogs and the 1992 doctoral thesis by Courtney Ann Shaw, *The Rise of the Artist/Weaver: Tapestry Weaving in the United States from 1930-1990*, document factors influencing contemporary tapestry weaving. During the 1990s, the two tapestry journals contained analytical reviews and commentary, but primarily it was a time for communicating through the imagery being produced and for coming together as a community. By its end, I still had questions and a need to better understand the dynamics of the medium.

It is important to understand that weaving in America has been predominantly a grass roots movement. Only during the greatest popularity of fiber art that occurred during the twenty-year span from 1965 to 1985 did the number of universities offering weaving expand noticeably. Pragmatically, since that era, art departments have consistently been unwilling to commit major studio space to bulky looms that can only be used for one student's work at a time. Those institutions that have invested in equipment have gone in the direction of computer-enhanced techniques. Whatever the focus of development, the work cannot be dismantled or put away at the end of a class session in order for someone else to use the same space. By comparison, since many students can use easels or potter's wheels throughout each day, teaching painting, drawing, and pottery makes more sense in economically driven art programs. The consequence of this lack of academic involvement in weaving in general, and specifically in tapestry, is that little research or commentary has been compiled about the artists and influences directing its current development. There is no faction within academic art exploring the dynamics of the contemporary tapestry medium.

When I attempted to write a response to the article brought to my attention, I discovered that there were very few accounts written in depth about influential American tapestry artists who began weaving before 1970. Also relevant, the major figures within the tapestry movement, even here in America, have been of European origin and/or training.

One fact about the years between 1985 and 1995 was obvious from my own observation. The dominant style of weaving to gain visibility in North America relied almost exclusively on traditional French tapestry techniques. Another concentration of weavers, especially those living in the southwestern area of the United States, were influenced by Navaho and Spanish American traditions. However, these weavers were not being included in tapestry exhibits, even though their work was of high quality. The dominance of a singular style piqued my curiosity. That, along with my increasing awareness of the minimal records accessible about the earlier American weavers, rekindled my desire to write.

The specific events precipitating the decision to research Muriel Nezhnie's role in our history came in 1999. I had recently moved to St. Louis, where she lived throughout her career. Having become friends with her last apprentice, I knew that Nezhnie was incapacitated with Alzheimer's disease. An exhibit of her work was to be mounted at the University City (Missouri) Public Library, where her large *Imprints* tapestries hang permanently. It would provide the opportunity for me to see a larger variety of her work and start my investigation there. I wanted to delve into her motivations and study her work in depth. It was time to get her story documented while information was hopefully still available.

Recalling her tapestries from the "Images of the Holocaust" exhibition at the Sazama Brauer Gallery in 1988 was enough to convince me that Nezhnie was worth studying. The visceral experience of circling the gallery in Chicago with almost life-sized figures looking out at me from their entrapment on the walls became an indelible memory. The content, repetition of images, and uniformity of the muted tone throughout the gallery distinguished her work.

At that time, I had rarely seen one-person exhibits of tapestries, especially of the scope I saw there. She had devoted a decade to the project. I was impressed by the commitment and the imagery that resulted.

Her husband, Sheldon Helfman, gave a half-hour slide lecture about her work during the library exhibit. Within moments after he began talking, I knew my instinct was right. His comments revealed an interesting woman who had insights to offer me. The deciding statement was that she had resolved, even as early as her four-month stint observing weavers in Germany in 1956, that she would start designs with the yarn selection, not the preliminary painting. It showed Nezhnie's grasp of the very different parameters that distinguish tapestry from the medium of painting.

When introduced to Helfman after the talk, I briefly mentioned that I was interested in writing about Muriel. However, it took me several months before I was ready to approach him for an interview. I was apprehensive that my inquiries might be too much of an invasion. Friends convinced me that it also might be a beneficial step in the family's grieving process, even a welcomed opportunity to reveal Nezhnie's talents. Finally I proceeded. Helfman proved to be very generous with his time, sharing her files and slides and patiently answering questions. Her children, especially Ilisha, were responsive as well.

Of course, observations from my own thirty-five years of experience would flash through my mind as I studied her path, with its obstacles, distractions, and rewards. I found I needed to address the struggles encountered by women striving to be taken seriously as artists, especially in the years between 1940 and 1970. Historical evidence was necessary so that her choices could be appreciated by a younger generation of women who matured after the women's movement of the 1970s. My own daughter avidly disputed my assumptions and sent me researching for valid explanations of facts I knew subjectively. I am grateful to her for that.

I never was ambitious or confident enough to expect that I could make a living as a weaver. However, I certainly witnessed the frustrations of colleagues who were trying to establish a financially successful career in weaving while enjoying the rewards and responsibilities of raising a family. I vividly remember a comment I flippantly made to a discouraged friend back in the early 1980s. I said it only takes one or two "Super Moms" to cause such discontent. Muriel was just such a mom. It was inevitable that I would observe her accomplishments from this perspective, and with a great deal of awe. It is quite easy for creative thrusts to be derailed by seemingly more immediate demands of the day. Muriel expended an amazing amount of energy sustaining all the parts of her life that she saw as important.

A second undercurrent kept emerging in my observations. She stubbornly resisted prevailing trends, whether in weaving or in the greater art arena, while also being a relatively conventional woman of her times. Nezhnie was typical of the majority of American tapestry weavers working in the second half of the 20th century in that she was essentially self-taught. Where she differed dramatically from many of her colleagues was that she had an extensive art background and exceptional confidence in her skills and talent. If I compare her approach to my own personal experience, there are some similarities and great differences. I have been as stubborn as she about going my own way, not seeking more than a rudimentary course in beginning weaving. Like her, I knew that understanding the basic principles could sustain me for a lifetime, as it did her. All this has influenced the commentary I have chosen to write.

One unexpected outcome of studying her life was that an issue from my own childhood surfaced. I felt that I understood how Muriel could have been so deeply affected by the suffering of the Jews at such an early age. As a young girl I grappled with the inhumane deeds from another perspective. I came from predominantly German lineage. My maiden name, Schult, was so Germanic I could not escape its heritage. I had to confront the reality that relatives of mine might have condoned or been perpetrators of atrocities. I spent many hours trying to imagine what bias or circumstance could possibly allow such an escalation of cruelty to occur in a society of people not so different from me. I know that the dilemma stayed with me and has affected my outlook about the capacity of mankind to do horrific, as well as heroic, deeds.

I could not have picked a better subject for beginning my quest about the influences affecting contemporary tapestry weavers. Nezhnie was very articulate and thought in great depth about the benefits and disadvantages of the medium. She used every platform available to communicate her ideas. Observing her sophisticated visual acumen and versatility has pushed my own boundaries refreshingly. I am deeply grateful that circumstances have placed me in this place at the right time to comment on the art and the woman, Muriel Nezhnie Helfman.

Acknowledgments

I am deeply grateful to Sheldon Helfman for his patience and generosity. He gave me an hour or two of his time on an almost monthly basis for two years, and plunged through files and boxes to make Nezhnie's records and photographs available for my use. I taxed his memory time and time again, but he was always willing to answer another question. Ilisha Helfman has also been extremely helpful, responsive, and thorough in providing information about family life and her mother's artwork. Thank you Shelly and Ilisha. Thanks also to other family members and friends: Jonathon Helfman, Dorothy Liftman, Alfred Gelfand and Maria Michaelides, to name a few.

I am also grateful to the many people who have contributed financially toward getting the book into print. Thank you, Lee and Walt Ingram for offering support and faith in the venture early in the project. Your contribution gave me the impetus to consider self-publishing the book when other alternatives failed. An equally big thanks goes to the Weavers' Guild of St. Louis, who stepped in with a generous contribution that also assured the book would become a reality. Further, I would like to thank The First Unitarian Church of St. Louis, Dr. and Mrs. Harold Joseph, Deann and Michael H. Rubin, and the many other contributors who have helped to ensure the project would succeed.

For technical assistance in production, I thank Julie Murkette for counsel on copious details during the process, to George Lestina of IPC Graphics for his cheerful cooperation, and especially, Julie McWilliams whose positive energy carried me through the final preparation when I had none.

A major thanks goes to the many collectors who graciously welcomed me into their homes to view the artwork in person. It was an essential element in accurately describing the individual tapestries. Indeed, the enthusiasm with which all the collectors discussed their pieces, and the pleasure they obviously derive from living with their objects of art, were an extra bonus to seeing the innovative work in its surroundings. They have provided valuable information.

I am indebted to Jan Garden Castro for the series of interviews with Muriel that she conducted during 1980 and the spring of 1981 in preparation for "The Holocaust Tapestries: A Talk with Muriel Nezhnie, Artist Weaver," *River Styx*, no. 9 (1981): 36-44. The series of conversations cover a wide variety of subjects and provides a major source of Nezhnie's own commentary about tapestry and her life. (See Citations)

Three apprentices have been major sources of content. Janet Jungkuntz provided many insights into Nezhnie's personality in an interview with me, conducted early in the fact-finding process. A report in the files, written by Jungkuntz in 1978 to acquire university credits for the apprenticeship, also added many details to the chapters on studio activities and family life. Christel Maassen provided me with a detailed written summary of her three-year experience as an apprentice. She has also enthusiastically contributed verbal commentary throughout my research. Deann Rubin also contributed both verbally and in an account written at the time of her apprenticeship in the late 1970s. Thanks, Christel, Deann, and Jan.

Also thanks to my friend, Janita Loder, who helped in many ways, reading chapters, photographing pieces, and being a sounding board often.

I have left my personal thanks to my family until the last. In writing this book I have come to value my father immensely for his gift of words. He threw them out to his children as other dads tossed softballs, challenging us to enjoy their uniqueness and use them sagaciously. I appreciate that my mother taught me about courage and to think for myself. It takes training. Understanding their special gifts to me allowed me to revitalize my memory of them. I am pleased to have siblings willing to share their perspectives with me for a lifetime. It was fortunate that my former husband gave me encouragement to develop artistically as we ventured through the years together. I believe that freedom to grow in my own development has been helpful in understanding another artist's progression. I am more than thankful to my daughter for being in my life. Among the many pleasures I have derived from her over the years is her wisdom and openness. I have been able to count on her to have good observations ever since she was a young child, from wry titles for artwork to her recent, frequently needed counsel for patience in writing this book. Thank you, Ellen.

Citations

For the most part, in citing published works, I have included the complete source in a footnote the first time the source is cited and then used the author and page number thereafter.

Because Richard Rubin is quoted from two sources, information from *THE SEEN* is referred to by title.

In reference to the Jan Garden Castro Interview, several quotes related to the Holocaust tapestries are from the printed article (referred to as Castro, *River Styx*). The majority of my information is taken from the transcript in Nezhnie's files (referred to as Castro). This forty-five-page typed transcript shows evidence of editing by Nezhnie and Castro. Another interview segment, (referred to as Second segment) is handwritten, and contains additional information. It is stored in the *River Styx* holdings in the Special Collections of the Washington University Libraries, St. Louis, Missouri.

Two other sources are not footnoted. They are the two limited circulation exhibition catalogues that provide historical documentation of tapestry weaving. The catalogue of the exhibit *Tapisserie de Lisse* was the source of information about the development of contemporary French tapestry weaving. The exhibit was a collection of contemporary French Tapestry organized by members of "le Clotet", presented by Rothmans of Pall Mall, Canada Limited, Montreal 1960, Winnipeg 1961. Material on exhibitions in the United States and the development of contemporary American tapestry weavers came from the catalogue essay by Courtney Ann Shaw for the exhibition "American Tapestry Weaving Since the 1930s and Its European Roots," University of Maryland, College Park, 1989.

I have quoted material from Nezhnie's answers to two questionnaires sent to her by authors of potential articles. One was from Nancy Crump for an article about Tapestry in *Interweave*, 4, no. 2. There was no specific information about Nezhnie in the subsequent article. The other survey was from Betsy Goldman for an article about families in the arts, although I am not aware of the destination for this information. Muriel's response is dated April 1987.

Information from Shelly Helfman was obtained through conversations in person or by phone. Material gathered from Ilisha Helfman was primarily from e-mail correspondence and an audiotape recorded in December, 2000. In addition, her patient reading of the manuscript in December 2003 verified many details. Material from Jon Helfman was acquired by phone and e-mail. Most accounts from other relatives or friends were by letter, e-mail or phone. Maria and Constantine Michaelides read portions of the text and offered commentary.

Information from contemporary tapestry weavers was from e-mail correspondence.

An Artist Who Listened to Herself

Muriel Nezhnie Helfman (February 28, 1934, to April 9, 2002) is best known for her series of six tapestries, "Images of the Holocaust," derived in part from actual photographs of victims of Nazi persecution. The commanding tapestries are a blend of expressive figures and calligraphic passages, unequivocally communicating their message. The richness of color and texture provided by the woven surfaces enhances their effect. Nezhnie's series first received national acclaim through an exhibit at the Sazama-Brauer Gallery in Chicago during the 1988 Handweavers Guild of America Convergence, an international conference of weavers. One of the tapestries, *Daughters of Earth*, had previously been on display at the American Tapestry Alliance (ATA) exhibition "Panorama of Tapestry" in Toronto, Canada, during the 1986 Convergence. Nezhnie had the honor of being the artist invited to represent the United States for that exhibit.

Although the Holocaust tapestries gained her international attention, Nezhnie had been producing innovative artwork for twenty years before starting the series. She actively pursued commissions but always needed to balance contractual work with projects for personal expression. Whether for commissions or her own interest, the majority of her tapestries were created for private collectors and religious institutions and were rarely exhibited in galleries. Thus, very few of her earlier pieces have received major publicity. Part of the intent of this book is to reveal the fascinating tapestries she wove.

Nezhnie fashioned her life through art. Those who came into her sphere stepped into a living work of art crafted by her sensibilities. In the recollections of a childhood friend, the impressions of an apprentice striding up the front path to meet Nezhnie for the first time, or of a mid-career friend who would casually drop by her studio, she was the consummate artist.

As a teenager, Muriel wanted to be a portrait painter. However, circumstances caused her to change directions as a young adult. Once she decided to work in fiber instead of paint, she defined a new challenge: to express her ideas in an authentically weaverly way. She sought new ways for interpreting form and for translating color that worked in yarn. In essence, her studio became a laboratory in which she explored a large variety of styles and ideas. During the late 1960s she was primarily concerned with creating tapestries that were free-form, not contained within a rectangle. In her mid-career she concentrated on weaving identifiable portraits that revealed their woven structure in innovative ways. She dedicated her later years to the Holocaust series.

She designed, wove, or supervised the production and marketing of 145 artworks during her thirty-five-year span of productivity. At least ninety were tapestries. Considering that some of the tapestries took well over a year to weave, the tally is impressive. Her commissions are in synagogues and churches on the East Coast and in the Midwestern states.

In St. Louis, Missouri, where she resided since the beginning of her career, two monumental curved tapestries, called *Imprints*, hang in the stairwell of the University City Public Library. It is the commission most accessible to the general public. Installed in 1971, it has been a source of inspiration for many tapestry weavers, along with the library patrons.

In 1992 she was awarded an honorary Doctor of Fine Arts degree from the University of Missouri – St. Louis for her contribution to art. The honor coincided with the end of her career. Nezhnie did not leave the world of the weaver, or the other roles that mattered so much to her, by choice. She was stricken with Alzheimer's disease.

Born on February 28, 1934, in Jersey City, New Jersey, she was the only child from the marriage of Jean Shiezer Liftman and Isadore Nezhnie, both widowed with children from their first marriages. Her mother's son, Robert, was twelve years old and Sarah, the youngest of her father's three children, was eight years old when Muriel was born. The family lived above their grocery store where both parents worked full time. A gregarious woman by nature, life was far more solitary for Nezhnie as a young child. While the older children were at school, Muriel was left upstairs to amuse herself with her mother checking in on her periodically. She learned to rely on her imagination to help pass the time. Activities such as drawing or observing her surroundings through a colored cellophane candy wrapper kept her entertained.

Young Muriel, looking ready for adventure.

Jean Shiezer had not been lucky in marriage from the beginning. Her first husband had died when Robert was only two and a half years old. Then Isadore Nezhnie died of heart failure when Muriel was six years old. There were many disputes in the household beginning even before Muriel was born. Her father had not wanted to have another child, but her mother was determined – a fact Muriel's mother impressed on her daughter throughout the years. Isadore's oldest child, Tanya, got married while Muriel was still quite young. His middle child, Nathan, chose to live with his sister but continued to work for his father. Apparently when Isadore died, the children from his first marriage sought to gain possession of the store. Bitter conflicts arose between family members. Robert secretly sold the majority of stock, leaving only a row of items at the front of the shelves to thwart the efforts of the others.

The family had been living in New York State at the time of Isadore's death. Nathan went his own way, and Muriel was unable to reconnect with him ever again. She and her mother, along with Sarah and Robert, returned to Jersey City where her mother remarried. Jean and her new husband operated a candy store. The marriage was very brief because the man turned out to be cruel. Jean continued to run the candy store with the children's help. When Robert went into the army in 1942, their mother was unable to keep the store operating. She then worked at an assortment of short-term jobs.

Life was continually a struggle for the family. They lived in a "cold water flat," meaning that the only source of heat was the kitchen stove. As an adult, Muriel could never tolerate the smell of

With her mother.

kerosene. The apartment was above a delicatessen, and vermin were a constant problem. There was not much joy in either of the girls' lives, not only because of the struggle to exist in such conditions, but because Muriel's mother fit the stereotype of an unsympathetic stepmother. She treated her stepdaughter almost as a servant. The history of conflict in the family may have caused her animosity, but more important, as a child in Russia, her family had servants. She experienced a very different lifestyle after immigrating but still expected people to do things for her. The memory of how her mother mistreated her sister continued to bother Muriel throughout her adult life.

Once she started school, Muriel blossomed, despite the unhappy atmosphere at home. Her sister-in-law, Dorothy Liftman, describes her as "always a warm, friendly, talkative person — from childhood to the onset of her illness. She made people feel comfortable in her presence and therefore had lots of friends." She was an enthusiastic child who seemed to genuinely care about people, to be genuinely interested in what they had to say. She joined in family activities, was a good helper and a good eater, too. Liftman felt Muriel acquired her social skills from her mother, who could be quite charming, while her artistic talent came from her father's side of the family.

In an interview with writer Jan Garden Castro, Muriel stated that she started drawing at a very early age by watching her sister draw. In fact, Sarah would get in trouble for spending too much time drawing. By the age of eight or nine, Muriel created very realistic images of her mother doing laundry or even sleeping. She sketched everything in the apartment.[1]

Unlike Sarah, who would hide her pictures, knowing her stepmother disapproved, Muriel sought opportunities to use her artistic skills. One favorite memory from childhood was when she drew a life-size skier as a backdrop for the school play and supervised her classmates in decorating the curtain with snowflakes. The snowflakes only formed a border as high as the students could reach. She was proud of the design solution to create a border, thereby not needing to use ladders.

She was introduced to weaving in sixth grade. Her teacher organized a project to make blankets for the Russian War Relief using small square potholder looms. Because Nezhnie was "blessed with dexterous fingers and a natural sense of organizing materials," she was the only one who seemed to quickly understand how to weave. Although the teacher was determined to produce some blankets, she could not sacrifice her other pupils' education, so she told Muriel to just listen during class and keep on weaving. Nezhnie learned about ancient Egypt and the Reconstruction period after the Civil War by listening very carefully while industriously making colorful woven squares. Thus, at an early age she became aligned with women throughout the ages with busy hands.

She knew all the children in the neighborhood and they knew her because of the candy store, especially since it was located next to a Catholic school. She was quite fond of the nuns who lived next door and enjoyed their friendly attention towards her. On the other hand, the children from the parochial school were the most boisterous in the store, once released from the disciplined classes of those same nuns. There was only one other Jewish student at the public school she attended. The neighborhood was predominantly German in heritage and not very supportive of the Jewish plight. Muriel learned how to adapt and get along with the children but still was the object of enough anti-Semitism to remember her identity.

Her mother was not overtly religious and eventually married "out of the faith" to Rudolf Johannsen, Muriel's last stepfather, several years later. She made no effort to seek any religious instruction for Muriel, who, nevertheless, was

---

1 From the handwritten second segment of the transcript notes for the Castro interview held in the River Styx Archives at the Washington University Libraries Special Collections, St. Louis, Missouri. Conducted in 1980-81, the interview was for an article, "The Holocaust Tapestries: A Talk with Muriel Nezhnie, Artist Weaver," *River Styx*, St. Louis, Big River Association, No. 9, 1981.

curious to discover what it meant to be Jewish. As news of persecution of European Jews filtered into her world, she took it upon herself to attend classes about the Jewish faith. The instructors were quite impressed with the child who had sought them out on her own and were very accommodating and attentive to her. Religious instruction never became a major part of her development, but at least she began to get a fundamental understanding of Judaism. In a broader sense, it shows a pensive nature that would not allow her to ignore events that might have gone unheeded by a less serious child.

A second family tragedy occurred when she was ten. Sarah, who Muriel credits for actually raising her, worked in a shipyard during the war. While returning home one evening, she accidentally fell out of a moving commuter train that had no doors and was killed. She was only eighteen. Robert was on duty in the South Pacific, so Muriel was left to console and help her mother as well as move on with her own life alone. Sarah had been her primary source of love and stability.

Radiant on a pony.

Muriel chose to continue using the name Nezhnie professionally after her marriage, primarily to keep the connection with her father and sister alive. According to her daughter, Ilisha, little was known of their history. The name had been abbreviated from its Russian derivation, Nezhdotnie. Muriel liked the Russianness of her name. In later life she tried to find her other brother, Nathan, but was unsuccessful.

Her mother never demonstrated much self-reliance and had the tendency to drag decisions out, pondering out loud about what to do. To make life easier for the two of them, Muriel actively tried to rectify her mother's dilemmas. In response to a vacillating, ambivalent mother, she became more resourceful and decisive herself.

Undoubtedly, any outside activities were welcomed respites from the sorrows at home and the loneliness of being the only child after Sarah died. It is not hard to imagine the impact of praise from the impressed synagogue staff or from the teacher who had singled her out to weave for the war relief and the special attention of not having to do written assignments for much of the school year. No wonder she had confidence later to trust her intuitions, and that initiating action towards a goal would bring rewards.

Conferring about the school yearbook. Note the striped shirt and pin at her collar. She enjoyed wearing jewelry even to work in her studio.

Relaxing while being photographed in her distinctive prom dress.

High school friend Alfred Gelfand commented that: "she always knew who she was." She defined herself as an artist, of Russian heritage, and Jewish. Muriel liked assuming responsibilities, such as being president of the B'nai Brith Girls Club. She was also editor of the 1952 yearbook during her senior year at Henry Snyder High School in Jersey City. She assumed responsibility for most aspects, including composing the text, creating the layout, and determining the print. Another of her creative involvements in high school was the yearly decoration of neighborhood store windows at Halloween. It was a common practice for schools and local businesses to hold competitions for the best window decorations. Muriel won at least once with a scene of two costumed skeletons dancing to the music of a black cat with a bass fiddle. [See photo on page 138]

In looking at photographs of the perky and petite high school girl, it is apparent that Nezhnie was already independent in her tastes. She had a penchant for stripes, as seen in her prom dress and school blouse. Another time she is pictured in a formal gown of obviously saturated color when all the other girls are in pastels. Photographs throughout the years show her in striped or patterned outfits.

By high school she spent her Saturday mornings going into New York City to take art classes. The teacher who had discovered her weaving talents years before, got her a scholarship for these classes. They were held at the Jefferson School of Social Science, a unique school providing adult education as well as classes for children. The school was sponsored by the Communist Party and had thrived during the alliance of the United States and the Soviet Union during World War II. However, according to the *Encyclopedia of New York City* by Kenneth T. Jackson, the school was considered subversive by the time Muriel took classes there in the late 1940s. She recalled walking down the hallway to her class flanked by poster-size photographs of Socialist and Communist Party leaders. The rows of faces watching her pass by made a lasting impression on her.

Encouraged by her art teachers to pursue a career in art, she applied to The Cooper Union School of Art in New York. In addition to drawing requirements, it had an extensive series of entrance exams lasting several days. Muriel was one of ninety students selected that year. Once accepted into the college, tuition was free.

While she was in art school she met and fell in love with fellow student Sheldon (Shelly) Helfman, who came from a traditional orthodox Jewish background. As a youngster he attended Yeshiva school where he was trained as if he would become a rabbi. However, by high school his life was less influenced by religion. After he and Muriel married and had children, they began to sort out their own belief systems. Both partners were intellectual and inquisitive. Matters of theology interested them as a natural part of their life. Questions naturally occurred about which rituals to keep, what to pass on to their children, even how to define themselves as Jews. Nezhnie took spirituality seriously, whether she practiced a formal system of belief or not.

The happy couple on their wedding day in 1955.

All the defining events that launch a child into adulthood happened to Nezhnie in the 1950s, several decades before the Women's Movement. In 1952 she graduated from high school and moved to New York City to attend The Cooper Union. She married Helfman in 1954, and when she graduated with a degree in Graphic Design in 1955, joined him in Germany where he was stationed in the U.S. Army. After his tour of duty, they moved to New Haven, Connecticut where he received a Master of Fine Arts degree at Yale University. Their two children were born during the years of his graduate work, Ilisha in 1957 and Jonathan in 1959. Shortly after Jon was born, the family moved to St. Louis where Shelly began teaching drawing in the School of Architecture at Washington University. The chronology is relatively typical for a woman of that era, but it does not take into account Nezhnie's determination to be a productive artist.

Many female students who showed artistic talent in high school in the late 1940s and early 1950s were encouraged by their male teachers to pursue their artistic talents in college. In general, however, women with art degrees were not expected by their instructor to actually become established, career artists. The consensus that a woman would not develop into a serious artist was magnified to a much greater extent if she chose to become a mother. Yet it was Nezhnie's goal to do both.

Compounding her drive to succeed, Muriel had been raised in a family whose struggle to survive depended on every member contributing their share. Once she made the decision to be an artist, she placed extensive pressure on herself to justify her deviation from a more commercial career such as occupational therapy, an option she had considered earlier. Her brother, Robert Liftman, continued to question how the pair of artists were to survive financially. Phone calls over the years were spent reassuring him that they were, indeed, not destitute.

To have married a man who also intended to be an artist imposed yet another layer of complexity to her picture of a future as an artist. While the alliance of two artists could provide the intellectual and creative stimulation on which Nezhnie thrived, the part of her that was very determined to be a good wife demanded she find a way of fulfilling her dreams that would not compete with his. She found that her painting endeavors did not meet with favorable reviews as Shelly came home from his hours of drudgery as a soldier. He tended to be overly critical of her work, and she could understand his frustration. While he was in the Army he had no time for painting. So Nezhnie's goal while living in Germany was to find a stimulating means to express herself that would not, as she perceived it, put pressure on their relationship.

She developed into a woman who listened to her interior self. Once she assessed a situation, she was decisive and had the drive to accomplish what she set out to do, employing whatever resources she could gather for that purpose. Whatever path Nezhnie took needed to satisfy the various voices within her. She wanted to be recognized as an artist and, equally important, to enjoy a full life as mother and wife. In addition, she aimed to make money and be a good businesswoman in the process. The way she became a tapestry weaver is a good example of her ability to define a direction and find a path to take her there.

She wanted a medium she could explore on her own at home. Despite having a degree in design, Muriel was not convinced that she wanted to focus on graphic art as she searched for her artistic voice in Germany. While there might be opportunities to freelance, she suspected that work in the graphics field would be limited to major urban centers. Not knowing where her husband's career might take them, it did not seem a practical outlet to pursue. Then, too, it had not been her first choice of concentrations in art school. She wanted to focus on portraiture.

The avowed mission of The Cooper Union was to train its students to be flexible and resourceful. However, because it was an era of abstraction in art, the instructors were not receptive to her interest in portraiture. In fact, she related being told that she would have to leave if she pursued that course. (Castro, 15) Truly appreciating the excellent learning environment and the free tuition, she decided to shift to her other interest, graphic design. The decision also relieved some of the pressure from her family to choose a lucrative occupation. She was quite skilled in calligraphy and word imagery, excelling in bookmaking and typesetting as well. It was a perfect choice for her, given the lack of support for her fascination with faces. She put the training to good use throughout her career. Many of her tapestries incorporated text.

Still, once out of school, she wanted to develop in a direction more in keeping with her original goal. During her search for a stimulating outlet, she chanced upon tapestry weaving. On a brief visit to Paris while Shelly was stationed in Frankfurt, they encountered an outdoor exhibit of contemporary tapestries by Algerian weavers. Discovering that tapestry was not a lost art turned out to be a pivotal experience for Nezhnie. However, she was not particularly impressed by the tapestries she saw that day, as she later stated in the ATA newsletter of August 1987:

> Confronted with these obviously contemporary weavings, my attention became acutely focused and to my surprise, I had an intuitively negative response. Their design seemed overly tight and mannered; the color too dark and without luminosity. And with the brashness of youth I thought that if I could somehow learn to weave, I could perhaps bring a more lifelike quality to this medium.

Even though she had learned the basic principle of weaving as a girl, she had never previously considered it in the context of contemporary art.

Soon after they returned from the trip to France, she enrolled in a craft school, Offenbach Werkkunstschule, in the Frankfurt suburb of Offenbach am Main. Despite the fact that she did not understand any German, she was accepted into the school because she had received her art training at The Cooper Union. Like Black Mountain and the Chicago Art Institute, The Cooper Union was one of the schools that had benefited from the influx of German Bauhaus artists who brought their approach to art to the United States. The instructors in Germany were curious to see if Muriel's training showed evidence of influence from their own culture.

Besides Nezhnie not knowing German, her instructor could not speak English. Fortunately, Muriel was a quick learner and had the rudimentary understanding of weaving from childhood to rely on. Through example and gestures, she learned the basic procedures for tapestry and how to prepare the cartoon, or scaled drawing used as the guide while weaving.

The town of Offenbach, which had been the center of Germany's leather industry, had two other institutions of interest to Nezhnie. One was a leather museum featuring, among its other rarities, beautiful sandals from Roman times and a painfully unforgettable lampshade made of human skin from a Nazi concentration camp. The other stimulating place she visited frequently was The Klingsphor, world famous calligraphy museum. Her time was thus spent productively in the museums and learning to weave. She also had the opportunity to meet Hermann Zapf, considered one of the world's finest type designers of the time. She had been referred to him by one of her teachers at The Cooper Union.[2]

By the end of Shelly's tour of duty, equipped with four months of training and an old upright loom she had purchased, Muriel returned to the United States with a career in mind that would suit her needs. She knew that she had found the medium for which she was searching. As a weaver, she could best express herself, while not competing with her husband. Her story is an important chapter in the history of contemporary tapestry weaving in the United States.

It is interesting to speculate that Nezhnie's first introduction to contemporary tapestry could have been very different. She could have stumbled onto a gallery in Paris that featured weaving designed by highly respected artists and woven at the best ateliers of Gobelins or Aubusson. One did exist. The first gallery to specialize in contemporary French tapestries was established in Paris in 1947 by Denise Majorel, who then joined with Madeleine David of "La Demeure" rue Cambaceres in 1950. "La Demeure" provided the venue for many French artists who were interested in creating art for tapestry. Along with artist Jean Lurçat, Majorel helped set in motion a movement, shortly after World War II, that was responsible for about 500 international exhibits of contemporary French tapestries over a twenty-year period.

Nezhnie's exposure could also have occurred in the United States because there had been exhibits of tapestries in New York as well. In 1948, when she would have been fourteen, the Metropolitan Museum of Art offered "Loan Exhibitions of French Tapestries: Medieval, Renaissance, and Modern." Other exhibits of French work followed – at the French Cultural Center in 1950 and one featuring the work of Lurçat at the Associated American Artists Gallery in 1953. Later, in 1959, the Museum of Contemporary Crafts exhibited the works of many of the members of the Association des Cartooniers-Peintres, the group of artists designing for tapestry that Denise Majorel had brought together in France after World War II.

In 1953-54, tapestries by British artists from the Edinburgh Tapestry Workshop were at the Arthur U. Newton Gallery. There also was an exhibit held at the Contemporary Art Association in 1955 that featured work of other European countries as well. Nezhnie could even have seen work by the German weavers she was to meet the following year.

Though the opportunities were there, her path did not cross that of French artists or even other Americans interested in tapestry. There is evidence that several American painters were using European workshops to produce their

---

2 Richard Marc Rubin, "Interview with the Helfmans", THE SEEN Newspaper of the Art Coordinating Council for the Area, St. Louis (January, 1977): 1.

compositions. While the interest in having their vision translated into the medium was increasing in the 1950s, Jan Yoors appears to be one of the few artists to learn to weave and set up his own studio. Like Nezhnie, he wanted to weave after seeing an exhibit of contemporary tapestries, these by the French artists. His first tapestry exhibit was held at the Montclair [New Jersey] Art Museum in 1956. In later years he recruited his wives to do the weaving.

Just as in art school where she felt pressure to work abstractly, Nezhnie found herself at odds with the prevailing trends throughout most of her weaving career. Her work was well received in the beginning and was included in reviews of several exhibitions in the early 1960s. Then interest in weaving took a dramatic shift away from function and content. The mushrooming fiber movement of the late 1960s that continued through the 1970s focused on exploring techniques and materials. Fiber artists concerned with sculptural forms and textures were garnering all the attention and press coverage because curators and critics were not responding to content or representational subject matter. Only later, as the interest in tapestry gained momentum, was Nezhnie's contribution really appreciated.

Thus, the impetus set in motion by the tapestry exhibitions in the 1950s was temporarily derailed as the interest in weaving took a very different path. When tapestry next gained the spotlight in America, the union of artist as both designer and weaver had occurred. Several weaving studios emerged by the early 1970s. However, as postulated by researcher Courtney Ann Shaw, it was the success of the San Francisco Tapestry Workshop, started in 1977, that turned the tide. Through the influence of French-trained tapestry weaver Jean Pierre Larochette, more than 300 students were exposed to traditional French techniques at the workshop in the early 1980s. They went back to their own studios in all the regions of the country to implement what they had learned and to teach others. Shaw presents an excellent summary of the history of tapestry in the United States in the catalog published by the University of Maryland in 1989 for the exhibit "American Tapestry Weaving Since the 1930s and Its European Roots." Muriel Nezhnie was one of the artists whose work was included in that exhibit.

During the 1980s, the type of work tapestry weavers produced shifted. As the decade progressed, fewer opportunities for major fiber art commissions surfaced and coincidentally more exhibits focusing on content and personal expression emerged. More studio time could now be directed toward the development of a style and for risk taking.

Nezhnie had little contact with other tapestry artists and developed her style independently. The very fact that she was comfortable with learning the techniques of tapestry weaving without being able to communicate with her instructor is evidence of her independent nature. Because of that language barrier during the period of instruction in Germany, she acquired no theoretical constructs to guide her. Of interest, too, is that she never felt the need to seek out further instruction later. She wanted to work out her own design solutions, unfettered.

Perhaps resisting trends gave her even more drive to succeed at what she was interested in pursuing. It is ironic that her failing health happened at a time when her insights and contributions began to have an impact on the tapestry community. Although she was finally at the forefront of the weaving world, she was not able to take advantage of the growing interest aspiring tapestry weavers showed in her work. Her last major public appearance, a workshop and keynote address at the "Tapestry Forum" held at the Oregon School of Arts and Crafts in April, 1990, fell short of her expectations even though she had tried valiantly to communicate her insights and love for tapestry.

Throughout her career, Nezhnie had been free to develop her own style and explanations for why the process of tapestry weaving appealed to her. She was very articulate. When she retired, she left a legacy of extensive written comments to augment her unique tapestries. Together, they reveal the rich imagery and complexity that characterizes the artist, Muriel Nezhnie Helfman. Her own commentary forms the basis for this study.

A Partnership of Artists

By their early thirties, the Helfmans were living in a three-story brick house with a large porch and a beautiful green tiled roof situated in an old established suburb with an excellent school system and an active artistic community. By the age of forty, Nezhnie had won three awards for major architectural installations. Her work was selected for an exhibit at the St. Louis Art Museum. Only two local artists per year received this honor, awarded to Nezhnie in the third year after the program was initiated. It is the kind of visibly productive lifestyle many women aspired to in the second half of the 20th century, but found daunting or logistically impossible to achieve.

She and Shelly started their lives together at a time when it became possible for a broad spectrum of the population to receive good higher education, a powerful tool towards advancement. They were savvy and made choices that gave them the leverage necessary to improve their lives.

Shelly's decision to serve in the Army is an example. Granted, he was accepted into graduate school because of his natural intelligence and talent, but it was a GI loan that enabled him to attend Yale and support a growing family, too. Graduating from a prestigious Ivy League university was a very marketable commodity. Subsequently, teaching at a highly regarded institution placed the family in a stimulating upper-middle-class environment. Yet, it took more than good timing and circumstances to so successfully accomplish the multiple objectives of artist, businesswoman, and caregiver that Muriel demanded of herself.

Like many other women artists, in discussing her accomplishments Nezhnie tended to attribute her success to external factors and to minimize her own role. According to her statements, she was in the right place at the right time to learn of a commission or to meet a woman who knew where she could find the kind of photos she was looking for. There is a modest omission of her natural talent, hard work, and the persuasive communication skills that she possessed.

Early in life, she understood that she was responsible for making things happen to meet her goals. She had a natural resourcefulness that allowed her to create situations that enhanced her options. One factor in accomplishing her objectives was to accept whatever opportunity came her way and not be limited by reservations. During her career, this self-confidence allowed her to accept an assignment even before she knew how to accomplish it.

Despite the strides made by women artists in the 1970s, being a mother and an artist continued to be an uphill struggle, even at the end of the twentieth century. For a woman establishing herself as an artist before 1970, the task was even harder. The history of women artists in the earliest decades of the century reveals that they were under pressure not to have children; even marriage was an indication that an aspiring artist did not take her work seriously.

Several women artists gained recognition in the 1930s because the management of major projects for the Works Progress Administration (WPA) was awarded to women such as Lee Krasner. According to Ellen G. Landau, in the essay "Tough Choices":

> Men had nothing to lose (economically, at least) by admitting women into their poverty stricken ranks. . . . Krasner, Alice Neal, Louise Nevelson, I. Rice Pereira and many others launched their careers under the auspices of New Deal patronage.[3]

By the late 1930s in a reaction to the WPA bias against non-objective art, the organization American Abstract Artists (AAA) was formed. The group had exhibits accompanied by extensive written commentary to define their objectives. Women, such as Alice Trumbull Mason, had a major role in the new movement because they were the ones articulating the theoretical tenets of abstraction. However, almost all of these females found themselves struggling for acclaim and support during and after World War II. An often-quoted revelation, expressed by a reviewer about work by Louise Nevelson in a 1941 issue of *Que* magazine, claims:

> We learned the artist is a woman in time to check our enthusiasm. Had it been otherwise, we might have hailed these sculptural expressions as by a truly great figure among moderns. (*Making Their Mark*, 32)

The incongruity of the situation for women has been that while their talent was cultivated by male art teachers, as Nezhnie's had been, they were not expected to actually become professional artists. As Calvin Tomkins stated in his essay "Righting the Balance":

---

3 *Making Their Mark: Women Artists Move into the Mainstream 1970-85* (New York: Abbeville Press, 1989): 30.

> At most art schools then [1963] it was taken for granted that the women students were not going to go out and become practicing artists, even if their work showed more promise than the men's. Jack Tworkov, who succeeded Josef Albers as head of the art department at Yale, actually begged them not to try. (*Making Their Mark*, 46)

The collective emphasis of the country after the war was towards giving the returning soldiers every opportunity possible to reestablish themselves in the work force. Despite the odds, there were some women who managed to achieve professional status in the post-war era. History does, however, show a correlation between their success and an alliance with an influential man in the art world. For Krasner, it was her partner, Jackson Pollack; for Louise Nevelson, the art dealer Karl Nierendorf; and for Helen Frankenthaler, her relationship with influential critic, Clement Greenberg.

During the 1950s, unfortunately, many of the women who had managed to break through the gender barrier were unable to sustain the high profile. As Landau points out, their fate was controlled by art dealers, frequently women, who felt that artwork by females would never be as commercially viable as that of their male counterparts. Gallery space was devoted to the more lucrative, collectible artwork of men. One response, exemplified by Lee Krasner, was to shift energy to furthering her partner's career rather than compete with him for fame. Ironically, many of these women artists have remarked that the only source of support for their talent came from the men in competition with them, not other women. It was not until the 1970s that the support system swung dramatically and women began looking to each other for validation. (*Making Their Mark*, 39)

The issue of being taken seriously as an artist while raising a family has not been resolved as easily as the issue of encouragement. In her essay, Landau acknowledged that several women chose not to have children and yet others "had to temporarily relinquish their parental roles." *In Strong Hearts, Inspired Minds*, Ann Mavor interviewed a wide variety of post – women's movement artists and concluded that women continued to work twice or three times as hard as men in order to accomplish the dual role of mother and artist.[4]

In this milieu, how is it that Nezhnie ever aspired to such illusive success? Of course, as she was commuting to New York City to take art classes as a teenager, no one was proclaiming the facts of the gender imbalance, and with each bit of recognition she was increasingly committed to art. Given her decisive and tenacious personality, her course was set.

Fortunately, besides being very talented, well trained, and intensely

---

4 Ann Mavor, *Strong Hearts, Inspired Minds: 21 Artists Who Are Mothers Tell Their Stories*, (Rowenberry Books, 1996): 251.

Three generations on an outing while living in New Haven, Connecticut.

committed to art, she also had a supportive partner. And, like Tom Sawyer, she must have learned early how to enlist help. Muriel communicated well, liked people, and made her opinions known. A good example of this is her relationship with the teacher who taught her to weave blanket squares and later found her a scholarship to take extra art classes. Perhaps, what inspired others to want to help her was Nezhnie's own enthusiasm and conviction that what she set out to do was important.

In any case, Nezhnie did have help, especially from her husband. He played a major role, helping physically in the process, financially as the main provider for the family, and emotionally as a personal confidant.

There is evidence that from the beginning Shelly saw their relationship as a partnership of artists. He could not enroll in graduate school immediately after his Army duty because The Cooper Union was only a three-year art school. Thus, to acquire more undergraduate credits before starting to study color theory under Joseph Albers at Yale, he did a senior project with Albers' wife, the famous weaver Anni Albers, as his advisor. Shelly's choice to create designs for weaving had started out as a way to connect Muriel with the renowned weaver, who had designed and taught at the Bauhaus along with her husband. Though he tried, Shelly was never able to introduce Muriel to Anni because Anni felt it was not necessary to interact with her, since she was only the artisan. As Muriel confessed much later to a friend, it was a difficult time for her, being perceived primarily as a mother with young children and not being taken seriously as a professional artist.

Nezhnie had no aspirations to gain acclaim through teaching art. Her ambition was focused on making a name for herself by selling her artwork. Soon after the Helfmans' move to St. Louis, Nezhnie took steps to create a more rewarding environment for herself as an artist than what she had experienced as the wife of a graduate student. In 1964 she helped to form Craft Alliance, a cooperative crafts gallery.

The gallery gave her a creative outlet and connection with her peers. It placed her in a setting with direct access to the markets for both her personal work and commission opportunities. It was also a way for her to actively help in elevating crafts to the status of art that only exhibition and acquisition by major collectors could do. Over the years, besides administrative duties, she wrote many reviews of exhibits at the gallery.

Participating in Craft Alliance was one of the great commitments that Muriel made in her life. At that time, women still felt a need to justify the time they spent outside the family if it wasn't in the context of a lucrative job or well-defined social cause. Without Shelly's sanction and cooperation, it would have been harder for her to accomplish what she did at the gallery and in her weaving. His contribution was not only as a founding member and willing worker, but as an active parent in the children's lives, giving Muriel greater freedom in fulfilling gallery commitments. Involvement in the gallery became a major aspect in the lives of all family members.

With Shelly's contacts in the Washington University School of Architecture, it is probably not a coincidence that several of the fifteen founding members of the gallery were architects. The architect who commissioned Nezhnie for the library *Imprints* tapestries was one of the founders. The gallery also brought them in contact with patrons and collectors who frequently became close friends. The venture provided a dynamic environment in which to market her work, made more viable through her husband's consent and participation.

There are many reasons why it is more likely for a married woman to be successful as an artist if her partner is also an artist. Certainly the confidence that your soul mate believes your pursuits to be valid is a major source of support regardless of profession. However, when both partners are artists, it is easier to have a dialogue; they speak a similar language. Her spouse can understand that success is not measured strictly by sales and not confront her with the "did you sell anything?" question that can be so deflating after an exhibition. Instead, he might ask something about the response to a specific piece or about what kind of crowd attended the opening. Having an artist as one's primary companion also means that there is a greater likelihood that you will exist in an artistic environment. Many women have discovered that their non-artistic partners are painfully uncomfortable at events where artists congregate. It is not that a woman cannot overcome these issues, it is simply the case that her life is made easier if she does not have to be distracted by an unresponsive partner. Some women decide not to have a permanent relationship and thus operate within a different set of parameters. Such a concept was never an option for Nezhnie. She felt a strong need for a family because of the many lonely hours she spent by herself as a child. (*THE SEEN*, 1)

In addition to the more abstract advantages of his being an artist, Shelly's physical help was ongoing. He photographed over ninety percent of her work with consistent, professional quality. No doubt his slides helped in presentations and competitions. Shelly relates having shot six roles of film of *The Daughters of Earth* and then Muriel decided she needed to change a small section that just did not look right to her. Facing one's husband with the request to redo the photographs because you changed your mind is a prospect most women at that time would have been hesitant to do. But they

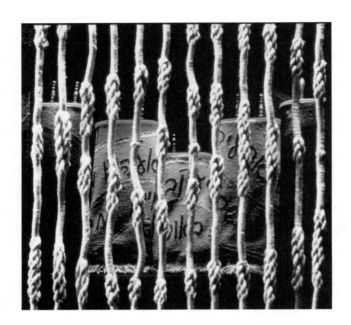

Detail of the ropes for the St. Louis version of Jacob's Dream.

both understood that there was no choice. Once she knew how the problem could be solved, she had to correct it. She had no aptitude for photography and he was good at it; thus, the task fell to him. Occasionally she had artwork photographed by a professional photographer, but Shelly did the majority of it. Frequently the tapestry was finished too close to the deadline to ensure getting the documentation completed on time by outside professionals. Also, there were few photographers really geared for photographing large artwork.

Shelly constructed armatures, crated and hauled works, climbed ladders to install tapestries, and even got involved in the weaving on occasion. He did all the wrapping of the ladder ropes for the St. Louis *Jacob's Dream* ark curtain. This involved tightly wrapping and knotting twelve sections 18 feet long, or over 200 feet of linen rope. His strength and ability to wield the weight of such long ropes was essential. In the end, when her health deteriorated he finished weaving a commission for her. It was his decision; he was not ready to confront her illness publicly.

The very cooperative relationship probably worked for the Helfmans not only because Shelly had a helping nature, but because they both were committed artists. There was no question that Shelly understood that the woman he married had an intense drive to succeed as an artist. He also valued her skill and shared the dream for her success.

He made an insightful comment that Muriel generously gave her time to causes she believed in, but she wanted her perspective to be implemented. She was not comfortable as a follower. Then reflecting, he said, "But her ideas could be so engaging!" One can infer that part of his willingness to devote time to her projects was because she provided a match for his own intelligence. She had a very inquisitive personality and was stimulated by conceptually complex issues and images. It is also said that her communication skills and outgoing nature brought him out of an introverted personality. They were indeed a pair that thrived on the skills and feedback of the other.

Shelly's fluency in Hebrew was a very valuable asset that came to Muriel's aid. He could go to passages that exemplified the concept she wanted to portray and transcribe the texts into various forms of Hebraic script. She incorporated many of his transcriptions into her imagery. It was of immense benefit in securing major commissions and in guiding her with the Holocaust texts.

Shelly was also a sounding board for Muriel. From his point of view this was, perhaps, the most difficult means of support he gave her. Muriel was an individualist, not only resisting trends, but other people's advice, even though she may have sought it. Shelly found it frustrating to be solicited for advice, then have his practical solutions ignored. After all, his profession was teaching design and drawing, and he was a successful artist in his own right.

His primary criticism was that she sometimes forced her artwork to conform to her idea rather than letting the nature of the elements dictate how to use them. Materials that were soft and pliable might be asked to stand firm, a hairy fiber perhaps used for an intricate detail. He was especially critical of complicated shapes that were challenging to mount because he had to devise solutions that would best counteract the limitations of the materials or shaping. Despite his consternation, the star-shaped tapestry *Constellation*, for example, is visually successful and dramatic in the setting for which it was designed. It showcases not only Muriel's skill in creating eccentric shapes, but her perception that the room would benefit from the innovative design. The problem was not in her daring to push the limits of her techniques, but perhaps in expecting him to deal with the technicalities inherent in deviating from convention.

Shelly installing Constellation. *Photo by Sharon Burde.*

Her results could be very exciting and beautiful, or at the other end of the scale, simply not work, though that was rare. It was an important fact that Shelly wanted to communicate. He wanted it known that some of her work was just "bad" art, not to be derogatory, but to emphasize her dogged need for completion of an idea. Her enthusiasm and conviction could carry her through an entire project without considering other solutions, leading to mixed results.

Surely the Helfmans must have had to learn to live with a high level of tension at times. Their son, Jonathan, maintains that arguments are an accepted part of the Jewish culture, originating in the teaching that it is one's responsibility to question the tenets of faith and deliberate on their meanings. This practice extends to family interactions in which voicing disagreement is not seen as threatening to the stability and love in the family unit.

From Shelly's account, when his suggestions seemed unrealistic or did not mesh with her goal, she would exclaim, "What's the point? It's too far away from what I'm doing!" No doubt there were many, many times when Muriel had been influenced by his perspective; but it is, of course, human nature to remember the frustrating interchanges when she could not accept advice. Despite his frustration, those times contributed to the refinement of Nezhnie's artistic vision. Great art is generated from the unknown. Ideas have to be tried, and they do not always work. Nezhnie's nature was such that once committed to a design, she tried to make it work . . . and she was used to resisting external input.

It takes more than natural talent in drawing to be a visual artist. Being an artist means communicating your own expression. The only thing an artist has to offer is that unique interpretation of what is seen. No matter how much encouragement or training is given, to be creative the personal perspective has to come from within. Nezhnie understood this notion instinctively. The best example of this is how she modified the design process specifically for tapestry, incorporating the selection of yarns in the early conceptual stage.

For example, while listening to her husband's comments she had to be able to picture his idea in an understandable way for her to accomplish. Nezhnie had a well-defined internal visual system of codes and tools with which to create woven images. Shelly's suggestions would have to work within her aesthetic system in order for her to use them.

It seems that Muriel did not perceive that Shelly wanted the same kind of dialogue regarding his work that she solicited. In a written response to a question as to whether or not they sought each other's opinion, Muriel wrote:

> I ask Shell for his opinions about my work and he asks for my opinions in general, but not about his work. However, he does listen to anything I have to say about a work in progress.

According to a woman who commissioned a portrait from Shelly, Muriel offered her input. The client is one of many who perceived the couple as having a partnership of alliance.

Indeed, it appears their relationship was a symbiotic partnership. The general consensus of friends and her apprentices is decidedly that Muriel consulted with Shelly about all aspects of her work. She would not mail a business letter without first having him check it over and contribute his input. One apprentice said she was always amazed at how much deliberation went on about what seemed the smallest of details to her. However, the Helfmans thrived on the dialogue and deliberation.

The receptive attention to her thoughts that Nezhnie received from her partner surely was a vital impetus to her creative process.

In the Studio

In tapestry weaving, images are not applied to the surface, but form the structure itself. The shapes and lines are built by interlacing various color *weft* yarns back and forth through the warp, or threads that are secured with uniform tension. A frame or structure is necessary to keep the warp taut. A loom designed for the purpose increases efficiency and enables more control of the tension. Every detail is laid in and manipulated by the weaver. The weft is packed in closely to the previous row in such a way that only these weft yarns show, hiding the warp threads. Designs emerge by using separate yarns of differing colors for each shape. The surface is characteristically uniform in texture. The process is slow but creates a unique pictorial fabric rich in color and texture well worth the effort.

The weaver can only work in one area at a time, unlike an artist in a medium where the details are applied to an existing surface. The act of actually building both the structure and the image simultaneously appealed to Nezhnie. In an interview she talked about the implications.

> . . . say you paint on a plain piece of white paper with black ink — when you make a stroke you immediately have some impact. Maybe not a great amount, but you do make some impact on the white shapes that remain. The Orientals were fantastically skilled in this form of art. They activated all of the space. And I think when you do calligraphy — when you work with letterforms, if you are not seeing the negative spaces that your pen is creating, then you are not really a good calligrapher. So what I love about weaving is that you actually have to make, physically construct, the negative spaces as well as the positive. It isn't like putting a brush stroke down on a surface that already exists; you have to make the whole surface. And that is very exciting; it also keeps me from getting bored when I'm weaving. I'm busy building the negative shape in order to support the positive shape. In fact, they all become positive as you weave each one. (Castro, 8)

In Germany, she observed the elaborate procedure of dying and blending yarns required to translate the colors of a painted design into a tapestry. This

*Inking in the cartoon.
Photo from the* St. Louis
Globe Democrat
*Archives of the
St. Louis Mercantile
Library at the University
of Missouri – St. Louis.*

approach seemed backwards to Muriel, so she decided to select the yarns she wanted to use first and then start working on the painting, matching the paint to the yarn colors. The decision was not merely because she had confidence in her ability to mix paints, although matching colors in paint does seem a less labor-intensive task than dying. More important, since she was aiming for a woven image, she had to approach her task differently than an artist whose goal was to create the image as a painting. Issues like the character of the yarn, the possible ways it might integrate with another, or perhaps the yarn's luster or non-reflectiveness were early considerations.

Although her approach was different from those of the weavers she studied, she was equally as meticulous about the process of taking an idea from the design stage to the final cartoon. Once she decided on the preliminary concept and specific yarns to use, she would make a small sample painting of what she wanted the finished piece to look like, generally in the scale of one inch equaling one foot. Even the little finishing knots that would show along the edge of the weaving were often included in the small-scale painting. She chose to use gouache, an opaque water-based paint, to ensure that areas remained true to the color of the yarn. That way, there would be no extra blended tones she couldn't reproduce with the selected yarns.

Once the painting was to her liking, either it was photographed and then projected to the intended size and traced, or it was superimposed with a grid and copied to scale by hand on the cartoon, section by section. A large roll of bond paper that measured five feet wide was used for cartoons. After the design had been transferred to the cartoon, it was again evaluated for distortion and adjustments were made. An apprentice might transfer the image to the cartoon, but Muriel would make any needed changes after it was completed. It was a slow and tedious procedure. The last stage of the process was inking the final scaled version with a permanent black felt-tipped pen. It was an important step in order to easily see the marks or lines once the cartoon was placed behind the warp.

The fundamental nature of tapestry is that a shape is created progressively from point A to point B, and the part already woven may not be completely visible. As the work progresses, earlier portions are rolled onto a beam at the front or lower section of the loom so that the weaver is still at a convenient position to work on the next shapes. Because the total picture is not visible at all times, weavers generally rely on a very accurate cartoon or scaled replica. There is an assumption, especially for beginners, that as long as the cartoon has been carefully created, and the materials and quantities carefully calculated, success is only a matter of skillful execution. The technician existing in the weaver takes over. Most tapestry weavers have a love of the actual repetitive building process; otherwise they find another medium to work in. The weaver settles into the pleasurable task of building and into the comfort of rhythm and regularity.

The majority of tapestry weavers today have learned methods used traditionally by French craftsmen to create shapes. Specific techniques were designed to enable the weaver to accomplish very predictable effects, such as creating a shadow or a smooth circle. Many artists rely on the prescribed formulas both to maintain the integrity of the style and to expedite the weaving. There is always the option to try something new, which many artists do, but the formulas diminish the amount of time it takes to create a conventional effect.

Nezhnie worked without the prescribed framework. It could be said that she wove "by eye" as a musician might play by ear. It meant that she worked in a trial-and-error manner relying only on her observation and previous insights to determine when the image looked the way she wanted it to. There were times when it might take an hour to get one curved line to look right. The weaver may muddle through several solutions, ripping and reweaving in what seems to be chaos. Most of the time a point is reached, however, when the line is right, the eye or the blade of grass depicted looks lively and like the artist intended. Order is reached from the chaos, but it has taken many decisions to get there. Nezhnie liked to create designs that gave her new scenarios for active engagement with her tapestry.

The artistic process doesn't stop as the weaving begins. The true artist must stay actively engaged in the image and the concept. There is a fine line between trusting the decisions made at the design stage and what is observed as the tapestry progresses. Also, as the composition comes together in yarn, there simply are new insights that need to be taken into account. Sometimes it is easiest to adjust an area on the spot; other times it requires looking at the finished work to best implement the correction. Despite confidence in the cartoon, there are times when the weaver/artist does make changes.

Few of Nezhnie's pieces came off the loom without the need for some adjustments or minor corrections. Her apprentices have many accounts of weaving and reweaving an area several times while the piece was in progress, as well as afterwards.

Her active participation as artist, not technician, manifests itself in the successful results she had, especially in terms of color. Apprentice Jan Jungkuntz recounts being asked to bring out black yarns as Muriel was determining the color combination for an upcoming piece. Jungkuntz searched and found three or four on the shelves and carried them back to the collection of yarns being considered. Muriel said, "No, I mean all the blacks, the red ones, the purple ones, bring them all!" In scrutinizing her tapestries, it becomes apparent that she used a large variety of slightly different shades to attain a desired effect or perhaps just to add another facet of interest to a tapestry. Some of these subtle changes occurred while the weaving was in progress, making it necessary to pull out a section already done to slip back in an only slightly different tone. Another apprentice, Christel Maassen, recalls:

> . . . There was one letter that I had to needle weave in and out three different times. Muriel, Shelly, and I kept feeling that this one red letter "popped out," as Muriel would say, from the tapestry and needed to be changed to a different color. We kept changing the color from the various reds and oranges that were used throughout the lettering. However, when we did this, nothing seemed to improve the word. We finally decided to needle weave it one last time and put the original color back. This was a lesson of importance to me. It demonstrated that if something doesn't read right, make the changes and continue to do so until the best option is found.

Time also influences the outcome of the piece. Part of the active engagement involves balancing when to change or accept the area in question. In general, unless an easy and clear solution occurred, Nezhnie went with her initial instincts. She has stated:

> I do not change approach in midstream, if I think of a better way or a better concept, my mind becomes full of it and thoughts grow as I work. It is the next tapestry that benefits.
> . . . Maybe it is because I have been weaving for 22 years, maybe it is because I plan so carefully before I weave but rarely am I surprised as I used to be when weaving was new to me. I remember tremendous excitement when a piece was to come off the loom but now I feel accomplishment or satisfaction instead.
> At times I am disappointed. The tapestry is not what I hoped it might be and at times I am delighted because it is more, much more, than I expected it to be but rarely is there amazement or wonder.
> Sometimes the color does not work as I intended. That can spoil the entire tapestry for me. Sometimes my colored warp does not mix as I intended and the work is grayer or duller than I like. Sometimes a work requires an exact aesthetic distance in order to read properly and I worry that it is therefore too limited and cannot easily [be] viewed or exhibited. Sometimes a tapestry is woven

poorly by an apprentice and despite my instruction reaches completion before it reaches my standards; that is always a disappointment. All of these examples obviously have their successful counterparts and on the whole there are more pleasures than pains.[5]

The Helfmans moved three times during the first five years they lived in St. Louis. By the time they settled into the large house in University City in 1965, Nezhnie already had three looms incorporated into the general living space. Besides the upright German loom with a weaving width of a meter, she had acquired a thirty-six-inch Leclerc floor loom, perhaps at a garage sale. Then she bought a large sixty-inch Nilas Leclerc twelve-harness floor loom just before the final move in 1965. The German loom would have made numerous journeys: across the sea, to the Midwest from New Haven, and two trips across town. Fortunately, it could be dismantled. Nevertheless, transporting looms and moving a studio is not a light matter. Many years later, at the end of her career, she bought a Shannock upright tapestry loom.

Shelly modified the weaving position of the five-foot Leclerc floor loom to reduce stress on Muriel's back. He mounted wedges under the base of the loom to tip it forward at least thirty degrees or more. Leclerc was interested enough in the idea to come look at how it worked. He thought it was an interesting innovation but did not pursue the idea for his production. The upright frame, or castle that supports the mechanisms for separating warp threads, needed to be about eighteen inches deep in order to accommodate twelve harnesses. Considering the weight and bulk of the structure, engineering the wedges to keep the mass from shifting must have been challenging indeed. As

At the tipped Leclerc loom before the studio was finished, from St, Louis Post Dispatch *clipping.*

seen in the various photographs of the uniquely pitched loom, Nezhnie appears to be at a comfortable weaving position despite how precarious the loom appears. Eventually, gravity did have an effect on the loom and the wooden harnesses started to bow because they rested at an angle in their grooves.

In the early 1970s, the basement was remodeled to create a studio measuring about 600 square feet. It was not spacious, considering the number of looms and paraphernalia it needed to house, but it was very functional. By excavating a portion of the backyard and creating an opening in the back wall of the studio for a double glass door, the area became an attractive and practical place to work. Without the renovation, it

---

5 From a draft of notes to Nancy Crump dated December, 1978, in which Nezhnie answers the questionnaire sent to her by Crump for an article in *Interweave* magazine. Notes page 6.

As she weaves in the studio. Note the upright German loom in the background.

would have been a somber, congested setting for working with apprentices. By that time, Nezhnie's workload dictated that she needed assistants.

Landscaping the reorganized yard was a family project for years to come, culminating in an inviting environment. The excavation left a big mound of dirt that they turned into a berm separating their property from the neighbors. Unfortunately, because the yard was so shady, it took quite a while for plants to get established. Mud would run off the berms during the heavy downpours that are typical of St. Louis rains. However, friends have remarked that Muriel was very persistent and never gave up. After a few false starts, the yard was transformed with leaf-shaped perennial gardens, paths, and a small pond.

Jan Jungkuntz has written a detailed and engaging account of her experience as an apprentice to Muriel. One interesting aspect relates to the importance of access to the backyard from the studio. The brick patio just outside the double doors of the studio improved the atmosphere. The basement could become claustrophobic when more people were working than the space could comfortably accommodate. As Jungkuntz expressed it:

> There was always a sense of connectedness with the earth, water, and vegetation that often soothed us during a pressured, frustrating job. Development of the larger context of the studio, its relationship to the outside territory was extremely important to Muriel. . . . When the interior would become overwhelming one had only to pass through the glass doors physically or visually, and recoup in the shady garden.

Christel Maassen also experienced that the contact with the outside setting was important. She liked working at the old German loom because it was situated by a window high in the wall. It had a beautiful wrought iron grill at ground level where glimpses of sunlight or shimmering leaves could refresh weary eyes. In winter, she related, "if you took time every so often from your weaving, you could watch the snowflakes fall, either to land and remain or melt before your eyes."

One small area housed tools for building and mounting armatures, and another small room was fitted with shelves for yarn storage. Detailed records were kept regarding sources and quantities. Apprentices have referred to Muriel as a tidy person who kept an orderly studio. However, she consistently had trouble keeping the yarns put away and organized in the right order by supplier.

Her tendency to want to examine a variety of options when choosing colors meant yarns were pulled from many areas for sampling. The task of regaining order was frequently left to the apprentices. Keeping her slides in order was also always a challenge assigned to them.

Despite a limited amount of wall space in the studio, tapestries could be hung for viewing and critique. There was a small office area complete with desk and typewriter, file cabinet, and storage cabinet with a light-table on top. Nooks and crannies were filled with interesting objects for visual stimulation, including an airplane propeller and a woven hat from Togo. Space was also needed for transferring designs onto cartoons and for the finishing work after a weaving was cut from the loom. A large Ping-Pong table was covered with orange fabric and became the primary work center. It could accommodate many people working at the same time, especially handy for completing last-minute details to meet a deadline.

Everyone available was enlisted for finishing work, especially if a deadline was near. All the loose ends of yarn on the backside of the tapestry would be tied, and the warp ends would be knotted into bundles of three. The warp knots were then turned to the back and the tails tacked down with a running stitch in two places to lay flat. It created a supple edge with no ridges or obvious bulges that occur if the ends are hemmed or sewn back into the fabric. Instead, it resulted in a decorative row of knots, referred to previously, which though visible, is surprisingly unobtrusive. The process is a distinctive trademark of work woven by or for Nezhnie.

Nezhnie's method of blocking tapestries was controversial and somewhat counter-intuitive. The procedure was to lay the tapestry face down on a surface of plywood painted white. Often more than one 4' x 8' sheet was needed. The tapestry was measured at the shortest and longest points on all four sides to determine the desired dimensions, which were then marked, using a square, on the plywood. Then the tapestry was stapled, adjusting the sides to the desired size. Stretching the fabric was a strenuous task. Using a pail of tap water and a large sponge or perhaps a hose, the entire surface of the tapestry was saturated. Puckers were soaked with warmer water in hopes of contracting the area, or boiling water was poured out of a kettle directly onto buckled areas. Shelly also remembers pressing a hot steam iron over a moistened towel on severely buckled areas to help them lie flat. The boards were then tipped at an angle to let excess water drain off. The house's long front porch provided a protected, clean area for the operation. Years later, a weaver who was first introduced to Nezhnie at a panel discussion during the 1988 Convergence in Chicago recalled Muriel telling how she used a hose to moisten the stapled tapestries. The weaver found the comment "both shocking and thought provoking."

Christel Maassen was among those who were skeptical of the procedure, but Muriel assured her that paint, rust or wood stains had never come through. On the other hand, an occasional incident of warp or weft colors running did occur, even though Nezhnie made it a policy to test all yarns she ordered for color-fastness by wetting each with both boiling and cold water and squeezing them between paper towels. The towels and yarn were observed when they had dried. In the three years Maassen worked with her, one shape did have to be rewoven in a commission because a warp color had bled through, dulling the surface.

The twelve apprentices Nezhnie trained had a wide range of skills and a variety of reasons for wanting to work with her. Deann Rubin had a solid background in graphic design but wanted to explore tapestry. Christel Maassen, her last apprentice, was already an experienced tapestry weaver who wanted more work with portraiture. Jan Jungkuntz had experience with primitive looms. Both she and Rubin had been profoundly influenced by Nezhnie's tapestry *Breath of Life*, exhibited at the St. Louis Art Museum in 1974. Others were interested in finding out about the process but were not necessarily committed to weaving as a career. A few were simply interested in interacting with the person capable of designing such moving tapestries. Nezhnie had to determine what each individual could accomplish and how best to use them. Apprentices might spend considerable time doing a portrait whose function was simply to get them to the level of expertise she needed. Their instruction and supervision was demanding, and it is debatable whether she profited from using apprentices in terms of the quantity of work produced. However, it was not in Muriel's nature to work in solitude. She liked people, and she felt it was important to share her knowledge and design concepts. She was a person who made herself available to others.

There was another more intangible way in which the process of working with apprentices benefited her. In order for them to successfully transfer images to a cartoon or know how to execute the weaving as she envisioned it, they needed to understand her intent in the design. The apprentices would have to enter into the visual dialogue, if not the conceptual stage of a project. Areas that were unresolved would become evident. The process of conveying what needed to happen would refine Nezhnie's understanding of how the image was communicating, as well as the apprentice's.

One experience early in her career taught Nezhnie the importance of close supervision. Without telling Nezhnie, a frustrated apprentice decided to modify the cartoon by decreasing the number of spots to be woven in a busy section. The apprentice balanced the changes skillfully enough that the alterations were not blatantly apparent. It was only after the tapestry was already off the loom that the altered ratio of background to dots was noticeable.

Although the experience was distressing, Nezhnie agreed that the tapestry was still successful despite the infraction. It was a lesson learned without major negative effects, but, it made her a more wary supervisor.

Another early lesson learned was to anticipate the difference in appearance that naturally occurs between weavers. Some people unconsciously weave more tightly, packing more weft into the piece than others do. For the weaving of the St. Louis *Jacob's Dream*, she contracted with two local weavers to supplement the work of the apprentice. One of the three produced a much more dense panel than any of the others, creating problems that had to be solved at the assembly stage. She learned to plan for such contingencies in the design. For example, in *Nader*, she used a yarn with very uneven texture for areas where more than one person would be doing the weaving.

There is no indication in the production log whether a piece was woven by an apprentice. If that information is known, it has been added after the fact. Only four of the twelve apprentices have been located: Jan Jungkuntz, Christel Maassen, Hannah Roth, and Deann Rubin. Another apprentice, Georgia Tewel, is no longer living. Of the four, only Christel has continued actively weaving although Deann returned to weaving early in the twenty-first century Two apprentices stayed with the Helfmans during the time they worked with Nezhnie. Robin Ulmer, a woman from Vermont, had a brief stay of only a week or so, but in that time won the hearts of the family and is fondly remembered. The other boarder, David Reigel, was the only man to work with her. He was there for a much longer duration and worked on at least one major commission, the St. Louis *Jacob's Dream*. He fit easily into the happenings of the family as well.

One of Muriel's greatest assets was her ability to draw people out to talk about themselves. It did, however, have drawbacks in that she was often interrupted by lengthy phone calls or by visitors. She was talkative, too, and could get caught up in a good story, extending the call even more. Often as she put the phone back on the receiver, she would comment that she should not have talked so long. However, she would soon be back on task in the rhythm of her work. She did not like to say no to someone with a problem or who asked questions about weaving. Her closest friend has stated that Muriel would never say no to someone with a problem, even if she were very near a deadline. She would make up the lost time later, perhaps working until four in the morning. She had the ability to stay focused for as long as needed and to exist on very little sleep. One notable exception to her sharing nature was that she was guarded in communicating with what she perceived as nosy inquirers, especially about the business and pricing details of being an artist. Friends were always encouraged to visit at lunchtime and they frequently did.

Both Jungkuntz and Rubin expressed ambivalence about combining a home and studio setting. For Jungkuntz the major drawback seemed to be in organizing one's time in order to keep a good balance between work and home activities. In Rubin's summation of her apprenticeship she stated:

> . . . Her weaving life is integrated with, not separated from, her personal life. An apprentice is treated as a family member.
> The advantage to the apprentice of the integrated approach is a total openness and involvement in Nezhnie's lifestyle. Because the apprentice becomes part of whatever events unfold, different apprentices experience different things. Aspects of my apprenticeship include guest artist visits (Theo Morman), visits to art exhibits (David Hockney's), Washington University's School of Architecture class critiques, and guest lectures. . . .
> The disadvantages to the home-studio location is that personal happenings become studio happenings. Studio work at times is interrupted or errands are run for non-studio related matters (company coming for dinner, family arguments happening during studio hours). On the other hand, if your studio is to be home integrated, then the interruptions could teach you coping strategy, a decided advantage.

Nezhnie took pride in writing inclusive contracts, but the task was an ever-evolving process as unexpected misunderstandings occurred despite the best intentions of both parties.[6] The apprentices worked under a contract that specified the number of hours per day they were to work and the amount of square feet of weaving expected of them at the completion of the contract, usually fifty square feet. In later years it also specified that if they did not accomplish the desired quantity, a certain dollar amount for the footage not woven should be paid to Nezhnie. In return, she would teach them all necessary techniques. It is unclear how tasks such as the transfer of cartoons figured into

---

6 Nezhnie's contract with clients began with a statement confirming the specific task. A second paragraph delineated the artist's responsibilities, including "to perform or supervise all work and also the supervision of installation." The third paragraph provided dimensions and the per square footage in order to determine a base price on which to set up the payment schedule, which was then itemized with the exact amounts for each payment.

A section followed that specified conditions regarding special adjustments in the fee, such as modification to the design proposal by the client, as often committee members did not agree amongst themselves about issues, or special installation requirements unforeseen at the initial agreement. Also, the limits of the agreement were specified, including a clause for the contingency that the contract be canceled. Once work was in progress, a contract could not be canceled. Another stipulation stated that the designs remain the property of the artist, but no additional tapestries could be executed from the approved design, thus ensuring its status as one of a kind.

At first she requested a five percent fee to initiate the agreement and a five percent fee upon the presentation of the initial design with another payment of forty percent at the time that the final design was approved and then the remaining fifty percent upon delivery of the completed work. Later she increased the two early payments to ten percent each and changed the other two payments so the first was fifty percent and the last would only be thirty percent. In actual practice, fees were not always on time, as each project had its particular set of circumstances. One essential part of being in business was the willingness to negotiate, but also to require that payments be made in a timely manner. Hence, skill in diplomatic correspondence was a valuable asset.

the agreement. Lunch was provided unless other arrangements were made.

As Maassen described, the first assignment for a new apprentice was to take an inventory of the yarn supply. Not only did it update quantities for Muriel, but it gave the apprentice an idea of what range of color was in the studio and a sense of becoming a part of the work atmosphere. Apprentices would type letters from Muriel's handwritten drafts, to be proofread later by Muriel and Shelly. It was an excellent way for the workers to become comfortable with the details of correspondence, a critical aspect in the promotion of an artist's work. It also gave Nezhnie more time to be weaving or preparing designs. She used a soft dusty rose stationery with a reprint of one of her weavings stretched across the top of the page in a two-inch band with relevant information about her address and focus just below the image. The letterhead served to communicate the nature of the weaving she did. Two images used frequently were *Nader* and a detail of the eyes in *Woman*, a tapestry that was later destroyed in a fire at the Sazama Brauer Gallery in Chicago along with several other tapestries and prints by Muriel and many paintings by Shelly Helfman.

Much of her design work would be accomplished at times when the apprentices were not there. She frequently worked at night. However, over a period of time, most aspects of the process would be visible to them. As Jan Jungkuntz explained:

> Designing was an always-happening activity in the studio and household, and could be observed/participated in at almost any stage on any given day - a photo or clipping tacked up in a strategic location feeding into some urge simmering just below consciousness, a stack of books being used to research an idea, a raft of watercolor mixes matching yarn palettes, sketches, sketches, more sketches, art work painted and repainted and repainted, lunch served with an elegant arrangement of pickles, sandwiches and sub-divided pear, planting in the garden, sea shells on a window sill, and so on.
> . . . During actual sketching and the pencil and paint on paper stage of designing, I learned to keep in mind the limitations as well as the potentials of the woven medium . . . Deadlines which might require quick weaving were considered at the design stage.

The studio was full of interesting objects and photographs that appealed to Nezhnie. As fragments of an image came together, the apprentices could see how she took a photograph or an idea and developed it into a design. Even though weaving was done from the cartoon, the small painted version was always in view during the weaving process for comparison.

The apprentices became involved in the entire process of being an artist. Nezhnie encouraged them to attend interesting lectures around town and meetings of the Weavers' Guild of St. Louis, including these activities in their scheduled work hours. She took them with her to openings and exhibits that she thought they needed to see. According to Maassen, who happened to be the same age as Muriel's daughter, Ilisha, Nezhnie took an interest in the individual. She was concerned that Christel, as a young person, could be engaged in a situation more conducive to interacting with others her own age, unaware that her protégée was completely entranced by the surroundings she found herself in. Apprenticing to Nezhnie meant, for one thing, interacting with other artists and intellectuals. Lunches frequently included guests and provided a learning experience in how to maneuver in an artistic environment. Jan Jungkuntz continued to be involved in the studio activities after her apprenticeship was over. She would offer to do typing or other jobs as birthday gifts or to return a favor.

Occasionally Nezhnie asked an apprentice to accompany her on a trip. In 1981, she participated in the American Crafts Council (ACC) Crafts Market in Baltimore, Maryland, and Christel Maassen went with her. In addition to loading up the car with tapestries, a portable booth, and luggage, they made a last-minute stop for pastries to be delivered to relatives in Ohio where they would stay overnight. Apparently, there was not a decent bakery in their town, so the transported baked goods were a cherished delight when the guests arrived. The next day they unloaded tapestries and the booth in Baltimore late in the evening and went to the row house of artist friends of the Helfmans. Nezhnie was invited by her hosts to give a talk at the Maryland Institute, College of Art where one of their hosts taught. The craft market was profitable for both her and Maassen as they seized the opportunity to look at the work of other participating artists and compare booths. Muriel made many connections and secured a show for the following year in Florida. For Maassen it was a wonderful immersion into the business side of art – an intense but stimulating trip.

Deann Rubin, although no longer an apprentice at the time, accompanied Muriel to Florida for the exhibit the following year. She relates how they arrived very late and tired at the hotel where a plush suite had been reserved for them, or so they had been assured by the gallery owner organizing the exhibit. No reservation could be found for them when they checked in at the desk. The clerk even suggested they might be happier trying a less expensive hotel down the street. Muriel was so sure she was at the right place and that indeed a room had been reserved that she continued to insist the clerk had made a mistake. The contact person could not be reached, either. She explained about the exhibit and the gallery to no avail. Finally, after extensive confusion, it was discovered that the reservation had been made in the name Helfman, not Nezhnie. The clerk's expression changed immediately, and the two women instantly discovered the meaning of "red carpet" treatment as they were ushered to their luxury suite.

Deann spent much of the time during the gallery reception watching Muriel interact with the gallery patrons. Within ten minutes of being introduced to someone, they seemed like best friends. She could joke or mildly chastise the formality of a man with a PhD for referring to himself as Doctor, or draw out a very shy person to reveal his life story. One couple invited them to a mansion for dinner the next night where they were treated as though they were long-time acquaintances.

Understanding that apprentices such as Rubin and Maassen were serious about a career in weaving, Nezhnie made sure they developed a business sense about weaving contracts, design contracts, and commissions with galleries and clients. One point she stressed to Maassen was that for every four commission proposals submitted, you would probably only be awarded one. She made it very clear that if a commission did not come through, it was not a personal condemnation of the work. Her philosophy was to accept it, learn from it, and move on. What was important to understand was the need to be compensated at the design stage.

Although she was very conscientious in working with apprentices, she only occasionally taught classes or workshops. Only a brief number are recorded, including one as a visiting instructor at Portland State College in Portland, Oregon, in July and August of 1966. A few regional lectures and demonstrations occurred sporadically during the 1970s. In 1975 she gave lectures at the Rhode Island School of Design and the Virginia Commonwealth University. She taught summer classes to young people for a few years in the late 1970s in conjunction with Craft Alliance's summer program, of which she was a director. She conducted a workshop at the Oregon School of Arts and Crafts in July of 1982, called "Designing for Tapestry." It was repeated again in April of 1990. Muriel was open to giving talks and teaching to some extent but did not rely on it as a major source of income or use it as a tool for success.

The workshop Nezhnie taught at the Oregon School for Arts and Crafts primarily focused on design but included a very comprehensive account of the process of executing a commission. Tapestry weaver Mary Lane recalls the experience:

Talking about the cartoon of Daughters of Earth. *Photo courtesy T. V. Vessell.*

> . . . She showed us examples of her commission work — which was incredibly varied — all sorts of furnishings — and she took us through the process that she used to deal with clients, make presentations, for example, how to read something about the client through a photo of a space. It was all very practical, as

I said, how to live in the real world, supporting oneself as an artist. Her head was definitely not in the clouds although her faith was ever present. We had to come up with a complete presentation for a commission, a scale drawing, a cost analysis. She gave guidelines for pricing, design fees, marketing costs, fees for managing a project that you design and someone else produces [as in the hooked ark curtains produced by Edward Fields, Inc. in New York]. Lots of very useful advice.

Lane went on to describe Nezhnie as a very involved teacher, good at critique. She was also impressed by the range of work Nezhnie did, how successfully she had carved out a career as a textile artist, and that upon meeting at various events in later years, Muriel always remembered her.

Nezhnie was very conscious of the need to educate the public about what distinguished handcrafted work from commercial products. Collectors, and anyone expressing interest in her work, were encouraged to visit her studio so she could increase their awareness of what went into the production of tapestries. A woman who bought Nezhnie's work while a volunteer at Craft Alliance recalls being invited to the studio. She was impressed with Muriel's organization, remembering the studio as being impeccable.

Despite the size limitations, the studio was a stimulating and productive environment. It was alive with activity and people, an environment that suited Nezhnie well.

Early Works, the 1960s

> WHEN DESIGNING + MAKING A TAPESTRY I TRY TO ALLOW THE CHARACTER + QUALITY OF WEAVING TO DETERMIN THE FINAL FORM. TAPESTRY IS FIRSTLY A WOVEN IDEA ONLY SECONDLY IS IT A GRAPHIC IMAGE. THIS IDEA OF TAPESTRY IS ABUSED WHEN IT DENIES WEAVING + IMITATES PAINTING. THE IMAGRY CREATED IN TAPESRY RESULTS FROM THE UNIQUE QUALITY OF THE STRUCTURE OF YARNS NOT PAINT, INK, OR COLLAGE.

Nezhnie wrote these boldly printed words in 1967. By the time she formulated this statement she had been weaving for a decade. Her goal from the beginning was to discover ways to create pictorial imagery that were unique to weaving. But first, she had to master weaving. While completely confident in her design skills, four months of watching and mimicking procedures in Germany was not nearly enough to make her proficient in weaving.

One of the earliest consequences of minimal oral instruction was that she acquired no information about how to select appropriate yarns. During the first few years of her career, in the late 1950s, Nezhnie wove seven tapestries depicting the days of creation that her husband, Shelly, had designed as his senior project. She selected weft yarns more for their color or appeal than their practicality. What was most available were knitting yarns, which she soon learned were too soft and fuzzy to be appropriate. Tapestry requires a lot of hand manipulation, and the yarn needs to be firm in order to withstand the handling. Also, she chose to use jute for the warp. Like other weavers of the era, she discovered that jute did not wear well, either. The completed tapestries were displayed in 1960 and subsequently sold. Within a few years, she had to repair them for the owner because the jute began to disintegrate. Nevertheless, the experience of weaving the tapestries was invaluable for improving her skill. After further problems with color fastness, she discovered good sources for reliable yarn and subsequently became meticulous about the quality of yarn she used.

She wove one other piece that Shelly designed, *Genesis*, 81" x 84", completing it in 1965. By then Nezhnie wanted to move on to pursue her own ideas. Explaining that it felt like she was being an apprentice to herself, she resolved to only weave her own designs from then on.

Burning Bush, *39" x 30", 1961*

Nezhnie did several medium-sized tapestries of three to five feet long in the early 1960s. Several were religious in nature, even though not commissioned. However, at least two of these religious tapestries were later fabricated in hooked pile for commissions. The earliest, *Burning Bush*, is an irregular "spade-shaped" bush of rusty orange. Its design was inspired by the cross section of a tomato. Within the bush, distorted "V" shapes suggest flames. The "Vs" are staggered around the trunk that spreads out at the base, forming roots as wide as the upper bush. Under the roots the ground is white. The intersection of the ground with the roots suggests Hebrew characters that say "and the bush was not consumed." The bush is enclosed in a series of very irregular outlines in a variety of colors. The free-form movement of the colorful bands creates a lively interpretation of the bush engulfed in flame. An especially effective dusty rose section expands broadly against the dark tones on one side of the bush and becomes only a narrow line on the other side.

The strong sense of composition that she brought from her years at The Cooper Union and her highly developed facility with color are evident in this early weaving.

Burning Bush
Woven version
39" x 30", 1961
Color plate 2b

Despite the sophistication of its design, however, the quality of weaving marks *Burning Bush* as an early work. About two inches from the start and finish of the tapestry, which was woven on its side, a half-inch segment of warp is exposed. One of the first challenges for any weaver is to keep the edges of the work an even width from start to finish. Leaving sections without any weft packed into them magnified the difficulty. The portions extending beyond the exposed warp might have been intended to fold behind the image as hem. Yet, since the piece is photographed showing the end sections, it is more likely that it served as an experiment to reveal how tapestry differs from painting. Exposing warp threads in designated sections emphasized the structure of how the woven image was created and thus was a place to begin implementing a key element of her artistic approach.

Burning Bush is one of the few of Nezhnie's tapestries that did not survive into the 21st century. Given as a wedding gift to Shelly's stepsister, it was the victim of moths, yet another incentive for Muriel to use high-quality yarns thereafter.

Preparing the warp for weaving, especially threading it onto the loom, was not an intuitive process for Muriel. Until she started working with apprentices, she needed Shelly's help. When they were setting up the German loom, she decided to alternate the colors of the warp to make it easier to keep track of the threading. In the process she observed that if "warm" and "cool" colors were alternated, she could affect the tonality of an area simply by letting portions of the warp show through.

The potential for greater variety of blending colors through warp effects led her to explore pattern weaves. The structure of "tapestry" weave is dense and even. Each row of weft yarn covers alternate warp threads. The next row covers the remaining half. By packing the second row down tightly, it fills in the spaces not covered by the first row, and a solid line of weft yarn is in place. The firm packing allows the piece to hang smoothly and keeps the rows of yarn in place so they will not shift or sag with time. The process is technically called "weft-faced plain weave." If the second row is not packed down, leaving as much of the warp showing as weft, the result is called "tabby." Weaves that do not follow the rule of covering only one alternating warp at a time fit into the category of "pattern" weaves.

A weaver who chooses to make tapestries is basically one who chooses to create a fabric that hides the warp and shows a uniformly textured, plain weave cloth. The excitement of the fabric is in the "picture" that is revealed by changing colors of weft yarn. Nezhnie made this decision but wanted more, too. She wanted nuance, to have the structure but with a bit of varied texture as well.

Any time the basic weft-faced process is altered, the density of the fabric is affected. Other types of weaves that have floats or warp exposed can result in a less stable material. Therefore, Nezhnie's challenge was to discover just how much she could deviate from the traditional structure and maintain an attractive appearance.

In 1964 she received a Louis Comfort Tiffany Grant for investigation of pattern weave in tapestry. Part of the money was used to purchase a massive, multi-harness Leclerc loom. It had sixteen harnesses that raised heddles with eyes through which the warp was threaded. The loom was set up in the fall of 1965. Just getting the cumbersome equipment to work was a time-consuming task. Also, it was immediately obvious that the mechanics of warping a complicated loom and the technicalities of the weave structures were not her forte. Nezhnie was dyslexic, and while using two colors might help the procedure, warping her loom would always be a struggle.

It is ironic that while she was intellectually drawn to complex permutations of an idea, some of the simplest procedures, like warping the loom, were hard for her to accomplish. Fortunately, she was able to find many ways of incorporating patterns that did not require special threading procedures or overly complicated weave structures. Throughout her career she relied on exposing warp to create surface interest, while effectively maintaining structural integrity.

One of the very last weavings she did, *Pogrom*, has subtle random horizontal orange stripes created by simply using the same "shed," or opening of the warp, twice or three times before going back to alternating sheds. The two or three rows of yarn would cover the same warps, leaving the uncovered orange warps to float over the weft yarn. Another distinctive trademark was that she enjoyed adding raised lines formed by looping the weft yarn around the warp in soumak technique. Most often, the ridges would be the same color as the shape, and frequently their placement appears to be random.

Foursome, *26" x 26", 1967*

There are two tapestries woven during the early days of learning about weave structures that contain elaborate patterns. Actually, it is believed that *Foursome* was not woven on the large multi-harness loom, but rather on a small floor loom that was already warped in a pattern when Nezhnie bought it secondhand. Three of the four implied faces of *Foursome* are woven in patterns. Each shape has an eye. The two outer profiles are part of the background pattern of black and creamy white. The pattern has bold white horizontal zigzags. The two central shapes share a mouth. The left side is black, and the right side, whose profile is highlighted in textured gray yarn, consists of a "pick and pick"[7] stripe pattern of rust and white.

Two versions of the tapestry were photographed. The first has a blue face instead of a black one. Nezhnie was not happy with the blue image and applied black India ink to the surface. Inspection of the back of the tapestry reveals the original blue color. The stained color has remained for at least thirty-five years with no apparent running or sloughing.

Highlighting the central profile with a slightly tapering line creates the focal point of the composition. The striped image has a mask-like quality because the line of the profile curves downward at the top instead of up as in the more natural skull contour. The dark side has a very round skull shape to it.

Foursome
26" x 26", 1967

Technically, the tapestry is successful in integrating pattern weaves with plain weave, and the concept of the mask is intriguing. *Foursome* holds its own in a room dominated by a large, graphic Alexander Calder tapestry. Though photographed hanging on a rod, it is displayed suspended from three points, presumably nails through holes in the binding tape attached to the back of the weaving. The resultant drape enhances the balance and liveliness of the bold image. In addition, short golden fringe drapes down at the sides, further defining the piece as textile. The tapestry is pictured in several exhibition catalogs and in the book *Creative Handweaving*, by Xenia Ley Parker.

In an era when abstraction dominated the art world, Muriel found a reference point in Picasso. Cubism formed a direct link between abstraction and portraiture. More important, the stylized face she adopted, consisting of a central profile line flanked by forward-looking eyes, served her needs well. Whatever imagery she chose needed to be simple, and the lack of shadow or detail in the stylized, two-color face provided large surfaces for patterns.

The problem in using pattern weaves in tapestry is that the warps at the edge of a shape may not retain the alternating appearance characteristic of weft-faced structure. Unwanted floats may occur, giving the impression of a mistake, as a slipped stitch in knitting might. Controlling yarn floats and defining the edges of shapes became her major technical challenge.

---

7 Pick and pick is a technique for creating vertical stripes. One color yarn is used for the first of the alternating sheds, and a second color is used exclusively for the other. When the second thread is packed down, its color is the opposite of that in the first shed, creating a single row of alternating colors. By repeating the two-color sequence, vertical stripes are formed.

Venus

57" x 24", 1967

Color plate 2e

Venus, *57" x 24", 1967*

Venus is a tapestry well designed to provide a few large areas in which to establish patterns while creating a fascinating image. Because the tapestry is woven on its side, most of the blocks of color and pattern sections could be woven easily without much shaping involved. The undulating patterns of the cape add to the dramatic presentation of a female encased in colorful attire. The beautiful combination of golden yellows, forming the folds of her garment set against the deep green of the arms, is an excellent example of Muriel's highly developed color sense. The rich red fringe, knotted on the side edges, emphasizes the erratic quality of the headdress plumes and the patterning of the cape. The background serves to anchor the figure, giving ground to the unadorned bare feet. Besides being successful as an experiment, Venus is an exotic and mystical image.

While the commission work she did at the time was formally designed and intricately woven, much of her personal work was in keeping with the more experimental trends emerging in the late 1960s. They are free-form, or non-rectilinear. Several pieces incorporate bulky yarns and are embellished with beads, melagros, shells, or buttons. Almost all of the non-commissioned work deals with the human form. The figures are abstract and exist alone without background. Most of them have cubist faces and fringe as elemental parts in the design. Although they look quite spontaneous, she used cartoons to indicate where the shaping should occur. She did not necessarily paint in the details on the cartoon.

Nezhnie created at least sixteen free-form figures in the 1960s. There are two major series in terms of shape and general character. She called one group "the little people." The majority of this group adheres to the rectangle except that the head and upper body have shape. The faces frequently have interlocking profiles, a style that appealed to Muriel. In the Castro interview she commented on the resulting ambiguity of whether images were of one or two faces:

> I did make one which I called "Embrace." Because it split so; it was clearly two. I simply love that in Picasso, Braque, and some of Matisse's things where the heads seem to turn and be pulled apart. (Castro, 12)

Some examples appear primitive, woven of loosely spun or textured yarns with blockish shapes. Others have more contours, especially with rounded heads and sloping shoulders, and are more tightly woven. Most are woven on their side. The main shaping occurs to one edge, forming the head and shoulders when the tapestry is rotated to its proper orientation. In general, fringe is either applied later or is an extension of the weft yarn. This is achieved by removing a few of the outer warp threads, leaving the weft yarn to form loops that are often left uncut. The tapestries are small, generally less than two feet in length.

Embrace
21" x 10", 1966

Large Embrace, *41" x 29", 1968*

Large Embrace is a good example of the little people and of incorporating the warm and cool interaction of colors. It depicts two opposing figures in profile. The female is woven predominantly in warm oranges, golds, and creamy white, while the male is in blues and greens. They form two distinct sides to the composition. The faces are set within a circle. Their profiles are outlined sharply in black against a magenta area between them. Both faces are framed in hoods that extend out to form points, not contained within the rectangle. Because the soft orange and the pale green-blue are similar in value, the hoods balance to form a hexagonal frame around the circle of the faces. The bodies extend out at an angle from the frame, creating the backs of the two figures. The bipolar nature of the composition is unified by a collar of magenta and lavender triangles that defines the base of the hood/frame. Also, a row of diamonds made up of warp floats extends across the two bodies. The top floats of the diamonds are green warp, and the lower ones are magenta. There is a second layer to this lower portion only slightly visible through the floating warp. The tapestry is very colorful and cheerful.

Tension is created by the strong outline of the profiles with the noses almost touching. Subtle distinctions in the hairstyles define the gender. Despite the simplicity of the faces, they are very effective. The lavender-blue male has a surprisingly expressive, "pouty" chin. The two figures look amusingly combative, despite the title suggesting they are in an embrace.

Because the principal at the high school where the tapestry hangs

Large Embrace
41" x 29", 1968
Color plate 2a

thought it looked so dated and crude, *Large Embrace* was almost thrown in the trash during the 1990s. A staff member rescued it, and now it is proudly displayed on the walls again. Teachers and other staff members seem to like its associations to a time when funky fiber was in vogue. One secretary was excited to show how the lower section was made up of layers, sometimes revealed, but mostly hidden.

Ilisha remembers her mother associating this tapestry with the movie "2001: A Space Odyessy," which was released in the same year the tapestry was woven. In particular, the reference was to the scene in which the two astronauts entered a pod to have privacy and talked at very close range. Most likely, Muriel was weaving the image at the time she saw the movie. The title certainly makes no reference to the movie.

The other group of tapestries created late in the 1960s focuses on discarding the rectangle completely. Most are curved female figures in which much of the body is implied with fringe. Many of these figures extend seven feet or more in height, including the fringe. They exist in space without background.

At least six figures were woven with the arms and body forming a circle. The head is also shaped, often in a bell curve. Although the eccentric shape of the weaving is not closely representative of a female figure, the curved upper body with a lower body of wispy textural fringe gives the impression that the figure is in costume, a symbolic figure on a float or in a parade. The imagery of this series relies more on the placement of color rather than texture or pattern, though many of the pieces are textural as well. The faces are occasionally Cubist in nature; others have long, stylized heads facing forward with pointed chins and elaborate eye treatments.

Loreli, *58" x 47", 1969*

Loreli is an interesting composition, typical of at least four of this group of figures. It has a strong bilateral balance without being strictly symmetrical. The balance is accomplished by repeating the general layout of color segments on either side of center, while allowing the specific shifts within each section of analogous colors to flow spontaneously. Most striking are the tapered

bands that enclose the face and extend down the figure. Each band has a light, off-white undulating line
edging shapes of gold and green. The effect is that of
a gracefully draped scarf or veil. The arms are
formed of similar bands, in soft magentas with a
reversed taper that is wider at the top, creating
broad shoulders ending in a short looped fringe
that is surprisingly suggestive of fingers. Other segments are lavender and eggplant, creating a colorful
lady indeed. The curved golden extensions of the
arms, the opulent collar, and the use of shells as eyes
and adornment contribute to a sense of pageantry
similar to that of *Venus*.

Loreli
58" x 47", 1969
Color plate 3g

Gypsy Moth, *90" x 40", 1969*

Gypsy Moth is similar in overall shape, but not in
theme. The concept for the large tapestry is reminiscent of the two "little people," *Mother I* and
Mother II, depicting a mother with fetus. The hands
are clasped below it. The composition is an excellent example of how Nezhnie used contrasting colors
to create a strong statement. Instead of the arms extending downward, they
are formed of alternating curved bands of red and black that surround the
fetus, which is also shaped of curving bands within the womb.

Two versions were woven and photographed. In the first, the womb
background color is red and the cubist face is gold and black. In the final
version, the red was ripped out and gold substituted as the fetus color with
a purple womb. The hair and lower body are also alternating colors of gold
and two shades of purple with the face half black, half red. Fringe drapes
down over the expanded circular arms. The tapestry seems to present a living
spiral, an archetypical shape fitting an image of fertility. It is a very graphic
composition; not primitive, as some of the "little people" appear, but primal.
The principles learned through her training in graphics proved to be very
appropriate for tapestry. The ability to convey an object within a very limited
color palette, in this case two alternating colors that form the details within
a section, seems equally desirable for both disciplines.

All the shaped figures were woven on the loom and curved supports
added later. Often, the yarn used to join the tapestry to the frame is used as
fringe. Shelly was responsible for devising these armatures. Many of the little

Gypsy Moth
21" x 14", 1966
Color plate 3f

people had very elaborate, though unseen, armatures suspended from small wire spiral hangers that swiveled above jointed, arched supports. They became less artistic as the weight requirements for the larger, circular bodied tapestries demanded heavier wire structures. Though generally not very noticeable from the front, the supports look quite professional if the backside is examined. A decade later, weavers were using hoops as the structure or loom on which to weave circular pieces, but Nezhnie did not explore this option.

Odyssey, *60" x 60", 1967*

Two of the most successful tapestries woven in 1967 did not fit either of the styles discussed above. Both were commissions for private individuals who left the decisions of style and subject matter to Nezhnie. *Odyssey* is typical of the style she was using for commission work at the time. It consists of images grouped loosely into segments within the whole composition. Impeccably crafted, it is one of the most literal interpretations of subject matter she created in the first half of her career.

The tapestry is vividly bold in color and displays Nezhnie's exceptional skill in balancing light and dark areas within the complexity of multiple images. It depicts a tightly composed juxtaposition of classical Greek figures. A procession is suggested through six linear segments. Each section has an obvious break, and no figure appears in its entirety.

Yet there is continuity, such as a curving line in one segment that connects to another line in the adjacent section, creating a transition that moves the viewer's eye from left to right across the tapestry.

The first figure is following the tail and hindquarter of a black horse. He has an olive branch in his hand, and his garment is woven in a pattern weave of lavender and white. The second segment is a female with tendrils of curling hair, wearing a generously draped garment. She is demurely looking down, as if trying to hide behind the next section — a fluted column with blue shadows. A soldier approaches from the opposite direction with a long stride. He holds a sword and shield with a snake on it and is wearing a helmet that totally conceals his face. The fifth segment portrays a proud female figure with head held high. She is dressed in a pleated toga and has an elaborate crown of leaves. The last segment is a pair of horses with just their heads and front legs showing. The black horse appears to be the same horse as is pictured in the first section, appropriately in scale. All the figures and horses are in profile with only the soldier and the snake on his shield facing left.

It is reasonable to assume from the title that Nezhnie was using the actual tale of Odysseus as her reference point. Also of interest, her loom was named "Penelope." The soldier is facing in the opposite direction from all other figures, suggesting he is returning and thus, is the older Odysseus. Within the tapestry, the two versions of both Odysseus and Penelope are depicted. It becomes a procession not only through space,

Odyssey
60" x 60", 1967
Color plate 2d

but time as well. The extended tribulations of the couple are resolved in the last section with the team of horses in step. The white steed is most prominent, suggesting the triumph of virtue in Penelope. According to Deann Ruben, the loom was named Penelope in homage to the slow rate of progress achieved in weaving a tapestry. Nezhnie might have chosen this narrative to affirm her underlying belief that tapestry was the right choice of medium for her, a virtuous choice.

The tapestry is beautiful. The details of the olive branches, the flow of the horse's tail, and the drape of the fabrics are all well executed. It also incorporates two areas of pattern quite effectively. Despite the fact that the piece consists of a wide range of vivid colors, there is a clarity achieved because the number of colors used in any one segment is limited to no more than five, including black and white. A lively orange and a deep terra cotta serve as the primary background colors, reminiscent of Greek pottery. The inclusion of white and black elements in all sections further suggests that tradition. The white line of the snake turns into a stem of a branch on the toga, which points to a white line descending to the horse's knee. Perhaps the exceptional vitality of the tapestry can be attributed to Nezhnie's interest in things Greek, stimulated by the close association between the Helfmans and Greek friends.

It is almost as if Muriel decided to prove her exceptional skill both in creating an intriguing design and in weaving a beautiful traditional piece so that she could then move on to her own exploration and wandering through the unknown.

Odyssey '67, *48" x 96", 1967*

Indeed, she wove another tapestry in the same year with a surprisingly similar title, *Odyssey '67.* In this piece the juxtaposition of images and shapes is quite asymmetrical and abstract. The clients were friends of the Helfmans, and their interest in abstract art was well known to Muriel.

Her palette is limited to essentially four hues: red, blue, black, and white. In general, the tapestry appears to be very bold and vivid. It is only when viewed at fairly close range that subtle details emerge, such as the shift from periwinkle blue to powdery gray-blue or from black lines to deep egg-plant-colored ones. Areas of blue are interspersed with lavender or reveal a hint of orange warp that complements the tones achieved in another place by delicate red stripes on a blue ground. Many sections are woven in twill patterns or soumak to form raised areas, with at least one face being formed by switching from plain weave to twill to form a white-on-white textural image. Most of the white sections are concentrated at the center of the composition. The viewer's eye moves to the striking confluence of white, rather than linearly from side to side. The treatment of white is especially responsible for the boldness of the tapestry.

There are seven profiles or three-quarter profiles in the composition. Many of the faces seem submerged within a geometric shape. Others are set off in sharp contrast to the background. The profile lines and eyes, whether subtle or contrasting, are the only features to define the faces.

An abrupt shift in color occurs just right of the vertical center of the tapestry where an edge of white angles slightly from top to bottom, dramatically dividing the tapestry in half. The bright white background emphasizes a vivid red profile facing the division.

In *Odyssey '67,* line becomes much more of a design element in itself rather than being used to create dimension or to establish transitions as in the first *Odyssey.* Vertical or slightly tilted clusters of parallel lines form shapes throughout the composition. The inspiration for these striped shapes came from a design of Shelly's in which he produced very interesting optical effects strictly through combining striped triangles.

This second *Odyssey* version presents a far less linear picture than the first one. Two of the faces are relatively the same size, decidedly larger than the rest. They are on the same plane somewhat above the others. They face in the same direction, left, but are separated by the vertical white division. One is the strong red female whose profile, especially the curve of the neck and chin, is reminiscent of a figurehead at the bow of a ship. The other is a soft blue profile separated from its more muted blue background only by a thin red line. It is positioned ahead of the female. It appears more masculine and, with its jutting chin, is very similar to the male profile of *Large Embrace*.

The remaining five faces are of varying sizes. They are placed at seemingly random heights, though clustered primarily near the center. Only one profile looks to the right. It has a diminishing white triangle extending in front of it towards the right edge of the tapestry where it is cut off before actually coming to a point. This face is positioned directly behind the strong red female figure. It extends from her eye down to the level of her neck. Also red, it is separated from the larger silhouette by patterns of white stripes. It has a pale blue eye, which is far more prominent than that of the large female. Actually, the large female's eye appears to be closed or looking down. Another face, a submerged three-quarter profile, also directed slightly towards the right, is positioned at collar level on the large red figure. This face is black with a red profile line and wide-open eyes looking out almost towards the viewer.

The meaning of the cone of light extending out from the face behind the large red female is open to interpretation. What are the fantasies alluded to as the face looks off in its counter direction? Does the cone represent a spotlight illuminating a hidden self? One of Nezhnie's greatest frustrations was the lack of recognition she received. She was intensely ambitious, and thus it seems plausible that she is expressing this sentiment. In any case, it does suggest a part of her has thoughts that yearn in another direction than the general consensus of the other figures.

A plausible interpretation of *Odyssey '67* is that Nezhnie reveals an innocent

Odyssey '67

48" x 96", 1967

Color plate 3c

expression of her desire to shed the virtuous woman role and be in the spotlight. It is revealed, but there is also resolution with her other aspirations to be a good wife and mother. The opposing directions of focus, suggested by the white cone pointing to the right, are balanced by the overall shape that the other white sections take across the tapestry. The white area that forms the background for the prominent female arches from the lower portion along the neck and chin across the dividing line and towards the left edge of the tapestry. Visually it brings with it a section of white stripes from the chest of the red female, connecting her to the activity on the other side of the line. The white shapes end in a point well before the left edge of the weaving. The white-on-white face of this section is tilted up, proud, leading the procession as did the white horse in the last segment of the earlier *Odyssey*. The tapestry appears to encompass both goals that Nezhnie wants to keep in balance.

The use of parallel lines as a key design element defines *Odyssey '67* as a transitional piece aligned with work woven later in the 1970s. Nezhnie had stated in the Castro interview that she was greatly influenced by Picasso. In addition to the obvious reference to his cubist style, there is a similarity to his use of stripes as a prominent design element. *Odyssey '67* and *Gypsy Moth* are the best evidence within the early work of the influence that Picasso had on Muriel. Although he used stripes dramatically throughout his career, the portraits from the late 1930s, such as *Seated Woman (Marie-Therese)*, dated January 9, 1937, are full of line patterns that might have informed Nezhnie's artistic vocabulary. *Dora Mar Seated* has a background formed exclusively of parallel lines. A third example from that same year, *Weeping Woman*, has hair formed of bands of alternating light and dark stripes very similar in style to some of Nezhnie's self-portraits woven later in the 1970s. There have been many tapestry artists who have translated portraits through line, but by incorporating the expressively fluid style of a master, Muriel became very effective in using banding and parallel lines in a distinctive way.

Other developments were emerging to shape her visual vocabulary, namely an interest in photography as a source for subject matter, and the major escalation in opportunities to do commissions.

In 1967 Muriel completed a large 11' x 7' commissioned tapestry, *Genesis*, and another one in 1968 as the 12' x 6' ark curtain, *Tablets of the Law*. Both received awards from the Guild for Religious Architecture, AIA, and set in motion a demand for her work.

Commissions
for Public Buildings

In a press release written by Nezhnie in the early 1970s she explains the special advantage of commission work:

> Tapestry should be "public art," art which is available to many. Tapestry should not only be conspicuous but functional and related to its surroundings. In designing a public piece, she always attempts to create something which is cognizant of its environment. Color, texture and form are all part of the design. They develop together within the framework of the architectural structure in which the piece will hang.

Her understanding of the balance between tapestry and its environment mirrors the sentiment of Jean Lurçat, the French designer considered most responsible for the revival of modern tapestry. Nezhnie owned a copy of his unorthodox book, *Jean Lurçat: Designing Tapestry*, in which most of the book is a discourse between THE AUTHOR and THE READER. Lurçat felt that tapestry did not really come alive until it was in contact with its setting and defends the positive benefits derived from external requirements by saying:

> It will draw from this apparent restraint on its liberty the particular advantage of having to decide which, out of the world of natural forms, shall be introduced into the building, and carried into its sphere. It will qualify then, and humanise in the final instance, the place and the abstract space which is given to it.[8]

An accurate account of how many of Nezhnie's works were actually commissioned is difficult to determine from her production records because only the collector's name is listed, not the manner in which it was obtained. However, the evidence shows that Nezhnie designed at least sixty-five pieces as commissions. Even though the above statement explains why she thought

---

8 Jean Lurcat, *Designing Tapestry*, (Rockliff, 1950), 4.

commission work was a worthy endeavor for an artist, it does not address the reasons why she sought out so many commissions and was so successful at working with clients.

Nezhnie was stimulated by the mental demands of solving problems and found interacting with people equally rewarding. She had exceptional communication skills and could encourage others to talk, whether it was opening up about their own interests or the dynamics of the project. Establishing and maintaining a good relationship with her clients was not only important to her professionally, but the kind of challenge she truly enjoyed. Commission work gave her the opportunity to interact with many people in a variety of ways, meeting many more needs than simply financial gain. The following comments by Jon Fields, current president of Edward Fields, Inc., indicate how skilled she was in business interactions.

> I remember her with warm feelings, because she was a truly dedi-
> cated, talented, and loving person. The many projects we produced
> with her were extremely successful and were developed with ease
> and excitement due to her resolute and considerate leadership. She
> was the ultimate professional, and her projects led to mutual learn-
> ing and fulfillment.

She produced forty-five commissions for institutions. Of those, thirty-three were for Jewish edifices, five for Christian ones, and nine for secular buildings. Only two of these commissions were for commercial establishments.

The preponderance of religious commissions could be interpreted as resulting purely from a domino effect; that once she gained a reputation with award winning designs, other religious institutions sought her work. Yet, as mentioned previously, several of her early tapestries had religious themes even though they were not commissioned for a particular client. Perhaps Shelly's early interest in theology stimulated her to explore Biblical topics. No doubt she had many hours to contemplate how she would express her own ideas as she wove the tapestries he had designed.

There are a variety of factors influencing her bias towards projects of a religious nature. In doing commission work, Nezhnie knew that she would have to balance the needs of the client with her own interests. Nevertheless, she intended to control as many of the aesthetic decisions as possible. She felt the majority of clients she encountered for commercial building commissions had too restrictive an approach to what the subject matter could be. Whether the perception was accurate or not, it caused her to reject many commercial opportunities. Religious groups seemed less set on what they wanted. The use of contemporary fiber art in temples and churches was a new concept. It was stimulated by the emerging trend in architecture to create large structures of concrete or brick that were essentially stark and without decoration. The congregations saw the need for something to humanize the austerity, yet most of these clients had no idea what such art should look like. They might suggest a broad theme, but they gave Nezhnie control of the design.

However, the primary factor influencing her bias was probably that religious art was well suited to her particular strengths and her interest in content. She always wanted the content of her work to be central to its purpose and she liked the meaningfulness of the message in religious art. Nezhnie also thought it was important to provide a design statement with each commission for the congregation or patrons to read. She wanted to share her interpretation of the scriptures and to provide a basis for contemplation. Religious art was also a way to incorporate her graphic prowess without being more commercial than she wanted to be. Text is a characteristic of almost all of her religious designs.

Her first commission, *Vesperal,* was created in 1962 for a Catholic shrine. It was a fish, appliquéd rather than woven, curved in the shape of the altar. A band of text extended across the body of the fish.

Genesis, *132" x 84", 1967*

For her first major commission, Nezhnie designed a version of *Genesis* rich in imagery, containing no text. The award-winning tapestry was designed for a small chapel, a new addition to the Plymouth First Congregational Church in Lincoln, Nebraska. The chapel walls were dark brick, interrupted only by an organ screen and lectern. There were no windows, only an amber clerestory near the white marble altar placed on a dark slate platform. In Muriel's words:

> The utter simplicity of the chapel demanded a radiant and absorbing imagery. . . . Its configuration was to be multiple and fragmented, with all of its diversity held together by a large central white cross that was barely perceptible upon first viewing. All the Days of Creation unfolded simultaneously around and within this central cross. The abruptly changing images range from water, crystalline rock, contorted strata of the earth, then to stars, the sun, the moon, a cherubic device suggesting divine presence, a microscopic view of the fertilization of wheat, sea life, insect life, blossoms, fruit, and the tracks of many animals leading finally to the hand and footprints of man, alluding to evolution. In this kaleidoscopic way I tried to express the spontaneous spirit of creation rather than a Biblical sequence. (Statement for award, October 22, 1969)

The project was of major scope to say the least. The tapestry hangs behind the altar, eleven feet high by seven feet wide. Woven primarily in weft-

Genesis
132" x 84", 1967
Color plate 1b

faced plain weave, it has a few areas of exposed warp, soumak, and knotted pile. At first she planned to use dark colors with a small brilliant burst of light, but she decided the chapel needed a luminous impact. She chose a middle-value palette and, in order to spread the light and create a dappled effect, included high-contrast black and white details in most sections, as well as the white ground of the cross.

The tapestry was woven in three panels joined horizontally, the height of the tallest panel being dictated by the width of her loom. The upper part of the cross, which is the central segment of the top panel, is predominantly white with zigzags of red and blue and squiggles of browns in an abstract pattern. The middle panel contains the horizontal beam of the cross, which is almost as long as it is wide. This thick horizontal beam makes an unconventional cross but a commanding composition. Its white background extends across most of the panel, flanked by narrow secondary sections with blue backgrounds. The focal point of the cross is the "cherubic device." It is formed of a stylized layering of wing pairs placed in a vertical, overlapping arrangement. The top pair of wings is inverted, with the lower two pairs pointing downward. It is an attractive and innovative symbol that unites the divergent imagery surrounding it. The bottom panel is slightly less than half the length of the tapestry. It is divided into five sections. The predominantly white middle section, depicting a crystalline rock pattern, forms the lower portion of the cross. Although the imagery of each segment in the tapestry is unique, the same color background is used in the two outermost sections of each panel, unifying the overall design. Each panel has one segment containing foot and hand prints whose intriguing patterns surely provide interesting stimuli for the congregation's contemplation. This first major commission that Nezhnie designed is lively, beautifully woven, and deserving of the Merit Award from the Guild for Religious Architecture.

Throughout the ages, religious communities have debated about how to depict their theology visually. Central to the dilemma was the degree to which a deity should be represented in humanistic form. Each religion resolved the question differently. In some Eastern religions, such as Hinduism, the visual depiction of deities has been central to the expression of worship. The

Islamic faith avoids representation by relying strictly on the art of calligraphy and decorative geometric patterns. Most Christian denominations have accepted figurative imagery, even though their specific conventions shift through time between literal and liberal interpretations of what the doctrines will allow. The Catholic Church has traditionally supported the most elaborate use of visual arts, while some of the Protestant sects are very conservative in the use of visual imagery.

In the Jewish faith, the issue of what role art should play and to what degree spiritual concepts should be represented visually has been debated rigorously for centuries. Consensus has traditionally defined text as the primary tool of communication, upholding the second commandment not to make any "graven images" of their God. It has been an essential element of Judaism from earliest times, and uprisings have been started over the issue, so important is it to the faith. Geometric or abstract decorations are generally accepted as the proper form of ornamentation to accompany written symbols. Thus, it has been the tendency to avoid pictorial imagery, even in a more general way, as the central statement of a work of art for a Jewish place of worship.

Of the thirty-three commissions Nezhnie wove or designed for Hebrew institutions, the majority were ark curtains and interiors. Occasionally she was commissioned to create Torah mantles only, rather than the whole ark presentation. Nezhnie was cognizant of the traditions and comfortable designing within the general parameters.

Tablets of the Law
Hooked version
84" x 60", 1976

Tablets of the Law, *144" x 66", 1968*

Nezhnie's other award-winning design, *Tablets of the Law*, was actually never woven. Later, however, it was converted into a limited edition of hooked ark curtains offered in a variety of colorways. Nezhnie decided, apparently after the concept had been submitted for the contest, that the original design was not appropriate for the setting in which it would go. The design was of two adjacent tablets, the Decalogue, rounded at the top and bottom with the commandments written in Hebrew on them. Both the background and tablets were of horizontal stripes. The transitions in the background move from dark at the top to lighter colors at the bottom, with the tablets reversing the gradation. Where the lettering occurred, one stripe color was used to form a larger block between the characters, disrupting the pattern of stripes. These blocks created interesting and unexpected color accents. The script was a solid color, generally beige or

Tablets of the Law
Tapestry version
144" x 66", 1968

gold, and a lighter value than the colors of the stripes. The design was a very traditional interpretation of the role of text and decorative elements.

The tapestry that was woven for the synagogue was a much-simplified version of this design. The ark had elaborate metal decoration on the wooden outer doors, with metal lettering above it. The scale was wrong for the original design. Nezhnie eliminated the tablets and used a more analogous color combination. The background was formed of predominantly purple asymmetrical triangles and quadrangles. The symbols were modified, using one of the first ten characters in the Hebrew alphabet for each of the commandments. In the early days, before the Roman numeral system was adopted, these first ten letters of the Hebrew alphabet had been used to delineate the commandments. It was an excellent adaptation of the original concept and a good decision on Nezhnie's part to abandon the earlier version for the specific project. The second design complemented the bold metalwork nicely.

As she became busier, she modified several tapestry designs or created new compositions specifically for rug-hooking techniques. Having her designs fabricated commercially was a way that she could offer a less expensive option to clients. She worked with one company most of the time, Edward Fields, Inc. Using a commercial fabricator also proved to be an effective opportunity for her to refine good designs even further. In the process of reworking the cartoon for the fabricated version of *Burning Bush*, mentioned earlier, she was able to clarify the interaction between the Hebrew text and the roots to convey more obviously the idea that the roots formed the letters. The adjustment turned a good idea into a refreshingly innovative image.

Imprints, *84" x 192" each, 1970-1971*

Imprints, woven for the University City (Missouri) Public Library, was the most ambitious of the nine commissions Nezhnie designed for secular buildings. It took fifteen months to design and complete at a time when she had another significant job in progress. She was able to accomplish an impressive number of commissions during the early part of the decade, proving her exceptional organizational skills and ability to shift focus from one project to another quickly.

Besides being monumental in scale, entailing 213 square feet of weaving, the two *Imprints* tapestries presented probably her most challenging design issues of any commission. The architect had wanted banners to drape below a long clerestory in the central area near a cantilevered stairway. The director of the library wanted a large metal sculpture in the open area. The architect left it to Muriel to come up with a compromise that would appease the director and still be fibrous and free-floating. Upon studying the space, Muriel felt that the area needed something to emphasize the curved movement of the stairs and their beautiful wooden banisters. She asked the architect if he could run a track around the clerestory from which to suspend curved tapestries. She envisioned two units, one higher than the other, to take advantage of viewing the artwork from several levels and angles in the library. The team worked with a tent maker to devise the best way to suspend curved metal support bars for the tapestries. Though a model had been made, once the final tapestries were installed, the two units did not hang at the predicted angles and moved to the center. Nevertheless, the presentation is very effective.

The most difficult parameter she had to work with was that the tapestries would be viewed from both sides. All the weaving she had previously done had the yarn tails exposed on the backside of the tapestry, as is the traditional European method of dealing with yarn ends resulting from frequent color

Imprints
84" x 192" each,
1970-1971

changes. She had no idea how she would solve the problem of hiding the loose ends but told the architect that would be no problem. She figured if the Navahos had found a way, so could she. It turned out to be a simple matter to solve. The yarn could be spliced together while weaving or, especially in small areas, darned in afterwards, a process that would take no more time than her normal method of finishing by knotting all the loose ends.

Nezhnie explained her initial design considerations:

> My response to that space was that it had to be so simple - with two spots on it or so complex that it would stand alone, because that space is complex. You have activity on both levels, and light above and color everywhere. . . . Yes, I really felt it needed something pure — a single color with two — and I knew I couldn't do that. I would go crazy. It would take a year and a half to do two spots. I'd just go out of my mind. So I went the other direction. (*THE SEEN*, 3)

The imagery of *Imprints* makes reference to writing and printing. (See color plate 1c.) Each tapestry has five distinct panels eighty-four inches long of varying widths, sewn together to total sixteen feet. One panel contains a stencil-like "R" the length of the panel with a hand holding a pencil super-imposed on the curved part of the letter. The hand and pencil are formed of narrow horizontal stripes in differing series to provide the definition. The area behind the "R" is a bold block pattern. Next to that panel is a narrower strip with four types of calligraphy on a background of broad horizontal stripes of irregular widths. The top character is Arabic, followed by a Chinese one; an Egyptian hieroglyph is next with a dancing female figure, derived from a South African rock painting, as the lowest symbol. The complex juxtaposition of imagery continues throughout the ten panels comprising the thirty-two feet of tapestry. The hours spent in the calligraphy museum in Germany must have contributed many inspirations for the imagery that emerged in *Imprints*. As Nezhnie wrote for the dedication commentary:

> Letterforms from many ancient and contemporary cultures have been worked together to suggest the variety of marks that man has made to communicate ideas. References, ranging from prehistoric cave drawings to the dot screening process used in publishing photographs, are joined with the letterforms to link man's expressions through both pictures and words. The deliberately compounded design of *Imprints* is suggestive of the way the multiplicity of ideas and images within the mind leap from one to another, generating new associations. Many letterforms have been reversed or inverted to stress the equal importance of all surfaces and to favor no partic-ular side or viewpoint.

How can such complexity work visually and not appear too busy? There is an interesting sense of scale that relies on very large and bold letters to balance the sections. The letters are attractively shaped and carry the eye through the areas that can be seen from any vantage point. What is a bold shape on one tapestry may be repeated to a lesser degree in a panel of the other. A second unifying aspect is perhaps created by the similarity of background treatments of the sections. It gives the appearance that the many interesting objects float just in front of the varied but balanced backgrounds. It is as if each item seems suspended, a ploy that enables the viewer to become engaged in the whole, to process the large forms immediately and then look further at smaller details. Her deliberate inclusion of faces and figures also helps people identify with the art.

The tapestries would hold together in terms of composition in black and white, but it is through the sensitive choice of colors that they are masterfully united with the rest of the library. When viewing the area from the upper floor where a railing borders the large open stairway, the viewer can see the lower stacks and seating areas, as well as the tapestries. It becomes apparent that all the colors found in the library decor are reflected in the hangings. The same shades are not necessarily used, but Nezhnie gathers together a wide range of colors to create rich blends that relate to the surroundings. The strongest color elements in the furnishings are the Dresden blue upholstery fabric and two prevailing wood tones. The sides of the black metal shelves are a rich orange fruitwood, and the furniture and stair railings are an attractive lighter blond wood. Several walls are brick.

Nezhnie used thirteen weft colors: four blues, two oranges, two yellows, lavender, beige, cream, white and black. Using these colors in combination with six warp colors (brick, "orange sun," gold, lilac, "toffee," and "barley corn"), she could create a subtle range of colors that went together to form a cohesive whole. There is the predominance of blue balanced by warm ranges of orange from brick to gold and all the neutrals, including lavender, that is effectively used in many areas.

Imprints is also a culmination of her understanding of how to incorporate pattern weaves and warp effects. Several letters, such as a "g," have either wrapped or exposed warps filling in the circles. Four of the ten segments were woven in four harness patterns rather than plain weave. The brick-colored warp, the darkest or most intense warp color, effectively creates rich tonality when used in pattern with another color.

In looking at the commission decades after it was woven, it seems surprisingly ahead of its time, especially in its thematic emphasis on letters and symbols. By the late 1980s and early 1990s, several fiber artists started using text as the primary subject matter of a work of art. Tapestry weavers Linda Hutchins and Archie Brennan and basket maker John McQueen, to name only a few, dramatized the visual impact of letters. In architecture, there is the innovative New Library of Alexandria, Egypt, whose granite exterior is to be carved in script and symbol to comment on the role of the library as repository for knowledge. Its construction began in 1995.

At least one well-known tapestry weaver, Kathy Sporing, has credited Muriel's tapestry as being her original source of inspiration to become a tapestry artist.

> I still have a black and white brochure from the library with an image of the tapestry, which reminds me of the woven letters and shapes that so enthralled me then. I can honestly say that it has been the image of that first viewed Nezhnie tapestry that sent me in the direction I have gone . . . to finally find out how it was woven, and to be at a point in my own life where I feel like it is within my power to create the images I want to weave.

Jacob's Dream, St. Louis version, *216" x 96", 1971*

Not only did Nezhnie create several versions of one design, as in *Burning Bush*, but she used the same theme, including the title, for very different designs. The *Jacob's Dream* ark curtain created in 1971 for Temple Israel Congregation, St. Louis, Missouri, is the first of three versions of this theme. Each version is distinctive, although the ones for St. Louis and Farmington Hills, Michigan share a similar dominance of warm reds and oranges presented in a spectral progression from dark to light colors. At the time she sought the Michigan commission, slides of the design for St. Louis were submitted to the architect as evidence of the style of work she did and might have influenced the congregation's choice of theme. The third, or "Boston," version is hooked and shaped in the form of a triangle. It uses many of the same colors, but in quite a different configuration with greater emphasis on the cooler range of blues and greens.

The St. Louis variation is the focal point in a chapel of high-gloss cream-painted brick. It covers the eighteen-foot distance from floor to ceiling. The presentation is dramatic. The depth and richness of color in the dense wool surface rivets the viewer's attention. A rope ladder of creamy white linen holds the commanding tapestry in balance with the chapel's austere walls. Several narrow, floor-to-ceiling windows of luminous alabaster add to the tone of elegant simplicity.

The tapestry is woven in four panels of curved shapes building upon each other. There is no attempt to match shapes where the panels abut. A pattern of red dots on gray and mauve shapes outlined in deep red form a large border at the top and a smaller base, visually anchoring the tapestry to the gray carpet. Rich red undulating forms meander actively across the lower half and meet with the lighter progression of orange and pink just above center where the lighter colors form a more calm progression until they reach the upper spotted border. There are bands of blue outlining the color segments. Each blue band tends to be near in value to the color area it defines, getting lighter towards the top. The effect of suggesting ascension through the color shift is most effective in this version, with the blues reaching a light sky blue around pale pinks and peaches. The undulation and vibrant effect of contrasting colors establish the appearance of movement.

The nebulous shapes shift randomly into wings of lavender in the lower area and pink ones higher up the panels. The wings are gestural, some thickly arched, others stretching out. Their tips are accentuated in a lighter color. Above the ark, Hebrew characters proclaim a portion of Genesis 28:12 woven in vibrant teal on a salmon and gold background. The letters are curved and fluid, in keeping with the overall flowing shapes. Stars are scattered across the curtains, mostly in green, but with an occasional red one. The backdrop in the recessed ark area is woven in arching shades of blue and purple defined by green bands. Vivid green Hebrew characters adorn three Torah mantles of vibrant orange and pink outlined in blue. The two outer Torah covers are in blue and purple banded in green.

The fore curtain of creamy white linen cables spans the ark, forming the ladder in Jacob's dream. (See detail, page 18.) The twelve cables are mounted on a traverse rod and can be drawn to the sides of the curtain to symbolize the gate to Heaven when the ark is open. Each rope is twisted and knotted at intervals of about fifteen inches. The fine threads of linen are lustrous and complement the similar high-gloss color of the brick walls. The richly colored curtains flanked by the contrasting ladder makes for a commanding presentation for the dwelling of the Torahs.

The rope ladder is a very innovative use of the kind of sculptural fiber art in vogue at the time. However, for Shelly Helfman, who constructed the ropes, there was a traditional reference that directed how he made them. Hebrew prayer shawls have long, knotted fringes, called "zizis," at the four corners, and he based the ladder on this fringe knotting style. It was the custom for men to do the knotting.

Jacob's Dream,
St. Louis version
216" x 96", 1971
Color plate 1a

In all, there were over 150 square feet of tapestry in the St. Louis project. Since the early 1970s were extremely productive years for Muriel, she contracted with two local weavers to work on this project with her apprentice.

Jacob's Dream, Farmington Hills version, *256" x 120", 1973*

In the notes pertaining to the design of the ark curtain created for the Adas Shalom Synagogue[9] in Farmington Hills, Michigan, Nezhnie defines the aspects of Jacob's experience that indicate why the theme was of primary importance and worthy of being interpreted in three very different ways.

> Apprehension, fear of death and unnegotiable darkness in an unfamiliar place are sufficient ingredients for a fitful dream. Instead Jacob has a surprising revelation of promise and optimism. A ladder with angels ascending and descending and the voice of God reassuring Jacob that his desperate state is the preface of prosperity, fertility and abundant blessings. Jacob awakes, his fears subdued, surprised that in his disorientation he had stumbled on a place where God is to be found.
>
> The imagery for such an extraordinary experience must not simply illustrate the stage prop of the scene. The tapestry must radiate the awesomeness of divine presence and, to suit the narration, be monumental yet transient and kinetic. I have used color transitions in a spectral sequence to suggest the ambiance between heaven and earth, pure concentrations of color to evoke the supernatural quality of the vision, and symmetry to intimate the formality and order of the event. The shifting colors deny the wings and the ladder any specific color identity causing these images as in a mirage to have presence but not substance.

The ark curtain of the Farmington Hills version is monumental in scale. A series of thick cement beams span the sanctuary ceiling, directing attention to the imposing tapestry. Textural, grooved cement walls flank the ark with wooden walls extending the rest of the way across the raised portion of the sanctuary. The ladder is not external, but woven into the curtain. It straddles the two sections with narrow upright columns in a variety of vibrant pastel tones. The rungs are formed of bands of light grayish chevrons, zigzagging across the inner part between the columns, wavy as a mirage might appear.

---

9 The name of the synagogue, Adas Shalom, was changed to Adat Shalom. As the original architect for the construction of the building, Larry M. Rockind, AIA, explains: "When the congregation was formed, the popular form of Hebrew used was Ashkenazic, or that used by western European Jews. With the founding of the State of Israel, the Jewish people essentially shifted to Sephardic or eastern. The Hebrew letter for Adas and Adat are the same letter, but in Ivrit (Sephardic, Hebrew) the 'S' sound becomes a 'T' sound."

These chevrons are actually quite random in shape, varying in thickness and angle as they extend across the ladder. Though suggesting gray, they are at least two colors, one reflecting the specific color of the column nearby, the other a silver metallic thread. The colors and high intensity of the ladder serves to balance the massive cement surrounding the tapestry. The ladder also stands in strong color contrast to its background of rich warm tones of orange, purple, and some red. Each area between the rungs is formed of subtle vertical bands of horizontal stripes using three colors from the progression. The stripes are staggered differently in each band, and only one color is common to all the bands in that section. Another color of each band is several steps away in the spectrum.

The backdrop colors extend to either side of the ladder, but with only one stripe pattern for the entire shape rather than being divided into vertical bands. The shapes no longer zigzag as the rungs do, but curve down. They are outlined heavily in blue, shifting to green near the upper part of the curtain. These drooping shapes form wingtips surrounded primarily by triangles of black sky with occasional stars popping out brightly. While each wing shape is unique, the effect is rhythmic. The way the contrasting outline separates the striped shapes into curved feathers is very effective and novel.

There is a shallow section representing heaven above the ladder and wings. It consists of more narrower chevrons of various colors including gold, green, violet, orange, and silver meandering across the entire width of the curtain, thus appearing to engulf the ladder in its firmament. Near the base of the tapestry, at the lower rungs, the columns of the ladder become darker in tone as they rest on the earth. The lower four feet of the curtains zigzag in narrow chevron stripes in alternating colors of purple, brown, and black to represent the ground.

Separating the upper area from the darker area below is an area of lavender that forms a pronounced visual break. The last set of rung-chevrons, appearing

Jacob's Dream, Farmington version
and detail showing scale
256" x 120", 1973

at the top border of this area, is less pointed than the rest. There is a small hint of black sky with stars sparkling across the tapestry just below the break.

Each curtain is twenty-three feet high and five feet wide. Two rows of dark letters, starting about twelve feet from the floor, extend across the ladder with the upper row stretching into the wing sections. The letters are bold in form, but also understated, fitting into the balance of the curtain. The Hebrew reads: "Surely the Lord is in this place and I knew it not." (Genesis 28:16) The rich absorbent colors and balanced patterns of this more formal treatment stand in warm contrast to the massive gray concrete and wood of the otherwise unadorned sanctuary walls.

Nezhnie received the commission after sending slides and newspaper clippings about her previous commissions to a Detroit architect who then referred her to Harry King, the architect of this project. King was looking for two ark curtains for the new synagogue he was designing. The contract to weave both curtains was awarded at the same time, with both designs needing to be finalized early in 1972. Nezhnie confessed in a letter to the architect of the project that it was difficult to work out a second design of the *Jacob's Dream* theme so soon after the first one was completed.

Both versions, as well as *Genesis*, attest to the impact of fiber in creating an atmosphere of reverence and contemplation. It is easy to see why a tapestry artist would seek out opportunities to create artwork for places of worship. The environment which includes other beautiful materials, such as the translucent alabaster windows or the dramatic marble and slate altar, enhances the already rich tapestries. An even greater incentive, tapestry has the ability to impact the mundane materials also present, such as concrete or brick, in such a way as to create a unified sense of splendor and spiritual presence. One observer, tapestry weaver Ann Schumacher, relates her response to seeing the Farmington Hills version:

> There is a texture to the cement walls that works well visually with the texture (visual and actual) of the tapestry. Next to the two cement sides is wood in horizontal stripes. The wood gives a very warm feeling and also works well with the warmth and softness of the tapestry. It is amazing how three different types of materials (fiber, cement, and wood) work so well together. You get a true sense of an architectural, spiritual, intellectual and sensual wholeness as you come into the room. . . so much so that it is breathtaking.

Jacob's Dream, Boston version, *126" x 132", 56 sq. ft., 1975*
Referred to as *Jacob's Ladder* by congregation.

The third version, a triangular hooked hanging, was created for Temple Israel, Boston, Massachusettes. This one is the most graphic of the *Jacob's*

Dream designs. The triangle is divided into five wedges from its apex in a bilaterally symmetrical color pattern. The outer sections of dark blue, purple, and black are interspersed with bright white stars and represent the sky. Mauve and soft pastel wing-like bands form the inner wedges flanking the central ladder. The base is divided into horizontal bands that repeat the light green, peach, mauve, and lavender of the wings. While the colors are not continuous all the way across the base, the pattern of light and dark does extend horizontally on either side of where the ladder rests, creating the effect of a desert below the very expansive and dramatic sky. Hebrew script spreads all the way across the base in a wide orange

Jacob's Ladder,
Boston version
126" x 132",
56 sq. ft., 1975
Color plate 1d

band on a mauve background, adding even greater weight to the image. The slender ladder rises up in the center in a spectral progression of maroon, red, orange, pink, and peach. Sections of two colors, one color darker than its mate, form rungs that "dovetail" up the ever-narrowing ladder until the apex is reached.

Horizontal color divisions in the sky and wing sections undulate in such a way that the surface above the base appears to ripple. Green lines define the segments that, though curved, are all parallel. Every other one of these outlines is a vibrant, almost strident green. In combination with the white stars, they create an exceptionally dramatic sky that seems to fold around the edges of the triangle three-dimensionally. Many segments of the dark sky repeat the parallel undulations with thin black lines in the blue or purple. The strong implication of wings is achieved with graphic parallel lines of white that curve in the same arc as the randomly alternating wing colors. As in a wing tip, the lower lines are shorter. Definition is given to all sections through the shaping of the hooked pile.

It is exciting to see the variety of designs that came from the one basic premise of representing the ascent in a gradation of warm tones, outlined and accented with the skyblues and vibrant greens.

In 1971-72 Nezhnie created the design for a large 415-square-foot ark curtain, *Exodus*, fabricated by Edward Fields, Inc. for the Congregation Anshei-Sphard-Beth El Emeth in Memphis, Tennessee. She supervised the production and hanging of the massive panels. Nezhnie especially enjoyed the potential for relief in the pile and interacted enthusiastically with the carver.

She also wove a reading table cover, *Tree of Life,* for the project of very fine, densely packed wool with metallic threads. The cover was worn out by the end of the century from years of use beneath the Torah during readings. The tree of life theme was later used for limited-edition hooked hangings and still later as the last woven ark curtain of her career.

Mt. Sinai, *168" x 48", 1972*

Mt. Sinai
168" x 48", 1972

The other ark curtain designed for the Adas Shalom Synagogue, *Mt. Sinai,* was the first to be woven. It was designed for the daily chapel. The ark curtain was woven with sections of gold and silver metallic thread to form a curve descending from the top of the tapestry. The curved metallic section starts with individually woven silver bands descending until every other strip changes to gold. It ends with all the bands in gold. A mountain peak emerges in front of the gold strips with a cloud of smoke swirling around it, repeating the semi-circular shape. There are hints of the gold strips within the rolling purple, black, and gray smoke cloud. Just below the billowy cloud, faceted angles of columnar basalt-like rock tip towards the center of the mountain. The facets are woven in purples, browns, grays, maroon, and soft orange, with a few bright orange accents. A large irregular orange mass extends across the curtain contrasting sharply with the dark mountain formation. It is placed with its upper edge approximately a third of the way up the curtain. The Hebrew phrase "We shall do and we shall listen" is woven in the orange section in silver. Nezhnie placed the text low on the curtain, to reflect that the statement was a commitment of man, not God. More faceted formations, in purple, blue, gray, and brown continue below the vivid orange portion. The curtain ends in a small border of silver and gold metallic bands of fringe.

After years of hanging, *Mt. Sinai* needed to be repaired. The metallic bands at the top started coming apart due to the amount of weight they had to support. The solution was to mount the tapestry on a black fabric. The weight was distributed better, and the backing did not show from the front.

The dual project, initiated in the fall of 1971, is a good example of the demands of commission work. The weaving schedule was hectic. The synagogue wanted this curtain to be completed before the New Year holiday that occurred in late September that year. Because of delays in payment and yarn delivery, Nezhnie only had six weeks in which to actually weave the fifty-six square feet of tapestry for the curtain. In a correspondence written on July 20, 1972, to the temple, Nezhnie commented: "I confess I find the unnecessary strain of this situation very enervating." A quick trip to the dictionary, if the recipient of the letter were curious, revealed that Muriel was sapped of strength or vitality, weakened in body or will, though this complaint was made decorously. The weaving was accomplished in time, by September 5, but had some technical problems causing it to hang about an inch lower in the left corner. She only noticed that it sagged when she hung it on the studio wall just prior to photographing it. It would take careful blocking and skillful mounting to achieve a professional presentation. In the end, the decision was made by the synagogue to wait until after the holiday to install the ark curtain, although it had arrived beforehand.

A shipment of yarns, twenty-six colors, to begin the weaving of the second curtain, *Jacob's Dream*, arrived within a month of Nezhnie's finishing the first curtain. It was a much larger tapestry, 230 square feet compared to the 56 of *Mt. Sinai*. Again in March, Nezhnie sent in another large order, along with a note expressing surprise at how greatly she had miscalculated the quantities needed for the project. She needed more of over half the colors. Yarn calculation is always a challenge, but the design requirement that some colors be used as secondary accents in many segments would have further complicated accurate planning.

Again, Nezhnie was feeling pressure to complete the second curtain quickly, this time because the family had planned their major European camping trip for that summer. The project was not completed until mid-July, thus delaying the trip. Fortunately, because Shelly Helfman had a sabbatical from teaching that fall, they had enough flexibility to accommodate the revised schedule. One of the last tasks Nezhnie did before leaving for Europe was to send in another order for twenty colors in preparation for her next project. She arranged to have the yarns shipped to a friend so that the supply would be available to start the next commission when they returned from the three-month trip and she would not have to worry about delays.

In the years between 1970 and the fall of 1973, Nezhnie designed five major commissions and wove or supervised the weaving of three of them. In addition, she wove a large tapestry for her personal expression, discussed later, bringing the total weaving to over 700 square feet in the three-year period.

Breath of Life, *84" x 286", 1974*

The tapestry whose yarn was waiting for Nezhnie's return was *Breath of Life*. The focus of the tapestry is a dove in front of a massive rainbow with waves

Breath of Life
84" x 286", 1974

below. An assortment of objects from nature and man-made instruments and symbols make up the side sections flanking the central rainbow. There are seven distinct visual divisions created by abrupt changes in background colors that alternate from dark to light. The border and several of the segments contain passages from the Old Testament. The composition is held together by the balanced relationship between light and dark elements. Nezhnie cropped the rainbow's arc uniquely, revealing only the thick center portion that dominates the entire sky from the sea up. The dramatic effect is heightened because of the abrupt transitions and contrast with its adjacent sections, calling attention to the pastel shades and novel view of the rainbow. In other areas, vertical symbols such as a sheaf of wheat deliberately straddle the transition lines, also presenting novel arrangements. All the objects are beautifully woven and draw you in to look more closely at their detail. Backgrounds have stripes and patterns giving greater complexity to the overall image. A numbered schematic drawing for identifying all the symbols was printed to accompany the design statement provided for the congregation.

Breath of Life had the honor of being displayed in the spacious central Sculpture Hall of the St. Louis Art Museum before it was installed in the temple. Its vibrant colors and monumental scale were well received by art critics and patrons. The two local newspapers featured reviews with glowing comments, referring to its "decisive design" and noting, too, that the tapestry "holds its own in the huge space of this hall."

Seed of Science, *30" x 30" each, 1977-1978*

Two secular commissioned tapestries, both completed in 1978, are of note. *Seed of Science,* created for the University of Missouri – Rolla, is a series of five square tapestries that are united in a very ingenious way. Each unit has two flat metal bars woven in as part of the design. The bars extend out past the edge of the weaving and are attached on an angle so that the series is bound together in a staggered arrangement that is bolted to the wall. The design was Nezhnie's solution to guard against theft, since the grouping would hang in a very accessible area of a busy building with minimal security. The segments of metal are randomly silver or gold colored, the "school colors" of this university known for its emphasis on metallurgic engineering.

Only two squares are displayed vertically. The other three are rotated forty-five degrees to form diamonds that flank the two upright squares. The side points of the diamonds line up with a corner of the adjacent square. The first tapestry is rotated to the left so that what would have been its lower right corner shifted up forty-five degrees to be at the level of the bottom of the second square at its left corner. The third square, rotated forty-five degrees down to the right, lines up with the top of the fourth square. The fifth segment is tilted so that its left point also lines up with the top of the fourth square.

The richness of the imagery gives the impression that Muriel must have enjoyed designing the units. Each is visually interesting, despite what might be considered unlikely subject matter for a work of art. Although the central diamond actually was derived from a chart showing the layering of the earth, it gives the impression of a curved road that drops off the tapestry to the right. It arcs across the diamond in rich blues with soft golden "shoulders" highlighting the curve in such a way that it aides the movement from the upper segments to the lower units. The scale of the imagery in the five tapestries is varied. The upper correctly positioned square is a close-up view of a face; the other lower square is a map indicating mineral deposits. The two end diamonds, which are the most detailed and intricate in scale, have a similar orientation of five bands of scientific patterns traversing across from lower left to upper right. They both have a light central pattern, one a handwritten formula, the other perhaps the pattern of a computer punch card. Along with the curve of light hues in the middle tapestry, they direct the viewer from left to right and give *Seed of Science* an ordered sense of balance.

Seed of Science
30" x 30" each,
1977-1978

The presentation is attractive and compatible with the imagery. The metal is not intrusive; rather it appears contemporary and lively. The staggered units appear much like the way molecules are connected, and the diamond format is reflective of the symbols and scientific notations. A predominance of blues interacting with orange, gold, rust, and brown seen in her other work is

again successful in this composition along with her inclusion of stripes or bands somewhere in all the sections. There is a quote from Emerson saying "'Wonder' is the seed of our science" in the last band of the fifth square. Originally, the hanging was mounted on a wall with chairs below the lower end creating a sense of movement that seemed to be directing the viewer's eye down to the resting spot. It has since been moved to a conference room.

Prairie Journey, *60" x 98", 1978*

Prairie Journey is the other captivating commission completed in 1978. Designed for the Macomb (Illinois) Public Library, it is a charming homage to the history of the Midwest. A map of counties in northwestern Illinois forms the backdrop for a horse carrying six children. The children are stairstepped from the very young girls, whose dark-stockinged legs barely straddle

Prairie Journey
60" x 98", 1978

the workhorse's neck, to the mature teenage boy astride the rump. The horse extends across the right half of the tapestry, blending into a golden segment of the map at the right edge.

The map, titled "Bounty Land," delineates tracts of land that were awarded to veterans of the War of 1812. The focus is on the area situated between the Mississippi River on the left and the Illinois River on the right. In the central area the quadrants are woven in medium and light green, whereas the areas on the other sides of the rivers are gold. Railroads in the central area are indicated in brown and elsewhere in rust. Beige or gold dots scattered along the railroads indicate where settlements sprung up. The dots provide an interesting decorative feature to the tapestry, as do the dark lines of the railways. Location names are skillfully woven in gold and rust. Many background areas are further divided into blocks of solid weft-faced weaving alternating with ones where light green warp shows, creating slightly lighter blocks.

The horse is positioned so that the curve of the Illinois River touches the horse close behind the tallest boy. This careful juxtaposition calls attention to the boy's tenuous mount. Judging from the bright orange ribbon in one girl's hair and the excited looks of the children, they are on their way to a special event. Perhaps the opportunity to be photographed was cause enough for the excitement.

The tapestry was commissioned as part of the Theodora Pottle Memorial Collection of Contemporary American Art. It is a straightforward design. Yet, surely, it must be a focal point for the library patrons. It attests to Nezhnie's ability to work within the parameters of a given task and is a lively combination of historical elements. Surprisingly, it appears she had some problems with a few of the faces, especially the youngest girl's.

No mention has been made of the many commissions undertaken for individuals. The majority were done during her mid-career and are more closely related to her personal artistic pursuits. She felt fewer restraints on her design parameters with private clients, who often were friends or were at least familiar with her style. In general, Nezhnie valued commission work, as the following response to the Crump questionnaire reveals.

> I absolutely do regard commission work as challenging. Many of my most important stylistic and conceptual discoveries have resulted directly from solving problems set by architects, clients, budgets themes or the architectural site itself. . . . The greatest limitation of commission is that it takes time and energy and there is often little left over for my own personal work, and the older I get the more important the personal work becomes.

In the 1960s her commissions and personal work were kept quite separate and looked remarkably different. The few commissions she did for private clients during that decade were, as noted previously, similar to the institutional ones in style and design, if not theme. By the 1970s, private commissions became a means for Nezhnie to reestablish her interest in portraits and designs more closely related to her personal calling. They also allowed her to continue her interest in the free-form techniques developed in her earlier experimental pieces. Considering the concepts and colors that suited the client's interests and space provided a specific challenge for each project. Still, the private commission could not afford the same degree of spontaneity that the earlier figurative work had displayed. Innovations needed to be limited to aspects that could be communicated conceptually to the client at the design stage, thereby avoiding surprises that might lead to later disappointments.

Nezhnie continued to do commissions throughout the 1980s, but many of them were designs for fabrication. Whether hooked or woven, she was still very much involved with the design modifications and special requirements that each assignment entailed. Using commercial fabrication had its own interesting design features. It was an excellent medium for creating sculptural forms and irregular shapes. It also enabled her to provide a less expensive option to a client than tapestry, not only in its production but at the design stage as well. Design fees were determined by square footage, like weaving charges were. A triangle has far less surface than a rectangle but can still command a large amount of wall space. Another ploy to cut costs was to design panels or units that could be separated to stretch the composition out, thus covering more space. Nezhnie was quite proud of working out innovative options.

Not all of the fabricated pieces were offered as limited editions. If they were, she provided more than one combination of colors, using as many as a dozen yarns in each choice. One of her strongest assets in designing commissions was the ability to complement whatever colors were in the surroundings without necessarily mimicking them exactly. A co-worker of hers at Craft Alliance commented on her acute attention to detail, to seeing the elements in the environment and knowing how to use the information. Her visual sensitivity to the components of the colors she observed is revealed throughout her commissions. This ability has the effect of making the total impact more lively than if she just reproduced the tones already in the setting. Indeed she understood the relationship between art and its environment as espoused by Lurçat, and that she reiterated in her artist's statement.

By the end of the 1970s, however, her focus was shifting to her personal creative endeavors. In part, the transition was influenced by the reality that commissions were very labor intensive. She was fortunate to have help from her husband and from apprentices who worked in return for their training. Still, careful calculation of the hours required by everyone to complete a commission, including copious correspondence, made her aware she could be earning more as a department store window designer, apparently her notion of what she could do out in the commercial world. The commission work helped Nezhnie sustain a balance between her various objectives. Certainly, commissions gained her respect as a businesswoman, and winning several awards for architectural installations validated her talent. Still, they could not really elevate her prestige within the artistic community. That would take a more cohesive development of her personal form of expression.

More important, as she matured as an artist she was increasingly motivated by a need to explore the stockpile of ideas gesticulating in her mind without the interruptions and shifts in concentration that commissions demanded.

Mid-Career/
Portraits

Creativity does not necessarily follow an orderly progression. An artist may have periods of struggling for ideas and other times when major developmental strides follow one right after the other. For Nezhnie, the challenges and success of the *Imprints* commission, finished in 1971, appear to have propelled her into an exceptionally creative state of mind. Besides designing massive commissions, she ventured into large and time-consuming personal works. She always liked to have an independent project in progress to balance the commission work.

By 1970 Nezhnie had become interested in using photographs as a design source. During the previous decade, a new trend had emerged in the art world. Several artists started incorporating images from everyday life into their artwork as a means to address growing concerns about contemporary society. Exaggerating the scale of an image, or perhaps repeating it many times, became a tool used to address the power of visual objects to communicate and to manipulate our perceptions. Photographs took on a new role in art as part of the subject matter.

The novel approach of using icons of mass production and pop culture appealed to Nezhnie. Its impetus, addressing contemporary commercialism and the fascination with superstars, provided the kind of content she wanted to explore. It allowed her to tap into her graphic background. She understood the power of advertising, having worked at an advertising firm during summers when she was at The Cooper Union. Besides, Muriel responded to photographs, internalizing their impact, as she had when passing the large reproductions of the Communist leaders on her way to art classes as an adolescent. More important, the work of controversial artists such as Andy Warhol, who popularized images of identifiable people, gave her confidence to return to her first passion, the human face.

It took a while for the impact of the changing attitudes in the art world to take effect. The bias against portraiture Nezhnie had witnessed in art school continued to inhibit her during the 1960s. Now she was a natural receptor of the new climate and ready to move on. She was able to start incorporating representational imagery in the commission work by the late 1960s. Photographs would have been the inspiration for much of the scientific imagery in *Genesis* and for the portraits in *Imprints*. However, when Muriel decided to use photography in her personal work, she did not start her journey of exploration tentatively.

Wild Cherry Charms, *60" x 138", 1972*

Her first tapestry based on a photograph, *Wild Cherry Charms*, is perhaps the boldest and most complex of her subjective pieces. The inspiration for the tapestry was a "Charms" candy wrapper she found lying on the ground while on a family camping trip to Canada. It brought back vivid memories of her own childhood when she loved looking at the world around her through the transparent magenta wrappers. Some details would be hidden by the rows of almost opaque dots on the wrapper.

Her design needed a second image as the object observed through the wrapper. At first she considered using a picture from her childhood, but she could not find one that seemed to work. After dismissing the idea, she found a snapshot of her daughter and friends dressed up for Halloween. She liked the concept of overlapping the merriment of the girls in costume with her own entertaining childhood pastime of viewing an altered world. It was a very appropriate choice, since candy is so inherently relevant to Halloween. Thus, she decided to create the appearance of looking at the girls through the candy wrapper.

Visually the tapestry is divided almost in half. The five girls are dressed as a masked vamp, cowgirl, clown, Native American, and lady. Approximately life

Wild Cherry Charms

60" x 138", 1972

Color plate 4f

sized, they are clustered together on the right side. To the left side of center, the faces of the vamp and clown are enlarged to the full five-foot height of the tapestry. The candy wrapper extends across the entire tapestry with all the lettering turned on its side. The background is a soft magenta. "WILD CHERRY" is positioned vertically just left of center, and the word "CHARMS" spreads boldly up the tapestry's right edge. The lettering is in dark burgundy. Four rows of opaque burgundy dots and the words "NET WT. 1 OZ." are in front of the enlarged faces. A series of translucent dots cover three of the life-sized girls' faces and, to a lesser degree, their bodies. All the dots are about the same size as the faces. The cowgirl has "ARTIFICIAL" superimposed on her body.

In the Castro interview Nezhnie talks of the insights and challenges she discovered while weaving the tapestry. When asked if there were ever things she discovered about her art she had not consciously known she was dealing with, she talked about this piece, saying:

> This image is of a candy wrapper superimposed over a photograph of my daughter and her friends when they were ten years old. I've always liked masks; I've always talked about people wearing them, putting up false fronts and facades. But I didn't realize I was talking about that when I designed this huge weaving. I just knew I loved the image; the combination of the two subjects, the graphics and the human together, and I loved the femininity of the girls.
>
> As time went on and I sat looking at the tapestry in daylight and night light, I began to realize I was talking about role-playing and how we condition our children to behave in certain ways. Each of the girls represents the different facets of a woman's role — a feminine role in this society.
>
> One is a clown, thoroughly covered up and behaving other than herself. There's a black girl and I had a very hard time getting her face right in the tapestry. There's a circle from the candy wrapper that goes over her face; her mouth came right at the edge. And every time I wove in the face it would look like she was crying. I ripped it out five times before I got her laughing with everyone else. And that was an ordeal in itself, because there's such little difference between the grimace of pain and tears and that of laughter. Another is a vamp. She has a mask, a red satin dress, a white fur collar, and high heels. One is an Indian, very natural, you know, with her tummy sticking out. *These are little kids.*
>
> . . . I took two of the heads and blew them up to monumental scale, and placed them at one end of the tapestry. It created a scale jump that was very unusual and optically exciting to me. In retrospect it also emphasized to me I was talking about masks and hiding behind them. (Castro, 1-2)

The original impetus in creating the design was the issue of distorting reality. Her idea was more complex than the whimsical overlapping of elements that had intrigued her at an early age. Manipulating the scale was a way to communicate another perceptual distortion she had observed personally. She had always been uncomfortable when people came too close to her during interactions. By her account, she thought it was the result of being far-sighted.

In any case, the level of discomfort would cause her to either pull back or be forced to have her vision dominated by the person. In creating the dramatic scale jump with the two faces, she is consciously providing a challenge to the viewer's comfort level as well. (*THE SEEN*, 3)

The tapestry had to be very large because she planned to submit it to the prestigious Biennale Internationale de la Tapisserie in Lausanne, Switzerland, which required that all submissions be at least five square meters. The piece was not an entry selected for the exhibition. Nevertheless, it was one of Nezhnie's favorite tapestries.

From the beginning, she had intended to keep *Wild Cherry Charms* for herself, and to pass it on to her daughter rather than sell it. Its commanding size and powerful imagery became an integral part of the family setting. It hung in the Helfman living room for many years.

It is a lively work that is exceptionally successful in communicating the essence of the photographic image. The project was a major step in sorting out how to incorporate text and photography into her visual vocabulary. Its strongest point is how convincing the girls' gestures are. They truly convey the kind of giddiness that dressing up inspires. The details of the weaving communicate well, like the fluffy fur collar, the smile of the clown, the awkwardness of a young girl in high heels, and the pudgy stance of one of them, so typical of preadolescent girls. The shift in scale created by the placement of the two enlarged faces to the left of the group is visually effective and serves to balance the overall composition.

Despite the innovative composition and skillful portrayal of the mood of the picture, the tapestry suffers somewhat for its complexity. The design presupposes the viewer understands that Charms candy wrappers were translucent with dots of color positioned in rows on them. For a viewer who does not recall what the wrappers looked like, the true charm of the girls is lost in the confusion of the superimposed dots.

The concept is exciting, but the piece could have benefited from providing a few more clues for the uninformed observer. In hindsight, it seems that Nezhnie needed to push the concept of transparency further. There are inconsistencies; none of the magenta of the wrapper covers the girls, so they do not really appear to be behind the tinted cellophane, nor are all of the dots in front of the girls. For viewers who have a strong connection to the wrappers, the innovative tapestry is powerful.

The tapestry is of major importance. It was quite a daring venture to have undertaken. She had woven work as large as this for commissions, but to commit such a major investment of money and time for an experimental piece required a lot of personal drive. Once she made the decision, she went straight ahead, directed by her instincts.

It reveals many aspects of Nezhnie's personality. The selection of subject matter illustrates the sophistication of her design sense and her bias towards complexity. She began with a concept related personally to her experience — the manipulation of visual reality. She had used photographic images in *Imprints* almost parenthetically, but in *Charms* photography was not only the means of acquiring an image to use, but also part of the subject of the composition. That relationship becomes evident to the viewer because she provided the second, enlarged version of the event captured by the camera.

That she had difficulty selecting the photograph to use becomes understandable. The one selected appears obviously posed for the camera and depicts an experience that most viewers can identify clearly as the documentation of children in costume at Halloween. It is probably the most documented aspect of childhood besides Christmas and birthdays.

The other factor revealed is perhaps the negative aspect of the great confidence Nezhnie had in the concept. As discussed earlier, an artist has to stay actively involved in all phases of the work. If Nezhnie had been less sure of the image once she had conceived of how to create the effect she wanted, she might have questioned the audience's perception of the overlay more. Instead, as Shelly noted, she went on her instincts. Her enthusiasm for the concept carried her through all phases, without her pausing to consider if the design actually communicated what she was trying to convey.

The complexity of the superimposed dots is its most risky aspect, and not tinting parts of the girls to indicate that the cellophane was in front of them is its weakest feature. Nevertheless, the composition she derived from the combination of the wrapper and photograph is a well-balanced blend of the words and figures.

Viewers either like the tapestry enthusiastically, or not at all. Negative reactions most likely result from the deliberate manipulation of the viewer's comfort zone. The majority of people do like the tapestry, and other than the Holocaust tapestries, it is the piece they refer to most often in discussing her work. They smile and remember its boldness and cheerful associations.

Nevertheless, it is probably the only one of her tapestries to receive any negative comments in print. ". . . its bad pop and trite material hardly justify the flawless workmanship, the profound richness of coloration and the inherent solemnity of the medium," one reviewer stated.[10] The harsh words reflect a

---

10 John Brod Peters, "Helfman, Seppa Works Displayed," *St. Louis Globe Democrat* (November 30-December 1, 1974): 4B.

bias that continued on throughout later decades, namely, art critics' dismissal of work depicting children as trite. (Mavor, 248)

In Nezhnie's case, one of the first comments made about the piece was that a man could never have created the image, an opinion even supported by her husband. Perhaps for that reason it was labeled "feminist," which she did not interpret as complimentary. She wanted a response to the perceptual issues that had been her motivation in creating the tapestry. She was trying to make a place for herself within the established art world, not work towards a redefinition of its structure. Even later, in questions directed to her by Castro about the subject matter of the Holocaust tapestries, she didn't really want to say she was focusing from a woman's point of view.

Spearmint Charms, *60" x 138", 1976*

Spearmint Charms, a male counterpart, was woven in 1976. A friend called her attention to a photograph of a group of boys posed in costume, reminiscent of the one she had used for the girls. Until seeing this photo, Nezhnie had not thought of doing a second version.

> . . . and the more I lived with it [*Wild Cherry Charms*], the more I realized I was talking about role playing. Still, I didn't think about a male counterpart until I saw Morton May's picture and saw the soldier with the gun. And then I knew I was talking about role playing and the more I thought about his picture, the more I wanted to do it. Finally I wrote to him and he was delighted and sent me whatever I needed. (THE SEEN, 2)

By that time she was interested in other concepts and not as committed to the project as she was to the first one; therefore it seemed to take more effort to weave. The design was not altered significantly; only the placement of the boys on the tapestry was reversed to the left side and the color scheme changed. The image was, however, modified from the original photograph because one of the figures had been a little girl. She substituted another boy and also turned the soldier's gun towards the viewers. There is a fascinating array of patterns in the beautifully woven clothing.

The tapestry background color is turquoise blue. Muriel tried hanging this tapestry in her living room, but the cool colors receded and seemed to need a much larger space. Interesting, too, the boys appear to be much less happy or giddy than the girls. They do not seem as comfortable with the process of posing in costume.

While weaving *Spearmint Charms*, Nezhnie discovered even more insights into the role of costumes, decoration, and gender.

I suddenly realized these males were covered with ornamentation. The soldier had leaves on his helmet. He had a grenade, he had a machine gun. And he had ribbons. He had medals. He had stripes. The Indian had stripes. He had feathers. He had war paint and he had a tomahawk. And on it went. I had a cowboy fully ornamented with a scarf around his neck, loops around the edge of his pants, chaps, a gun, and boots, and spurs. And again, I said, "My God! Are the men in this society really, you know, the colored birds?" I didn't set out to say any of this; I wasn't making a conscious statement about male and female differences. Yet there it was. (Castro, 3-4)

During the weaving of *Spearmint Charms*, a revealing interview with both Muriel and Shelly was audio-taped by Richard Marc Rubin for a local arts publication, THE SEEN. Much of the discussion was centered around the two tapestries, especially deliberation about the differences in projected role fantasies between the sexes that might have led to the lack of joyfulness on the faces of the boys.

Spearmint Charms

(detail)

60" x 138", 1976

As Muriel pursued incorporating photographic material, she became fascinated by the work of weaver Helena Hernmarck.[11] The contemporary subject matter caught her attention, especially Hernmarck's rendering of *Little Richard* in 1969. Her interest was also peaked because Hernmarck used calligraphy freely. However, what was most exciting about Hernmarck's work was the element of surprise created by the discrepancy in what the viewer saw from a distance and at close range. From a distance of twenty feet the weaving looks convincingly like a photograph. The opposite effect is true at five feet. At close range, only the woven multicolored, textural surface of yarn is visible, without any reference to identifiable objects. This phenomenon meshed with Nezhnie's own

---

11 Monica Bowman & Patricia Malarcher, *Helena Hernmarck: Tapestry Artist* (Byggforlaget, Kultur, Stockholm, 1999).

Helena Hernmarck is known for her large tapestries derived from photographs. She enlarges the photo enough that the image is broken down into units of color much like in pointillism. She then creates the yarns bundles to match each segment. The yarn appears as thick groups of threads laying across the tapestry with the warp exposed in rolakan, or Swedish tapestry weave. Pattern rows primarily of soumak strengthen the color density. Variety of color is further manipulated by the ability to rotate the weft bundles of soumak to accent parts of the combination of yarns. As many as ten weights of yarn might be included in the bundle.

It is a fascinating experience to view one of these tapestries and see just how realistic it looks at a distance and how very unrecognizable it becomes at close range.

commitment to creating images that conveyed their woven structure and also her interest in perceptual phenomena.

However, Hernmarck's style of weaving with bundles of yarn was not compatible with Nezhnie's interests. In this method, each bundle contains about ten fine yarns. The colors within each bundle are added or replaced systematically to match a specific color indicated on the greatly enlarged photograph. One tapestry demanded over 700 separate hues of yarn. (Bowman & Malarcher, 70)

Hernmarck's style of realism was most dependent on her creative, highly sensitive skill with yarn blending. She used enlarged photographic images as a code for getting an accurate color palette. Nezhnie preferred a more spontaneous manner of color interplay and manipulation of the photograph through the design. Fascinated by Helena Hernmarck's imagery, but eager to continue her own journey, she explored a variety of ways to attain the visual effects she sought.

A photo clipped from a magazine or bulletin might catch her interest and claim a prominent place in her studio for years. Its availability for study was a definite benefit. She could evaluate the subject as a light and dark composition or consider how the shadows or highlights might translate into shapes and lines. She could study the impact of the various features and what aspects were responsible for her attraction to the picture.

The *Charms* tapestries are woven in a "painterly" manner, i.e., color blocked in with frequent transitions to imply contours, as a painter might to convey a realistic face. Many of the other portraits that Muriel designed in the mid-1970s more closely resemble drawings. The number of colors is limited, and details are defined by lines.

A straight line in the direction of the weft is the easiest way to add a new color in tapestry weaving and therefore is the first building block of forming shapes. Her graphic background prepared her to interpret imagery with lines, as pen and ink drawings, wood blocks, and etchings have done for centuries. Several sections of the 1971 commission, *Imprints*, incorporated the technique of creating dimension through parallel lines. In 1975 she wove several free-form portraits in this method.

While making use of the straight line became her primary tool for translating the potency of an image from the photograph to tapestry, her choice of what to emphasize was equally critical. It is interesting to note that for all the years she reacted defiantly to the trend towards abstraction in art, she understood its potential. Her most effective portraits were abstractions of the photograph. She tended to select only a portion of the face or a dominant feature to work around. Even if she included all the features, the face was frequently cropped in close to the eyes and mouth, not extended out to the full shape.

Constellation, *84" x 84" (star shaped), 1975*

Technically, *Constellation* is the most ambitious of her non-rectilinear tapestries. It is a complex star shape with twelve points that extend out from the body of the piece. The configuration could perhaps be considered as a ten-point star overlaid by a smaller five-point one. Each point is divided, one triangular side being light, the other dark, creating a faceted effect. Some of the inner points appear as pyramids, and the overall light and dark triangular facets give the illusion of dimension. Of the thirteen dark triangles, five are forest green containing occasional lines of red, four have a measure or two of musical notations in black on a rust background, and four are deeply saturated solid black. The twelve lighter triangles are evenly divided between white and gray randomly striped shapes, solid lavender ones, or ones with faces woven in olive green lines on a gold background.

All of the shaping occurred on the loom, with some of the angles being quite acute. The tapestry was woven in two pieces. The cartoon was cut in two and placed so that the straight edge of the cut followed one side of the warp. Keeping the cartoon secure and accurate was critical to the effectiveness of the design. The join is quite indistinguishable in the woven star. When mounted, the tapestry was rotated about thirty degrees clockwise in order to locate the figures at the best angle.

The faces do not have specific references for the client; they are faces that appealed to Nezhnie, each distinctive in features. One is derived from a detail of Pontormo's *Annunciation of the Virgin Mary* that she saw in a book about the restoration of the Church of Santa Felicita in Florence, Italy. Only one face is looking towards the viewer; the others are three-quarter profiles looking more towards the center of the tapestry. Nevertheless, the eyes remain the focal point. Much like in *Odyssey '67* the faces are contained in triangular shapes. Two females are suspended out at the very edges of the composition.

The tapestry was commissioned by a young doctor who had seen her work at galleries and at a local temple. He had no specific concept in mind; he just knew he wanted a tapestry. She came to his home to see the space and to interview him about his interests. His interest in music inspired her to use the notations, although as seen in the photograph of her high school window

Constellation
84" x 84", 1975
Color plate 5g

decorations, she had used musical symbols in her artwork before. In *Constellation*, the segments of musical notation provide a novel and very effective element to an already innovative composition.

The wall the tapestry was to hang on sloped gently at the ceiling, dropping from about ten feet at one corner to eight feet at the outside wall. She felt the space needed an irregular shape rather than a rectangle. The tapestry is right for its location. The star shape and the rich colors enhance the sloping ceiling line and bank of floor-to-ceiling windows of the room.

The shape was clearly very labor intensive, not only in the weaving, but in the finishing and mounting as well. Once it was properly mounted with Velcro stapled to the wall, it became a very successful piece, drawing onlookers into the room.

The design was a chance for Nezhnie to work on some ideas that interested her. During the 1970s weavers were highly motivated to push the limits of traditional weaving. Nezhnie proved that she could successfully produce a very complicated, eccentric shape; that materials or techniques would not daunt her. Part of the genius of the composition was in the way the well-rendered and very realistic faces are integrated into the fabric. That they are merely parts of an interesting whole creates a sense of mystery about them that would not exist in a more traditional presentation. It was one of Muriel's favorite pieces along with *Wild Cherry Charms*. She liked adding complexity to the weaving. Hence, the challenging task of shaping created excitement and interest for her during the process.

Stella
29" x 29", 1975

Stella, *29" x 29", 1975*

Stella, the other star-shaped tapestry that she created, was probably the first of the two to be woven. It clearly has the appearance of an experiment where Nezhnie couldn't quite anticipate how the various elements would come together. It is much smaller than *Constellation* and woven in one piece. There is less consistency in how the points are faceted, so that the two most horizontal ones appear to be on a very different plane than the others. The piece may have been photographed before it was completely finished because fringe is left hanging on the lower sections, but not on most of the upper points, detracting from the impact of the star shape. A sorrowful female face, derived from the same cartoon as that of *Prisma*, fills the entire central area. In fact, it extends into the points in some areas. The transition between the face and the points is awkward. It also appears that the process of shaping might have distracted Muriel from executing the features of the face as attractively as she normally did, especially around the mouth. There are some beautiful areas of shading around the eyes, similar to the style she successfully used in the later piece, *Portrait of Dr. Richard Ferry*, but in general, the tapestry is of interest primarily as documentation in the process of exploring an idea. It underscores the cleverness of embedding the faces of *Constellation* within the faceted shape.

Although most of the shaped pieces woven in 1975 were more conventional portraits, Nezhnie started experimenting with using lines as a design element separate from the function of creating form or detail in the imagery.

Circus, *126" x 60", 1975*

There are two tapestries with stripes in both the figure and ground. *Circus* is like a shaped banner. It is flared at the top, then tapers to the lower half, which is very narrow and straight edged. The entire piece is made of horizontally striped images and background. Two female acrobats fly above a man balancing on a galloping horse holding a hoop in each hand. The luminous disks could also suggest spotlights tracking the action. The figures are formed in a series of wide horizontal sections of warm orange or greenish gold. Both colors are further elaborated with large repeats of yellow or gray stripes. The stripes in the figures are relatively uniform in thickness and spacing.

Circus
126" x 60", 1975
Color plate 4b

Like the figures, the background consists of horizontal bands of colors interspersed with narrow stripes, but they have more variation in color than the figures. Lavender and blue dominate the upper flared portion, with some light brown sections as well. The narrow stripes are dark red and extend across the tapestry, except in the area where the two trapeze artists meet. The banding and striping is staggered in this area of activity.

The middle area, starting near the man's waist, has both light and dark brown background sections with a few navy blue or dark red ones. The thin stripes interspersed in these central bands are mainly white, placed at relatively uniform intervals. The spaces inside the hoops are also white with navy blue stripes. The rims of the hoops are navy, too.

The lowest portion of background returns to the blue, lavender, and light brown segments, but has white and navy stripes instead of the red of the upper section. In this lower section, where the horse's legs and big hoofs are, the white stripes are staggered, effectively creating the impression of movement.

In general, the white stripes are most bold just under the rider's outstretched arms, in striking contrast with the dark background colors. In this section, there is very little difference in thickness between the contrasting color units and both are bold. The background stripes are used throughout the tapestry to create tension and convey a sense of motion. In addition, the repetition of the colors in the figures implies the flickering or dusty, filtered light that might be seen in a circus tent. This effective use of line and color makes for a very dynamic tapestry.

Designed to hang in a circular stairwell, the tapestry was suspended on a flexible rod that enabled its gently arched top edge to curve with the contour of the stairwell. Curves within the design, especially the round muscles of the horse, reflect the curves of the railings and stairs.

The couple that commissioned the tapestry, friends of the Helfmans, gave Muriel free reign at the design stage. Their only stipulation was that it be appropriate for the specific site: the stairwell. Muriel arrived at the unique shape by reversing the form of a long-necked Tiffany vase that sits in a recess in the wall of the stairwell. Surprised by the circus motif in the drawing, the woman was a bit skeptical, but in consultation with her husband, she decided to trust Nezhnie's judgment and didn't make any comments. The clients were pleased with the finished tapestry. Muriel had been enthralled by a large sculpted Chinese horse she had seen in a hotel lobby and was happy to have an opportunity to translate it into tapestry.

Acrobats, *24" x 126", 1976*

In *Acrobats*, she chose to use bands of bold patterns to delineate a row of five gymnasts silhouetted in various feats of agility. Both the background and figures are in stripes reminiscent of southwestern motifs. The patterns used are diamonds, chevrons, and ovals contained in vertical bands within the figures. The yellow, rust, peach, mauve, teal, and sky blue colors could be considered southwestern as well; a decade later they would become very popular, reflecting Native American motifs.

The girls, in colorfully patterned leotards, are very skillfully woven. Nezhnie was able to achieve smooth curves to the body forms, despite the difficulty of maintaining the two differing pattern sequences. *Acrobats* is a good example of the appeal popular culture had for Nezhnie. It depicts America's newly found fascination with gymnastics and the dramatic changes happening in sportswear at the time.

1

a. Jacob's Dream,
   St. Louis
b. Genesis
c. Imprints, detail
d. Jacob's Ladder

Plate 3

2 & 3

a. Large Embrace
b. Burning Bush
c. Odyssey 67
d. Odyssey
e. Venus
f. Gypsy Moth
g. Lorelei

c

f

g

a

b

f

Plate 5

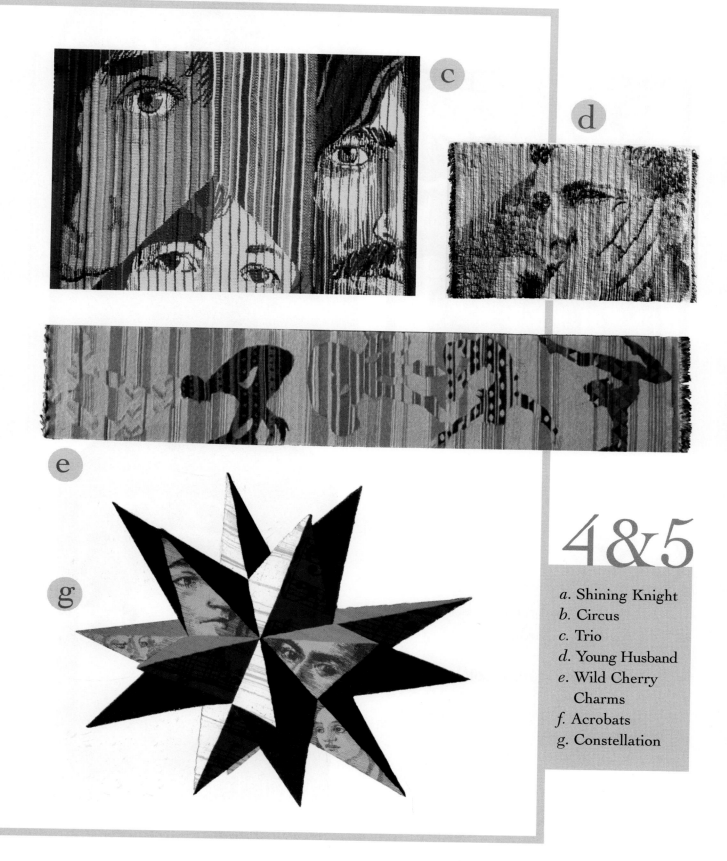

c

d

e

g

4&5

a. Shining Knight
b. Circus
c. Trio
d. Young Husband
e. Wild Cherry
    Charms
f. Acrobats
g. Constellation

6&7

a. Daughters of Auschwitz
b. Daughters of Earth,
c. Liberation
d. Daughters of Earth, detail
e. Lodz
f. Pogrom
g. Deportation
h. Ghetto Child

Plate 7

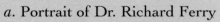

a

b

c

d

e

8

a. Portrait of Dr. Richard Ferry
b. Evangelos
c. Eliot Again
d. Phil Ochs
e. Zelda

The tapestry, over five times as wide as long, was designed to wrap around a corner of the owners' room above a couch and end table. It was Nezhnie's decision, but the owners liked it. In subsequent houses, they displayed it flat on a wall and even draped it over a banister when no other space for it was available. Even draped with only a portion showing at a time, its appealing colors and patterns are visually enticing.

Nezhnie did not restrict her designs to conventional proportions. The nature of her commission work often demanded long narrow tapestries, especially for ark curtains, but her natural preference, as seen in many of her personal constructions, seems to be for long horizontal pieces. *Acrobats* and *The Nader/Trio* diptych are good examples of unconventional scale.

Another way she explored the potential for creating shapes with lines was by varying the character of the line itself, such as allowing it to be thick and thin. Magnifying the size of a photo many times was a good tool for determining the critical details and where lines needed to remain or could be eliminated.

Acrobats, detail,
24" x 126", 1976
Color plate 5e

Nader/Trio *(diptych), 39" x 188"/ 39" x 47", 1976*

Nader is a huge enlargement of Ralph Nader's eyes and meandering brows. Extending over fifteen feet in width, it is an uncompromising and daring composition, perhaps fitting the man portrayed. Muriel succeeded in making an attractive abstraction in the process of depicting the eyes. Obviously, the design had to take into account that the viewer would not be able to perceive the extreme magnification as eyes until looking at them from a great distance. Some other source of interest was necessary to engage the viewer at close range.

Nezhnie created an interesting surface by using very textural yarn and establishing a repetitive pattern. While the background was essentially two colors, white and rust, there was a wide range of tones within the two colors. She chose to weave the features predominantly in shades of blue. At least seven shades were used, some close to purple, others near green. They ranged in value from muted to intense and from middle to dark in tone. The randomness and variety of colors give an exciting richness and activity to the image. Both the white textured background and the enlarged features are interrupted at regular intervals of about one inch by narrow vertical stripes of varying shades of rust. The majority of the surface is simply the rhythmic stripes. Here and there, squiggles and random shapes of blue appear to straddle the stripes. The shapes cluster and "hang" around the orderly progression of lines across the long expanse and ultimately form the eyes.

The design, with so much of the surface woven in textured white yarns and unspun fleece, allowed for apprentice Jan Jungkuntz to weave it during the day and for Muriel to take over the process at night. The textured nature would diminish any differences in tension in the weaving of the two.

Trio is the left panel of the diptych. It is much more humble in size and easily viewed as three faces, even at close range. The face on the right side is derived from a photo of George Harrison. It spans the height of the tapestry, with only the right half of the face in view. It has a strong beige ground with detailed blue features. The eyebrows and moustache are textural, formed by raised lines of brilliant cobalt blue. This face is visually separated from the other two faces by a section of patterned blue bands with slender white stripes. The face of a female, cropped into a triangle from the top of her forehead to her nose, spreads across most of the lower part of the tapestry. This segment, woven in a soft powdery blue with deeper blue and teal details, is of poet Constance Urdang. The left side of the tapestry is dominated by the left half of Nezhnie's own face. Only the eye is delineated in much detail.

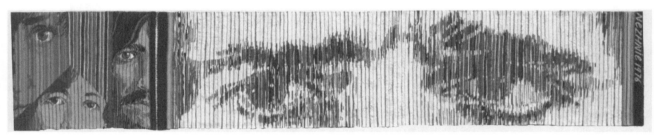

Nader/Trio
(diptych)
39" x 188"/ 39" x 47",
1976
Color plate 5c

The beautiful blue eyelid and focused bright, white eye provide a dramatic contrast to the rest of the face, which is basically bands in shades of tan with the nose and mouth suggested by dark blue lines. The left edge of the tapestry is predominantly cobalt blue.

All of the eyes have pure white grounds and command the viewer's attention. Rust and occasionally brown stripes traverse all sections except the central area of light blue with its white lines. The subtle use of white in the repetitive stripes in the central area of *Trio* is essential to establishing the rhythm of the parallel lines across the diptych from *Nader* to *Trio*.

Curiously, from a distance, the diptych reads from right to left instead of the classic Western convention of left to right. The viewer's glance goes first to the light ground and large-scale eyes of *Nader,* then on to the pleasing detail and color of the other panel. The fact that the features of the face on the right side of *Trio* are more detailed and that the face appears to be in front of the other two also draws the viewer's attention there before moving on to the ones to its left.

Although the two pieces of the diptych were displayed together, *Nader* was sold separately. Drawn to the tapestry immediately, the buyers had to wait for many years before being able to afford it. Surprisingly, the commanding image is right at home in the dining area of their house. It is mounted where it can be seen at a distance from the entry hall. A long table is placed in close proximity to the tapestry, allowing the diners to leisurely appreciate the beautiful, abstract surface. The design works successfully close up at the table, at mid-distance in the seating area where the impression is of an active color field, and at the greater distance of thirty feet in the entry hall where the eyes connect with the viewer.

Eliot, *64" x 60", 1976*

Three tapestries were woven from one cartoon derived from a photograph of William Greenleaf Eliot. He was an important historical figure in the St. Louis area as the founder of the First Unitarian Church of St. Louis and later of Washington University and even a private girls' high school, Mary Institute. Muriel became intrigued by the photograph that appeared on the cover of a publication from Washington University. The clipping hung in

Eliot (detail)
64" x 60", 1976

her studio for a long time while she pondered how to use it.

Eliot was purchased by the church he founded. It was woven by Hannah Roth, a new weaver. Muriel designed a large woven frame around the 17" x 17" portrait to be woven of Rya, a pile weave structure popular at the time. It was a way to provide her new apprentice with practice. Muriel figured that by the time the novice got to the face, she would have enough experience to follow the cartoon accurately.

The tapestry face is designed with minimal detail, and yet the information conveyed by its horizontal lines of irregular thickness convincingly reveals a man with very penetrating eyes. The design relies on the established fact that humans visualize incomplete details they see as predictable objects. A bright spot of light on a dark round shape flanked by more light is interpreted as an eye and helps define other more ambiguous details into a face. The face is cropped in to only show the area from the forehead to just below the mouth. He appears to be peaking out of a small window, seeking a response from the viewer.

The choice to work in pale earth tones for the pile and predominately white, coarsely spun wool for the face adds to the understated quality of the piece. Even the blue and red used for the features are muted. The softness of most colors gives more impact to a rich dark brown used primarily for heavy short lines that create the eyes and nostrils and hint at the mouth. The tapestry is finished so that it can be displayed with either the pile or flat weave side showing, and the church has alternated its orientation over the years.

Shining Knight

43" x 36", 1976

Color plate 4a

Shining Knight, *43" x 36", 1976*

In a far less tentative depiction of this notable man, *Shining Knight* has a luminous woven Mylar background surrounding the face of Eliot. There is more definition and variation in thickness of the lines, especially those forming the eyebrows and nostrils. All the details are in brown and dark blue. The main filler yarn for the face is brown cotton roving in its natural ochre hue. Its uneven tone and non-reflective surface are an exciting contrast to the silver Mylar of the frame. The warp alternates blue with one of two browns. It weaves in and out through the flat strips of Mylar, creating an attractive frame.

As in *Nader*, at close range the weaving does not communicate a face, but a textural delight of contrasting materials and vivid linear shapes. It is a very successful and contemporary work of art, giving stature to the commanding face.

Prisma, *29" x 29", 1975*

One other portrait was framed in an expanse of Mylar. *Prisma* was woven the year before *Shining Knight*. The female face is enclosed in a circle, cropped in close to the eyes, and not including the entire mouth. The face is multicolored and executed in Nezhnie's classic horizontal line rendering. The original owners, parents of its current owner, had a large collection of Fornasetti plates that might have been the inspiration for the stylized face. The plates feature large round portraits with round eyes and an exaggerated Cupid's bow upper lip.

Prisma (detail)
29" x 29", 1975

While the face is colorful, it is muted and very delicate. The base tone is a golden beige used by itself only to delineate the central area. It highlights the area around the upper lip and defines the long nose and contour of the forehead. Elsewhere the beige alternates with stripes of muted prismatic colors. The stripes at the lower part of the circle begin the progression with magenta used alone to form the upper lip. The shadow below the nose is in solid orange, and the striped cheeks are orange shifting to gold. The eyes are pale green with blue shading that changes to soft purple stripes for the forehead. The formal linear pattern is broken up only to form the contours, like the prominent nose and an area just below the eyes where the horizontal lines become distorted. Gaps of beige meander vertically to suggest protruding eyes in a relatively flat face. There is a break in the lines going down the left cheek that hints at a falling tear.

The curved edge around the face created a slightly less successful transition between the Mylar and soft yarns of the face than in *Shining Knight*. With a vertical edge, a precise triangular turn in the relatively inflexible polyester film is accomplished; when the turn is not straight, the bend of flat Mylar is not quite as attractive. Yet, it is only a small technical caveat in a definitely charming blend of materials. The decision to use a prismatic palette works well with the Mylar, which reflects all the changing light cast upon it. There is a thin curved fringe of delicate multicolored warp threads that subtly reflect the tones of the face. The scale of the fringe adds to the success of the piece. Like many of the other privately collected tapestries, it is beautifully suited to its surroundings, a shimmery dining room of chrome, silver, and opalescent details.

Valentine I, *20" x 28", 1977;* **Valentine II,** *36" x 44", 1977 (not pictured)*

Had this discussion of Muriel's work been organized differently, there might have been an entire category about whimsy. Many of the little people were whimsical. She had a playful side to her that balanced her very serious nature. In the two *Valentine* pieces a heart-shaped female face is woven with the letters "Be My Valentine" surrounding and forming its features. The eyes are within the "a" and first "e" of Valentine, along with the mouth which is

The Door
59" x 58", 1968

Doll Baby
19" x 16" plus fringe,
1977

the last "e." The composition was inspired by a painting Ilisha did as a child.

The Door, *59" x 58", 1968*

Muriel's clever presentation of whimsical imagery also allowed her to express controversial issues in very palatable ways as the earlier work, *The Door*, illustrates.

The tapestry is divided in two with the exterior of the door on the left and its interior view on the right. The distinctions are made obvious by details like the mail slot and doorknocker on the outside and the chain catch on the inside. A small window in each door reveals a face peering in from outside and peering out from inside. At first the concept of the faces looking through the window seems an amusing comment on curiosity. However, upon further examination, a more poignant statement is revealed. The highlighted side of the interior face is pale; that of the exterior face is a darker tan. The safety latch securely in place alludes to the exclusion of people of color from opportunities and the security afforded those of lighter skin. As the owner of the tapestry pointed out, Nezhnie was very aware of the inequalities present in society.

Doll Baby, *19" x 16" plus fringe, 1977*

Doll Baby seems stylistically similar to work woven in the 1960s, especially the primitive, free-form images with fringe. It is also the only example reminiscent of a style of tapestry weaving that was popular in the 1970s, sometimes referred to as Polish weaving. Images woven in this style are built in overlapping irregular lozenge shapes of generally analogous colors. Woven in vibrant wools, *Doll Baby* is oval, papoose-like, with short curved fringe at the bottom. A variety of golden and coppery tones surround a deep green face, with plumes of yellow accented with bold dots of magenta rising from the head. The middle area has horizontal bands of greens and magentas to either side of a coppery shape on which rests a magenta heart with a green hand at its center. The lower section is divided into the overlapping curved shapes identifying it with the Polish tapestry style. They are of varying shades of magenta, accented by a slash of golden yellow. It is a charming little primitive of beautiful, cheerful colors.

Portrait of the Artist as Young Woman, *60" x 43", 1977;*
Young Artist, *36" x 80", 1978;*
Young Wife, *64" x 38", 1978*

Muriel designed several self-portraits from old photographs that she used specifically for training apprentices. One cartoon of a greatly enlarged face was used several times. It broke the image into bands and stripes of color, with no pretense of subtle shading. While most of the design consists of straight vertical stripes, some areas, especially in the hair and eyelids, are angled bands. These bold deviations from the vertical pattern transport the image from being mundane to visually effective. A pensive and attractive young woman emerges from the woven surface.

Portrait of the Artist as Young Woman
60" x 43", 1977
Pictured on cover

Young Husband, *40" x 58", 1979*

A counterpart, *Young Husband,* was woven predominantly of white textured yarn, similar to the background of *Nader,* with its features in soft brown. His attentive face, propped up by his hands, appears to be listening and looking. Behind the face, on the tapestry's left side, the textural background changes from the vertical white ridges to what appears to be the slope of a roof and side of a house woven in a brick pattern of tans and rust. It is a delicate composition revealing many details, with very minimal lines of color or areas of shading. For example, a small curve of brown at the edge of his left eye is all that indicates where the little finger is placed. Deann Rubin wove the tapestry. It is not known exactly which apprentices

Young Husband
40" x 58", 1979
Color plate 5d

Zelda
8" x 11", 1977
Color plate 8e

wove the self-portraits of Nezhnie, but it is believed that Jan Jungkunst wove *Portrait of the Artist as Young Woman* and that Georgia Tewel wove *Young Wife*.

While the scale of many of the portraits was greatly enlarged, Nezhnie also began to weave small silk portraits in the late 1970s. In general, Nezhnie designed portraits and figures to be woven on their side, as in the conventional European tapestry tradition. Thus, what appears as vertical stripes in the finished tapestries are actually woven in horizontal bands. Nezhnie believed figures appeared in better proportion if woven sideways. Sometimes in the packing down of weft threads, the figure distorts and becomes squat if woven in the vertical orientation. It is more flattering to err in the direction of figures that are more elongated than foreshortened. However, many of her designs are exceptions to this practice, such as *Circus* and the two Mylar pieces, as well as all of the silk miniatures.

Most of the miniatures have a border and fringe of nubby brown silk flecked with natural white and interspersed with lines of purple. The faces are no more than six or seven inches in either direction. All but *Phil Ochs* are woven in very fine, lustrous silk yarns.

Zelda, *8" x 11", 1977*

Zelda is the face of a mature woman in three-quarter profile. It is woven in six colors: dark red, deep purple, pale pink, and three closely related shades of straw yellow, light yellow orange, and light terra cotta. The oranges and pink work together to form the base color of the image. If the color of the portrait had been applied in layers, as in printing, the foundation color for the face would be the medium yellow orange, with the first layer of detail added in the soft terra cotta to create the mouth, eye socket, and cheek. The hair is predominantly the lightest straw yellow, with most details in red. Highlights are created in pale pink; shadow and definition are established with deep red and purple.

An interesting effect is created by using the dark colors primarily in single horizontal lines. They frequently traverse parts of both background and figure. Because the silk is very fine, the lines appear delicate and wavy. Occasionally, the lines leave the horizontal plane to curve into the outline of the mouth, then thicken to form an earlobe, or to create some other detail. The only boldly solid area is the hint of a red collar that narrows to form the back of her neck and ultimately defines the earlobe. It continues the diagonal movement above the ear, coming close to eye level. The back of the hairline and the profile are effectively delineated even though the background color is essentially the same as the head. The portrait is one of the few of Nezhnie's in which the eyes do not dominate the composition. They communicate never-

Eliot Again
8" x 10", 1978
Photo by Janita Loder.
Color plate 8c

theless, revealing age and a very human quality to the face.

The colors complement each other well and appear lively set against the textured dark frame. There is a small area of yellow to the side of the face with a few purple lines in it, giving the portrait space within the frame. The face is not centered, but has a wider border in the direction it is looking. It is an exquisite rendition of a beautiful, mature face, perhaps only surpassed by one of the faces in *Daughters of Earth*. What Nezhnie accomplished in weaving the little faces, influenced the larger works to come.

Eliot Again, *8" x 10", 1978*

Eliot Again is the most minimalistic of the miniatures. It is as stunning as *Zelda* for its ability to capture the luminous beauty of woven silk. The central portion of the face is golden, most likely the same combination of silks described previously. The nose is a column of lighter straw yellow. Dimension is established on the left cheek by adding a tanner gold to the primary golden tone. The eyes, and whatever other detail is included, are rendered in brown and some purple. Very fine lines of purple are used sparingly on the face's left side and more densely around the eyes. A series of purple lines curve out from the right eye. There is only a thin line of mouth positioned close to the lower edge of the image. The right ear and surrounding hair are conveyed, almost parenthetically, in brown and purple. The nubby border on that side is very narrow and combines with the dark details of hair to visually equal the wider border on the other side of the tapestry.

The sparsely detailed composition directs the viewer to contemplate the golden luster of the surface. The warp is many times wider than the thickness of the weft silk. Vertical ridges are formed, each ridge reflecting at least three intensities of golden light. The effect would be impossible to achieve in most other materials, except perhaps, if gold leaf had been applied to a similarly textured fabric.

Evangelos
11" x 10", 1980
Color plate 8b

Evangelos, *11" x 10", 1980*

Evangelos is as bold a composition as *Eliot Again* is subtle. It is a much more challenging combination of colors, even though it is woven in several of the same colors as were used before. The face is essentially divided in two unequal sections, with the side closest to the viewer composed of highlights in orange. Its features are defined in two shades of blue. The orange is actually the same coppery gold silk used in previous pieces, but because it is surrounded by blue, it appears more intense. The left side is almost hidden behind the large curving line of chin, nose, and forehead. It is accented in natural nubby gray silk, with red and purple definition. The face is set apart from the frame with a narrow section of yellow also used with purple to create his striped shirt. The nubby gray of the background frame blends down into the face at the top of the forehead, emphasizing the large features.

The strident orange and blue combination makes the tapestry harder to look at than the other two, but it is an equally exciting composition. It defines a man of bold features, given an earthiness by the integration of the nubby silk with its fine cultivated silk counterpart.

Phil Ochs, *9" x 11", 1978*

Phil Ochs was woven in an inlay technique. It is rich in color and texture. A variety of fibers including wool, brown cotton roving, and silk are banded across the portrait. Most features are in a dark purple, with highlighted areas in cotton ranging from ochre to almost white. The hair and shadows are pronounced bands of green, blue, and purple. Very close up, the green is bright, seemingly much brighter than the other bands. Yet, it all blends together convincingly when seen from five or six feet away. Nezhnie was exceptionally skilled at selecting the right values of color to produce a desired effect. In this case it aids the transitions between bands and controls the light-dark relationship. The image is placed on top of a tan raw silk background and held in place with fine brown silk "tie-down" threads. It is surprising how lifelike the image appears, despite its textural quality and limited detail.

Phil Ochs

9" x 11", 1978

Color plate 8d

Muriel was fortunate to have the chance to use private collection commissions to explore ideas and techniques. The 1970s proved to be an especially fertile time. She took advantage of any opportunity that came her way to investigate a range of styles. In general, she tended to do at least two pieces in any particular style, although *Phil Ochs* appears to be the only one to use inlay. Her versatility in style and size was remarkable. Because so many exhibits at the time had size requirements that restricted small works from being included, weaving miniatures was as daring, if not more so, than creating monolithic tapestries.

Portrait of Dr. Richard Ferry, *24" x 26", 1978*

Nezhnie wove one larger, though still not big, portrait in 1978. It has the most elaborate patterning of any of the portraits, and yet is as realistic as any other. This Ferry portrait is comparable to *Acrobats* in the concept of using pattern in both foreground and background, but the treatment is very different.

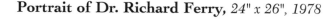

Portrait of Dr.
Richard Ferry
24" x 26", 1978
Color plate 8a

About half of the face, its flat planes, is taupe with broad highlights of beige and taupe horizontal stripes. The shadows are delineated in both horizontal and vertical stripes of blue or gray and taupe. The multiple combinations of stripes give a coarse or weathered look to the mature face. Exposed, light-colored warp threads that appear to be both taupe and beige are responsible for some of the textured effect.[12] The gray upper lip is the only solid detail. Shadows near the hairline are woven in two grays, and even the taupe surfaces that appear uniform are woven in two very similar shades. The eyes and lids are a darker taupe and black mottled with gray. There are many contours consisting of vertical and horizontal stripes used to form the eyes and brows. The "whites" of the eyes are taupe. The hair is alternating strips of mottled black, blue, gray, and dark tan to imply waves.

There is a small portion of medium-value blue background extending vertically beyond the left side of the face. This uniquely solid section of blue is crucial to the composition because it defines the space, giving the face a sense of depth and distancing it from the asymmetrically patterned frame. A good balance occurs between the more intricate, linear stripe patterns of the frame and those of the face. The predominantly tan and black bands in the frame convey solidity and structure. It all combines into a very masculine image.

Nezhnie's acquaintances have remarked that they would find her in her studio mired in the weaving of some detail that was too complicated to accomplish without a great deal of patience and guesswork. This tapestry might have been just such a piece, although it has none of the appearance of a struggle whatsoever. Its size is helpful because all of the face, approximately 20" x 15", could be seen as it progressed. Nevertheless, it had to be woven spontaneously. It would have been impossible to predetermine each pattern shift, either in the face or frame. She would have indicated where shading needed to occur, but how to achieve the proper density of any color would have to be worked out at the loom. She had to be actively engaged in every row of every shape of the tapestry's progression. Muriel liked this kind of active involvement. On the other hand, such focused concentration required to continually make creative decisions is shockingly exhausting. It is quite

---

12   The current status of the tapestry is not known, despite a thorough attempt in 2003 to locate the owner. Therefore, the description is from the photograph and one brief statement by Michael Buchman in her files: "by showing the light warp Muriel infuses the piece with a glowing sense of life."

possible that she would emerge very tired, or sometimes frustrated, from even a short session of weaving such intricate designs. Nevertheless, for her, there was more reward in exploring an elaborate idea than there was in settling for easily accomplished designs, even in commission work.

One of the most regretful aspects of Nezhnie not being closer to the forefront of weaving at this time is that other weavers were not exposed to her mid-career work. Even her most experimental work was often for private commissions and therefore rarely in exhibitions. Had she been on the workshop and lecture circuit or featured in the weaving journals more frequently, these works would be better appreciated.

Early in her career she had successfully gained national recognition in weaving exhibitions with two pieces featured in *Craft Horizon* in 1962, but the predominance of interest in sculptural weaving emerging in the late 1960s afforded her only rare acceptance into national weaving exhibits or articles in magazines in the 1970s. She did continue submitting photographs, but the response, such as that from Jack Lenor Larson, coauthor of *Beyond Craft*, published in 1972, was mainly that her work was too traditional for the book's focus. One opportunity for national exposure did come her way. Photographs of several of her tapestries, the most recent being *Springfield Genesis*, 1974, were featured in the book *Creative Handweaving* by Xenia Ley Parker in 1976. How Nezhnie and Parker connected is not known. Perhaps the author placed a call for photographs of current work in the weaving journals. Nezhnie was active in submitting photographs to whatever leads she discovered.

Her experience entering *Wild Cherry Charms* in the 1973 Lausanne Biennial was, perhaps, the most frustrating attempt to compete during those years. She actually attended the exhibit while the family was traveling in Europe. The work that had been accepted for the exhibit was so far removed from the direction Nezhnie wanted to pursue that it was a shock. Ten of the fifty-five items were not even woven. As one reviewer describes the entry from Magdalena Abakanowicz, *La Corde*:

> It greeted you at the entrance, ran along the floor of the first gallery, over and around an eight-foot cable reel in the second gallery, back down to the floor, up to the ceiling in the third gallery, down to a heap of ropes, up again, and — out the window! — whence it was suspended above a pond, over a wall, and out of the exhibition.[13]

Another entry, this by Sheila Hicks called *The Preferred Wife Occupies Her Nights*, was a very colorful disk wrapped in linen with thick cords wound

---

13 Meltzer, Marilyn, "But is it tapestry?" *Shuttle, Spindle and Dyepot*, Handweavers Guild of America (Summer, 1974): 39.

in silk extending over it and onto the floor. The experience left Nezhnie feeling deeply isolated from the mainstream of weaving at the time, but still driven to pursue her own interests.

Even without the impetus of competing on an international scale, she had plenty of challenges to keep her stimulated. It was a time of intense exploration, not only with the use of photographs, but also with new materials such as Mylar and natural fibers other than wool. Muriel discovered new techniques and formats like those utilized in the miniatures or reversible tapestries. She executed over forty-five tapestries in her studio during the 1970s, including many monumental commissions. She also did the design work for several very large hooked commissions, all involving a huge amount of correspondence and trips to the sites or to New York to confer with the fabricators. In addition, she began her journey towards creating the Holocaust series, completing *Daughters of Auschwitz* in 1979.

Where Nezhnie was most innovative was in pushing the way lines could define images. Focusing so exclusively on portraits in her personal work during that period allowed her to delve deeply into the options possible for creating form in ways other than mirroring painting. The progression from the *Charms* tapestries to works like the equally innovative *Shining Knight* and *Zelda* reveals a transition to an ever more obviously woven image. The viewer becomes aware of the path of the yarns. The more present that path, the more the essence of the face is captured. It is this kind of progression, from the imitative to the imaginative, that an artist strives to achieve, and Nezhnie obtained.

Striving for Balance and Perspective

Nezhnie was never willing to sacrifice any of the goals she had defined for herself. She sought to carve out a total life that met her standards. It was not enough to be a successful artist if her personal life was suffering, nor was it enough to be a good wife and mother if she could not express herself artistically. Her need for a high level of interaction with people was a third driving force shaping how she channeled her energy. If anything had to be sacrificed, it was her time for regeneration — time to sleep. It all had to add up to success. It is fascinating to observe how she maneuvered all the facets of her life to that end.

Even though she craved involvement with others, Nezhnie never considered teaching as a major component on her path to success. In terms of a career, her ambition was directed primarily to discovering venues where she could sell her art and to investigating whatever opportunities were available for commissions.

It did not take Muriel long to realize that St. Louis lacked opportunities for local craftsmen to show and sell their work. A few venues offered imported crafts and heirlooms, and the public purchased them enthusiastically. The response showed that the climate was right, but that local work was being ignored. She knew there were plenty of skilled craftspeople in the area. The public needed to know what was being produced locally. Her idea was to have an exhibit that showed not only the work, but also the tools and processes, so that the public could be educated about objects made by hand rather than machine.

She met with five other women who were also interested in promoting local crafts. An organization for craftsmen already existed in the area, but it was faltering. The women decided to start over on their own. They began raising funds and looking for exhibition venues. An architect offered them temporary space in a building he had just finished. Then a theater company, whose building renovation Shelly was designing, wanted the group to display their work in areas where the theater patrons would congregate, providing a ready-made audience. It did not take long, however, for the women to see drawbacks to either option in terms of security and the logistics of selling the work.

At this time there was a movement in progress to revitalize a section of St. Louis known as the Central West End. An architect, responsible for developing many of the new galleries in the area, was interested in establishing a craft gallery there, too. He called Nezhnie and said he knew of a perfect space for such a gallery and thought it would be fun to open with a Christmas exhibit. In her words:

> And we all went bananas because we were thinking about a little show with the Gateway Theater, and suddenly, we were in business. We had four months to open that place, to rent it and organize ourselves. And we did it. (Castro, 36)

In order to incorporate in the state of Missouri, they needed to have fifteen members. Spouses and friends were enlisted along with both architects who had shown interest in the cause. Craft Alliance opened on December 13, 1964, to an enthusiastic public. The gallery was organized as a cooperative, with exhibiting members paying $5.00 a month. The plan was to have ten exhibits per year, with the gallery closed for two months in the summer. Any person actively producing crafts was invited to submit items to be juried by a rotating selection committee. By the second year, they began having classes in the summer. They also published a bimonthly newsletter called *The* CRAFTSMAN, which Shelly and Muriel designed and produced together.

Nezhnie was on the board of directors for sixteen years, actively hanging shows, exhibiting, and participating in policy decisions. She was the type of person who could get totally immersed in a project. Along with the architect, Richard Cummings, she worked through two nights to get the initial exhibit ready. They were still cleaning up and getting into party clothes as patrons arrived. Along with several other women who exhibited extensively in the early days of the gallery, she was considered a mentor to a generation of young female artists beginning their careers in the late 1960s and the 1970s.

Nezhnie's gregarious nature and interest in problem solving propelled her into a role that was a major time commitment. Many hours were spent on the phone dealing with Craft Alliance issues and many more at the gallery hanging shows. In the late 1970s, Nezhnie co-directed and taught summer programs for children.

It is hard to overestimate her appetite for human contact. Very high on the list of her priorities was an unconditional commitment to giving time to anyone in need of advice or support. No deadline of her own came before dealing with a request for attention from a friend or colleague in need. Consequently, she frequently found herself working into the wee hours of the night as one of her deadlines approached. She had the capacity to go for several days with only a few hours of sleep, without sacrificing the quality of the work that resulted. She was selective, however, when it came to social events and didn't hesitate to decline an engagement when it threatened her work time.

Muriel could "think on her feet." When a problem came up at the gallery, whoever was in charge often called her for a quick solution rather than deliberate over it or appear vague to a customer. Another interesting phenomenon was that she could quickly extrapolate what a person's personality was like. It was a trait she had fun with, especially at gallery openings or large social gatherings. She liked to tease someone she perceived as being pretentious. That was one quality in people she couldn't tolerate.

Nezhnie's contribution, according to collectors and artists alike, was monumental. As one of the other founding members of the gallery suggested, without Muriel and her tireless work, there would have been no Craft Alliance. It has been said that all six founders were strong women. Most had long careers in other fields, such as law and journalism, while maintaining an interest in the crafts. Nezhnie was the one most single-minded about her art and the gallery.

Her colleagues claim that no one else was as dedicated as she was to seeing that details got done. And yes, one admitted that although Muriel was her good friend, she was a difficult woman. She made enemies along the way; their perception was that she always thought she was right. Nezhnie had very high expectations of herself and was in the habit of pushing to accomplish whatever she wanted to see happen. She could lose sight of other approaches. Thus, she presented a different side of her personality to her co-workers than she did socially, where she could relax and be charming. It is said that she might come in after someone had finished hanging an exhibit and insist that objects be rehung, not necessarily her own work, but anything she felt could be displayed in a better way. It was hard for her to let go of the authority she had earned through countless hours of dedicated work and the countless interruptions she had tolerated over the years.

Despite overstepping her role occasionally, her commitment to art was a model admired and emulated. Many of the women whom she influenced learned how to maneuver in a professional and very persuasive way from her example. Others were grateful for the time she gave to them. Recognizing the potential of one weaver not accepted the first time she applied to exhibit, Nezhnie went to her house to encourage her to continue weaving and to expand her skills with design classes. The woman was impressed with Muriel's thoughtfulness, took her advice, and forged a very successful career in weaving.

In 1970, Craft Alliance moved its gallery to a rented space in University City where the second floor was converted into classrooms. Throughout the decade, the emphasis gradually shifted away from being a cooperative gallery. As a cooperative venture, energy was directed towards making sure that members were actually producing enough items and working their quota of hours in the gallery. Dissention started to mount. Pressure was placed on members to keep their work current and share the responsibility of staffing the gallery. A proposal gained momentum to restructure the gallery as an enterprise with paid staff.

One of the most convincing tenets of the Women's Movement taking shape at the time was that women be paid for the community services they did. It was a valid expectation, but it also was the demise of many excellent endeavors that could not be fully funded and needed to rely on volunteers. Supporters of the reorganization believed that it was imperative to select exhibits from a larger field of artists, especially relying on the work of established artists, in order to attract a greater sales appeal. It was a direction that Muriel resisted tenaciously. Members were divided into factions by the shift away from providing a viable way for local artists to exhibit their work. After sixteen years on the board, Nezhnie left with feelings of defeat.

The legacy of the cooperative venture can be seen in the enduring creativity of the early participants. Many have sustained a lifetime of artistic expression and passed their love of art on to their children and a new generation of artists. An interesting phenomenon related to the shift of emphasis was that the majority of members who activated the change moved on to other interests, relocating to other places quite quickly, leaving a new staff to rebuild community support. The gallery has survived to celebrate its fortieth anniversary in 2004. Very few craft galleries have endured that long. Craft Alliance was able to withstand the schism because of the emerging emphasis on classes and a reliance on grants to spearhead new programs. It has changed, but so have the times. St. Louis still has a place to view and acquire well-crafted items, though not as many are of local origin.

There were other changes in Nezhnie's life that coincided with her struggles and eventual withdrawal from active participation in the gallery. By the late 1970s both of her children were away in college, affecting her role at home as well. Also, her mother's health and mental stability faltered, and she died early in 1979. Thus, Muriel's position as both mother and child changed during this period, too. Nezhnie saw the transitions as a time to redirect her professional focus and concentrate more on her personal artistic endeavors, leading to the Holocaust series.

Of all the goals Muriel strove to accomplish, perhaps the hardest to evaluate is that of being a good mother and wife. Devoting time and energy to the family was a crucial component of her life that she had to balance with the demanding involvement necessary for her professional commitments.

She loved her children enthusiastically and was definitely proud of their achievements. Nevertheless, she was demanding, having equally high expectations for them as she did for herself. An artist friend described her as a perfectionist. Whereas many creative people choose not to let clutter or mundane household duties distract them, Muriel needed to exist in a very presentable, attractive environment. Household accessories and her own personal appearance, though casual, were always well thought out. She enjoyed choosing her clothes in the morning, for example, with an eye for an interesting presentation, even for a day in the studio. Though small in stature, her dynamic personality and tenacious drive made her a force to be reckoned with, even on the home front.

Happy Chanukah photograph, 1966

It is tempting to generalize that in the Helfman family, Muriel's needs came first. A more accurate statement is that her assessment of what needed to be accomplished took priority. She was a very giving person, quite capable of sacrificing her own interests for those of others. Yet, she brought much more intensity to implementing her way of doing things than others in the family could muster. If she had figured out how to approach an issue, it would take a very clever rebuttal to change her mind. It was the natural outcome of the personality she had developed with each successful assertion of her will and her resourcefulness since early childhood. Also, even though she did not condone her mother's demanding personality, it was the example of motherhood that she knew best. Thus, it is not surprising that she set the rules and demanded a lot from the other family members.

It is also not surprising that Shelly chose to take a lesser role in structuring the dynamics. His mother died when he was eleven, and his father, a strict, deeply religious man, raised him in a very authoritarian manner. Shelly wanted to be a different kind of father than his had been. Muriel would have liked for him to take more initiative, but determined that his children not face a judgmental father, he often deferred to her about discipline.

Everyone had responsibilities and duties. The children understood that family events took precedence over spending time with friends. According to Ilisha:

> We adopted a friend's "Communist House Cleaning" system for a while, and I totally hated it. It involved two hours of cleaning by everyone in the family at the same time, each to his/her ability every

week. Mom liked how the short people would dust the baseboards while the tall people would dust the doorframes, etc. It was torture. I remember helping with the cooking quite a bit and in fact became vegetarian at the age of twelve with the understanding that I'd have to make nourishing meals for myself or go back on the family diet. The family ate my food, which was fine with me. . . . I appreciate that my mom gave me the power to make that kind of decision for myself at such a young age.

The family went to movies, played games, or watched favorite TV programs together in the evenings. Much of their entertainment time was spent socializing with one family in particular, most often involving a meal at one house or the other. Vacations were generally camping trips, frequently cross-country car trips. Both children have many memories of the camping trips. According to Ilisha:

We used to do a lot of art projects with Mom when we were kids, and she always encouraged creativity. . . .When we camped across the country and back the summer my parents taught at what was then called Portland State College [1966], we would sit at the picnic tables and draw portraits of each other. (I remember my brother and I drawing my dad.) We used to take turns reading aloud when we went camping.

Jonathan remembers trips to Mesa Verde, the Grand Canyon, and when he was four, to Mexico. The three-month European camping trip when he and Ilisha were in high school was routed so that the family could see as much artwork and architecture as possible. He considered it an amazing experience.

They spent time in Greece and then purchased a VW camper van. They paid for the van with money from the commission that caused their delay in embarking on the trip. It was an embarrassing transaction. The funds had not yet been deposited into their account as they had expected. Everything was straightened out, and the family was off on their adventure. The van was shipped back to New Orleans when they returned. It turned out to be a very convenient vehicle for hauling tapestries. Vivian Alpert Thompson, who interviewed Nezhnie in Atlanta in 1982, recalls Muriel pulling the early Holocaust tapestries out of the back. She was amazed that such valuable tapestries had been stashed in the back of such a humble looking van.

Shelly and Muriel had a flair for finding unique objects, not necessarily valuable or

Jon and an intent audience as he prepares to fish.

pristine, but noteworthy. Shelly especially enjoyed discovering antiques in unexpected places. Even when they were a newly married couple with young children, they did not deny themselves the pleasure of buying artwork. They preferred to scrimp in some other way, perhaps making bread rather than buying it, or stretching other supplies in order to acquire something of beauty.

Muriel was exceptionally resourceful. Her creative problem solving amazed her closest friend, Maria Michaelides. In fact, when asked to comment on Muriel as a mother, one of her first statements was that she was imaginative. She also stated that Muriel could make a meal out of almost nothing and so was always comfortable spontaneously inviting folks to stay for a meal.

Muriel and Jon with a Chanukah gift.

Eating the proper foods and having a well-balanced diet were very important to Muriel. She made a point of being informed about the ingredients of products she purchased. Maria remembers that she was very concerned about the presence of strontium 90 in milk and used powdered milk for quite a while. Though she didn't read novels frequently, she was an avid reader of newspapers and magazines, especially concerning health and scientific discoveries. She particularly enjoyed magazines, like *Scientific American*, that were visually stimulating as well as informative on a wide range of subjects.

The preparation of food definitely was a form of expression and communal activity that gave Muriel great pleasure. Everyone who spent time with her relates that food was always attractively presented, a work of art. Elaborately arranged fruit platters were a specialty, and anything served was always garnished. The Helfmans enjoyed collecting interesting dishes, teapots, and glassware that they used daily or for special occasions. The children, even when very young, were encouraged to prepare attractive snacks, learning that how food looked was as important as what was served.

Ilisha referred to her parents as having adventurous tastes. They were avid collectors of cookbooks and enjoyed cooking together. Some of the exotic dishes she remembers her mother making on a fairly regular basis include steamed eggplant slices with a delicious thickened sweet soy sauce with minced candied ginger on top, saffron rice with butter-sautéed pistachios, stuffed cabbage with raisins in light tomato sauce, and a "sort of baked cracker out of sauerkraut and caraway seeds thickened with a little flour." The meals often started off with fruit, especially grapefruit or avocados. Sometimes the grapefruit halves were baked with a dab of jam in the center, which surely awakened their taste buds for sensations to come. On the other hand, they also had such mundane fare as frozen pizzas and fish sticks, since fresh fish was hard to get in St. Louis at the time. Since their closest family friends were Greek, shared meals often featured Greek cuisine.

Most of the twelve apprentices Nezhnie trained joined the Helfmans and any guests for lunch. The family got used to sharing their space with whoever was working at the time. From the accounts of several apprentices, the meals were always a highlight of the day, with interesting food elegantly presented and enjoyable conversations. Christel Maassen recalls sandwiches such as avocado, red pear, and sweet onion slices with mayonnaise and a sprinkling of bacon on top, or a poppy seed bagel with cream cheese, red onions, and sardines that broadened her culinary tastes. She also came to appreciate canned tomato soup because it was served in such an appealing way, perhaps in a colorful blue bowl. It was not uncommon for Shelly to prepare the lunches if he was at home, and the children routinely helped in meal preparation.

Both Ilisha and Jon agree that the presence of apprentices enriched their lives. Some became very close to the family. A few chose to bring a lunch and spend their break alone, but in general the apprentices interacted with family members. They were able to let themselves in through the basement studio door in the morning, but many chose to give greetings to whichever family members were around before settling down to work. Those who boarded with the Helfmans while they were working for Nezhnie were made to feel welcomed into the family routines. Being gracious and hospitable was part of the family dynamics.

When Nezhnie had a deadline to meet, everyone was put to work. A prized family photo is of Jonathan as a young boy, sewing slits for his mother. He enjoyed the process. Ilisha recounts a gallery opening where she and Jon sat behind a tapestry, tying knots as people walked by them on the other side, a novelty they thought great fun. Both children recall spending hours in the studio, playing and feeling the communal spirit in their mother's workspace. As a young child, Jon was

The view from behind the loom looking through the warp.

fascinated by watching the warp threads go up and down as he lay beneath a loom. They also spent many hours at Craft Alliance. Jon was of kindergarten age when his mother became involved in organizing the gallery.

While lunch was a social event, he muses, "Dinner was always as a family, just us and the Vietnam War on TV. Watching the news was important, but I found the body count unappetizing." His primary complaint about chores was that he hated to shop, even for things for himself.

A friend of the family stated that Muriel felt she was a good mother and noted: "She was also proud that her son Jonathan knew how to sew and that Ilisha could use a hammer and nails. She wanted them to be self-sufficient."

They were encouraged to participate in whatever activities they chose, such as music lessons, but the logistics of getting to classes, rehearsals, or social events was their responsibility. Nezhnie went to performances and school functions but did not feel it was her obligation to chauffeur her children. It was not an unreasonable attitude for a woman who had spent hours commuting to art classes in her teens. For the most part, because the house was centrally located, the two could ride their bikes to whatever activities they were involved in. When Ilisha wanted to take oboe lessons from a teacher further out in the suburbs, however, she had to wait an hour and a half after her lesson for the ride she had arranged. She gave the lessons up after ten weeks. In Muriel's defense, at times it seems that some mothers lose their own perspective as they get caught up in seeing that their children acquire as many skills as possible. It is ironic that at the same time, the one practice they are not exposing their children to is the commitment to their own pursuits, to structuring time for their own meaningful outlets as adults. Ilisha and Jon lived in an environment where adults challenged themselves, too.

Nezhnie believed strongly in public education and felt her children needed to grow up in a multicultural environment. She had observed friends, who were raised in ethnically unified neighborhoods, experience painful cultural shock when they left their community to go to college or relocate for a job. Ilisha recalls that her mother took them to hear Martin Luther King, Jr., and to some civil rights demonstrations when they were young.

While the school system included a broad spectrum of society, their neighborhood was relatively insular. Although it had a large percentage of Jewish families, its defining feature was less ethnic than cultural. It was an enclave of artists. A neighbor has recounted that there were three members of the St. Louis symphony orchestra, several architects, as well as many poets and visual artists living in the few winding streets of the limited-access subdivision. Being in close proximity to Washington University, many academicians lived there as well.

Both children were already pursuing artistic endeavors in high school.

Ilisha, radiant at her graduation from Yale Graduate School in 1981. Jon graduated from Harvard that semester, too.

Jon had a pottery studio set up in the garage, and Ilisha was selling textile designs commercially in New York through her own agents. When it came time for them to go to college, they benefited from a policy Washington University had for faculty children. It paid the equivalent of half its tuition toward that of any other college. Thus with a combination of Washington University's funding, tuition payments, work/study programs, and student loans the Helfmans were able to have two children at prestigious Ivy League universities at the same time. Ilisha went to Smith, graduating in 1979 with a major in art. She specialized in the study of pattern with the curator of rare books and the departments of art and math. She received an MFA in Graphic Design in 1981 from Yale. Jon graduated from Harvard in 1981 with a double major in electrical engineering and environmental design. He went on to get higher degrees through his employment at Bell Laboratories.

From all accounts, Ilisha and Jon were very normal, adjusted offspring. Children devise their own way of charting the path to take in order to keep themselves on reasonably smooth footing with their parents. A family friend remarked on their differing personalities. Ilisha was the less talkative of the two. Nevertheless, she was the one to challenge her mother most directly. She seemed to approach issues head on, deciding to comply with whatever was being disputed, or not. Jon, who had the benefit of being the second in line, could observe the consequences of the direct approach and chose more fluid tactics. He got in less conflict with his mother, partially because he was very quick to react and chose less interactive solutions.

Ilisha has stated that there was a lot of pressure placed on them to accommodate the personality and high standards of their mother. At times, it resulted in anger and resentment. She identified strongly with her father, feeling her mother placed far too many demands on his time. She was very conscious of Muriel's frustration about how slow tapestry was and about her mother's persistent regret at not having fulfilled her desire to be a painter. A parent who works outside the home has the opportunity to vent frustrations to co-workers, rather than to family members. Someone working primarily in the home is more likely to express dissatisfactions to the available children, which Muriel apparently did.

The different angle of discontent expressed to the two children is also interesting. To her female child, Muriel emphasized the sacrifices she made to keep harmony in the family; to defer, magnanimously, to her husband's painting career. According to Jon, the thrust of complaints appeared to be the sacrifices made as a mother. Were it not for all the time required to nurture her children, she could be producing more artwork. She enjoyed talking about her ideas for future projects, and he was a good listener, picturing her ideas in his mind. Jon recalls a wonderful series of people sitting on couches that she envisioned as a future project.

His interpretation of how he could best help his mother was to become solvent as soon as possible so she would not have to do so many commissions and could get on with her own work. He felt pressure to find a job at the age of fourteen. He was frustrated to discover that his mother continued to spend energy working on commissions well after he left home for college. He wanted to see all the images she had so vividly described to him come into being. Her motivation in sharing her creative side with him might have originated from a desire to show that she still was a stimulating, intellectually sharp person lest her male child forget that aspect and see her primarily in the role of caregiver. Her message to her daughter, however, might suggest that she be prepared to make some concessions for harmony. Such expressions of discontent may well serve as a form of instruction that is the way family values are informally passed on. While the issues women might currently direct towards their children in moments of reflection have evolved, the tendency to grumble to their children about missed opportunities most likely remains a potent element in family dynamics.

More to the point, from her children's perspective, Muriel's gregarious nature conflicted with their desire for her attention. She would get overly involved in external matters. At times, long telephone conversations about gallery matters or the personal traumas of various friends would postpone or eliminate the time she had to share with them.

It is important to mention that for all of Nezhnie's outgoing nature, she had another side that was not necessarily upbeat. As a mid-career friend, photographer Sharon Burde characterized her:

> I wouldn't call her optimistic. She always felt the weight of her family's relative poverty, the death of her beloved sister in a freak accident, and, more than anything, her mother's Alzheimer's disease.

Her children most likely experienced the persistent sorrows that were her heritage. Muriel was a woman of complex personality who, more than anyone else, shaped the family dynamics. With her as the energetic leader, the entire Helfman family worked as a team of artists, with gracious and productive living as their goal. Her success was a general concern of all its members.

Nezhnie never really resolved the issue of her missed opportunity to be a painter. For one thing, her personality was such that she did not easily give up a path she had chosen. Part of her self-worth remained attached to the dream of succeeding as a painter and emerged in moments of frustration. As a child, painting and art were synonymous to her, and since she knew she wanted to be an artist, that meant she would become a painter.

It is tempting to make judgments, to assume that she could have shifted to painting at some later time in her career if she wanted to. However, some of her friends have stated that she tried painting at various times and continued to feel that it would put a strain on the family to have two painters in competition. Even though their styles were completely different, she believed a sense of rivalry might exist that would be counterproductive to both. Neither partner could have contemplated life without the other and therefore had to find the set of compromises that would be most beneficial to coexistence and family harmony.

It is also tempting to suggest that there were other options she could have chosen that would have bypassed the actual weaving process and would have therefore given her the time for creative work. It would have been possible to be a designer, such as California artist and tapestry designer Mark Adams, and have the images woven in a workshop in France or several other countries. There were also a few American artists, even in the 1980s, who were creating works for major exhibitions intended to be woven by tapestry workshops, not displayed as paintings. These artists had become intrigued with the difference in effect caused by translating their images into fiber, but they were not interested, for the most part, in participating in the actual weaving process. That approach did not appeal to Nezhnie at all. In fact, she had the opportunity to see the work of famous artists being woven at Aubusson during their trip to France in 1973 and had a decidedly negative reaction to the concept.

For all Nezhnie's lamenting about the missed opportunities, the reality is that she had a great affinity for tapestry. Her actions showed an emotional response to weaving that could not be denied, as she described becoming intently alert and focused upon first discovering the tapestries in Paris. Perhaps, if it had not been for this strong affinity, she might have been forced to risk competing with her husband for self-expression in the painting world.

From the start, Nezhnie had decided to learn to weave because she thought she could contribute something to the medium and do a better job than what she saw. She was intrigued with the notion of creating the structure along with the image and committed to making images that presented art differently than in other media. There was no need to acquire a theoretical construct from which to proceed. She came to the field already equipped because she saw instinctively what the medium offered visually.

Further solidifying her direction, she simply was too good at what she did to discard her career as a weaver. There was a steady enough demand for her work to make it hard to shift gears along the way. She was much more advanced in balancing her design skills with her technical prowess than the majority of tapestry weavers emerging at the beginning of the fiber explosion and for many decades to come. Tapestry has never been a concentration given much attention in art schools in the United States, even in the peak of interest in weaving. Therefore it was not a part of the traditional exposure to techniques offered to art majors. Most American tapestry weavers have taken circuitous routes to becoming artists or shifted from another medium to tapestry. She did not have as much competition as she would have had in painting. Furthermore, since the kind of painting she wanted to do was not in vogue, it would have been an even harder struggle.

Even with her talent and intuitive understanding of tapestry's strengths, fame was still illusive. Nezhnie's frustration with the lack of recognition was not just an issue of ambition. She sought validation for her vision. What drives an artist is the act of bringing into being some form of expression that is fresh and personally exciting, to feel the surprise of seeing something emerge that is even more interesting than expected. That process is as honest as the individual can be and therefore is an intriguing and powerful incentive to continue being creative. Her discussion about the content of *Wild Cherry Charms* is an example of the kind of revelation that can occur. It is natural to want that excitement reciprocated.

Unfortunately, if what emerges does not coincide with the view held by most of the artist's colleagues about what is innovative, it is hard to sustain the euphoria of discovery. It is a fate Nezhnie shared with many artists throughout history, one that has never been easy to accept for the individual experiencing such a fate. That she could not secure a niche, either in painting because of her subject matter or in weaving because of her choice of technique, remained a recurrent frustration.

Perhaps her tendency to write extensive answers to inquiries and to revise her own comments so thoroughly can be explained by this frustration. She was driven to explain her perspective and to gain allies for her enthusiasm. Late in 1978, in a written response to the Crump questionnaire she expressed some interesting concepts about abstraction and the nature of content that show her maturing perspective. When asked if her work was decorative or more than that, and how she would define decorative, she stated:

> All visual art is decorative to some degree because it is concerned primarily with esthetic considerations. (This is not to be confused with the fact that the visual arts are most often "used" in decorative ways: when they are installed in shows, hung in rooms, placed in landscape, reproduced on a page; that does not mean the work itself

is decorative, only the use to which it is put.) Abstract art moves closest to the decorative. One has only the beauty of the medium and the composition of the color and forms in their metaphorical behavior to appreciate. There is little to distract you from this basic intellectual and visual adventure. It is the quality and degree of subject matter that moves art toward or away from decorativeness. When subject matter is added one becomes more or less engaged in its imagery rather than in the abstract elements. The strength of the image and the successful synthesis of it within the composition determines the nature of the art's ability to go beyond the decorative. In short, one will focus on what is being said more readily than how it is being expressed when subject matter is present. The decorative is usually thought of as the frivolous, pleasurable or ornamental rather than the tragic, awesome, sober or threatening. I've tried on all of the hats.

A gradual evolution occurred during her mid-career, shifting her focus away from establishing a reputation through commissions to putting more effort into her own creative direction. As she gained experience during the 1970s, she came to understand that she needed to expose her personal vision more openly. She was after an expression that would make the world stop and look at what she produced. It had to come from within herself. By the end of the decade, Nezhnie was primed to take personal risks.

The Holocaust Tapestries

In 1979 Nezhnie embarked on a series of tapestries that focused on the victims of Nazi persecution of Jews. The concept for the series took many years to evolve, but the seminal idea occurred during the Helfmans' trip to Europe in 1973.

The trip was a pivotal event in Nezhnie's career. Besides affording her the opportunity to visit the Lausanne Biennial, it gave her the chance to observe myriad tapestries woven throughout the centuries. In the Castro interview, she recounts her impressions of the beautiful old weavings and the Bayeux embroidered "tapestry" she saw. The account provides an interesting look into her thought processes and her rationale for undertaking the Holocaust project in the medium of tapestry.

> . . . There were the 11th century tapestries that we saw in Basel which are called "upper-Rhineish". They are primitive, and beautiful, and figurative! And they have kings and queens. They are little tapestries, they are patterned everywhere. And they are gorgeous! And then you get to the Angers 1373-1380 14th century.
> . . . they are most superb; they are the highest form for me, and after that most of the weaving gets much fussier. You go to the Cluny. You see the "Virgin and the Unicorn" tapestries, and they are already too removed. They become too mannered. They're gorgeous, but they are not as direct as the earlier works. (Castro, 19)

Seeing the beautiful early tapestries deepened her appreciation of the medium at a time when she most needed it. Once she realized having two painters in one family might create conflict, Nezhnie channeled her energy into weaving to such an extent that it would have been hard to change direction. Weaving proved to be a stimulating profession, yet because of the slow pace of production, moments of despair occurred all too frequently. At the time of the European trip, she was exhausted from working so rigorously for two years to complete the Adas Shalom commissions. A career as a painter must have looked quite appealing to her at the time. Witnessing the exhibit at Lausanne, where she felt like an outsider within her adopted field, did not help her morale, either.

Fortunately, the insights she gleaned through observing traditional tapestries allowed her to shift her perception from a dismal outlook about her future into an affirmation. The experience that influenced Nezhnie most profoundly was discovering the Bayeux tapestry.

> The Bayeux tapestry, which is actually a stitchery and not a tapestry at all, was remarkable. It was so literal. It is 10 or 11 inches tall and 110 feet long. It just keeps going and going and going around this old church — it's beautifully executed, and it's the history of the whole Norman invasion. And tied in with that experience was finally finding some of the American gravesites [from World War II]. . . . Bayeux turned out to be the town which sits right on the cliffs of Omaha Beach; it was the town that the Americans liberated first.
>
> There I not only found the Bayeux and the German bunkers but I found the largest cemetery that I had ever seen in my life. . . . I was sort of struck by that, realizing that this same spot had been invaded more than once. I also realized that tapestry has traditionally been a teaching, literary, extension. And that tied back to my interest in books and the written word and letterforms. I wasn't interested in telling the story of the Second World War, but I was interested in talking about the Nazis and the Jews. So Bayeux synthesized a lot of things that were important to me. (Castro, *River Styx*, 38)

Instead of coming home dismayed, she understood how well equipped she was for this field of endeavor. She began processing what content she wanted to develop. Much like when her interest in pop culture had been aroused earlier, she wanted to address historical topics that were relevant to her own experiences. Still, understanding that the impetus drawing her to the subject of the war was the desire to expose the catastrophic results of anti-Semitism proved to be an unsettling conclusion. It sent her into turmoil.

> And I was so afraid of my idea that I literally buried it for over four years; just terrified — that to deal with the subject would — would depress me to the point that I might not be able to function. I had no confidence that I could handle it; it kept haunting me; it kept coming back and coming back. Gradually I clarified some of my ideas. I have very strong feelings about genocide and racial prejudice. (Castro, *River Styx*, 38)

Her closest friend, Maria, admits that she tried everything she could think of to dissuade Muriel from taking on the project. She could not understand why someone would put herself through so much anguish, particularly at a time when she was free to stop driving herself so hard. Both children were away in college, and she was no longer involved with the gallery. Perhaps this new freedom was the key ingredient giving Nezhnie the energy needed to face the emotional consequences of the commitment.

I became obsessed with the idea of weaving tapestries that deal with the Nazi destruction and suffering. I didn't experience anything directly, or personally, but I did grow up in a community which had very active German-American BUND. And I did experience anti-Semitism in my father's store, and when we moved away from there, after my father's death. I was young, six years old and later in Jersey City I experienced more of the same. It was frightening, and the war was going on which was also frightening. (Castro, 17)

The war years were not just frightening to her; it was a time of personal tragedy in which she tangibly experienced the disintegration of her own family. Within four years, she lost both her father and her older sister, with whom she had a very loving relationship. Muriel was deeply affected by their deaths. The extent to which she identified with the plight of the Eastern European Jews at such an early age can be understood in the context of her own personal tragedies. It is not hard to imagine Nezhnie weighing her own sense of loss against the magnitude of loss suffered by the Jewish people collectively. She may have been able to assuage some of her grief through the transference of her sorrow to the far greater suffering of the Jews in the concentration camps.

Even with conviction compelling her to deal with the subject, the Holocaust tapestries required a long gestation period before Nezhnie was ready to proceed with the project. The earliest written reference to her interest in the Holocaust appears in the dedication commentary for a tapestry that was commissioned in 1976 for Temple Beth-El in Hammond, Indiana. The piece commemorated the temple's former rabbi, Ulrick B. Steuer, and his wife. In the dedication brochure, she singled out what was relevant to her, stating that she used a portion of Psalm 126 that "suggests his Holocaust experience and his salvaging and restoration of what had been destroyed." She began to reveal her interest in the topic quite simply. In calling attention to the rabbi's efforts, Nezhnie brought the subject to light for her to use.

Besides her own apprehension about confronting the issue, she was aware of a strong response from the survivors to inhibit the appropriation of images from the internment. After liberation, they reacted to the experiences they had endured with silence. Collectively, they perceived it was impossible to put into words or images what had occurred. Their inability to find adequate forms of expression was compounded by wariness that the actual process of description would lessen the impact. They feared it would facilitate a gradual forgetting and its inevitable absolving of the horrific deeds.[14] Despite the

---

14 Charlotte Crofts, "*The Peanut Crunching Crowd* in the Work of Sylvia Plath: Holocaust as Spectacle?" Semitism and Anti-Semitism in English Literature manuscript, Internet, 2/22/01.

survivors' initial response to remain silent about the atrocities, a larger ripple effect inevitably occurred as the extent of the cruelty surfaced, shaping the perceptions of distant sympathizers.

Nezhnie's mother died in January 1979. While she was in New Jersey, after handling the details of her mother's death, she ventured to the Yivo Institute in New York City in search of material and images to start addressing the Holocaust issue. Having the strength to cope with her mother's death gave her the assurance she needed to proceed with the task. As Muriel expressed in a letter to Nobel Peace Prize Laureate, Elie Wiesel,[15] in November of that same year, other reactions are as compelling as silence, especially as the human capacity to perpetrate such atrocities continues.

> . . . "If we do as you suggest, listen to the "tragic silence", "open ourselves to the silenced memories", there *is* something to be heard. I have been caught by that mournful sound since my childhood. Although I am American born and have no knowledge of my European family which must have surely been caught and lost in the nightmare, I feel, that by accident of place, I am a survivor. Not a survivor as you are, yet my response is impassioned and genuine.
>
> I believe that art can embody the experience of the Holocaust. Perhaps art is the only expression that can keep the vision, horrible as it is, alive in a positive and constructive way. Your se[a]ring books and articles, the words and images of others, perhaps music yet unwritten are all creative responses to the reality of the Holocaust. Echoing answers made not to fill the silent void but made to dissuade the i[n]humane imp[ulse] to implement anti-Semitism and genocide as a solution to human problems. It is the accumulation of all these efforts that stands as a body of resistance.

Nezhnie was 45 years old in 1979, when she completed *Daughters of Auschwitz*, the first of seven tapestries in the series. She had allowed her ideas to mature and had spent the intervening years productively exploring techniques. She honed her skills and refined her vision while pondering the significance of the insights she had gained abroad. Feeling empowered that tapestry's narrative potential brought all her talents together, she was ready for even more challenging endeavors.

> As I grow older, I care less, and less whether it fits into what is happening in tapestry in this country now or not. I don't give a damn, and I used to care a lot. You know, I felt like an outsider, I wanted some kind of recognition. I never thought when I was twenty that

---

15 Elie Wiesel, b. 1929 in Romania, survivor of the Holocaust, Nobel Peace Prize Laureate, 1986, for his dedication to the cause of human rights. His first book, *Night*, was written and published in 1958, shortly after he broke his long silence in an interview with a French writer about what he had endured during his internment.

I would ever feel this way because I didn't understand how one
could. Now I don't give a damn. I just want to work and get to it.
And cut out a lot of distractions. (Castro, 27)

In retrospect, Nezhnie's decision to commit the years from 1979 through
1989 to the development of the series was remarkable. One tapestry the
scope and size of the works displayed in "Images of the Holocaust," typically
requires six months to a year to complete. Therefore, one-person exhibitions
by tapestry weavers rarely take place, especially with a unified theme. She
began weaving the tapestries with no specific idea of their reception or sales
potential. She only knew she wanted to create them.

I have an instinct to bring to light pictures which are lost in these
archives or even closed in a book somewhere on a shelf. And I want
to make some tapestries that are hard to dismiss. (Castro, 26)

Nezhnie went to Washington, D.C., to research the topic, starting at the
Library of Congress and continuing at the National Archives. A researcher at
the National Archives directed her to the Pentagon, where the majority of material relating to the war and the Nazi persecution of the Jews could be found.

I spent two days looking at everything at the Pentagon. It was just
incredible. . . . In fact, almost everything you handle is stamped
U.S. Army, and some of it had been classified and then declassified.
And I handled things that dealt with the Americans who fell behind
the lines early. Either flyers or spies who had been tortured to
death, and the French had smuggled the pictures out. (Castro, 24)

As Muriel studied the documents and photographs, she made a list of
items that she wanted reproduced. She had access to many valuable historical documents. Being able to touch the physical evidence from the war made
an impression on her. While at the Pentagon, Nezhnie sifted through many
pictures of bodies stacked in piles, occasionally finding an image so compelling
she selected it for her collection. In general, however, it was not her intent to
document the atrocities. She was interested in individual human responses.

I found that I avoided the horror pictures. I really was looking for
some strength and dignity in the people. And there's plenty of it. But I
did select one photograph of a pile of bodies; it was the most incredible
image I had seen among the hundreds and hundreds of that subject.
This pile of bodies had one figure, on a diagonal, which looked so much
like a Christ figure that I was really struck. The head was tipped, with
a ruff of hair around it — like a crown — and the arms were stretched
out and limp, and the legs were raised and bent like Christ is often

depicted on the cross. And then I realized, in absolute shock and amazement that I was looking at a female. It hadn't been obvious because the bodies were emaciated. I knew that I would use it. I don't know when because it will take me longer to deal directly with the subject of death. The kinds of images I've begun to weave are less searing. (Castro, *River Styx*, 44)

She also went through the holdings of the Yad Vashem archives in Israel that are on microfiche at the Holocaust Museum and Learning Center in St. Louis, Missouri. Then she hired a photographer in Israel to take pictures of items she thought useful.

Nezhnie acquired a large variety of photographic images to work with. They were not pleasant to look at, being the documentation of genocide. Indeed, while she had defined her mission to create tapestries that were hard to dismiss, her challenge was to present the horrific details in a manner that people could find aesthetically compelling. She needed to achieve a balance between revealing the aversive injustices incurred and constructively attracting the viewer's attention.

This dilemma, and her plan to select images that conveyed the dignity of the individual, may have prompted her to choose a photograph of women for her first tapestry, *The Daughters of Auschwitz*. She found it buried deep in the archives. The tapestry was completed before the interview with Jan Castro. In answer to Castro's inquiry about whether she was focusing from a woman's point of view, Nezhnie replied:

Well, I don't know. Certainly, it's true the earliest images I am dealing with all happened — just happened to be women. In my recent research trip to Washington, D.C., I found some strong pictures that deal with men. But quite frankly, the strongest still are of women.
I found one set of huge, full 8" x 10" heads of women with the most incredibly strong, determined expressions on their faces. All the Army information stated about the pictures was that they were a group of Hungarian women and that they were all artists, professionals, writers, and poets. Women and children also symbolize innocence and that's an important factor in my response. (Castro, *River Styx*, 44)

In designing the holocaust tapestries, Nezhnie discarded the traditional conventions she had adhered to in her commission work for synagogues. Her new approach was to represent the human drama literally, as it coexists with religious expression. A shift emerged in the Holocaust compositions that placed the scriptures potently within a relevant cultural context, not abstracted into a ritualized religious format. A primary theme that surfaces in the tapestries is human solace in a belief system.

Once the image and corresponding text was determined, she called on all her design skills, first to create a color palette that was subdued but appealing, then to hone the images down to the essential details in order to give potency to the message.

Daughters of Auschwitz, *60" x 54", 1979*

The backdrop for the women is the gate at Auschwitz. An authentic rendering of the curving metal band of words above the gate declares in German, "ARBEIT MACHT FREI" ("work makes you free"). The patterned surface below the women contains a passage from the Hebrew daily prayer book. It translates: "And now we were made a few from many." Thus, the voices of perpetrator and victim vie for attention in the piece. The base of the tapestry is reminiscent of how the roots of *Burning Bush* (1961) form Hebrew letters.

The women are clad in the scratchy, striped pajama-like outfits of the camp. The tapestry is dominated by the figures in the overly bold stripes. Nezhnie had been experimenting with the use of parallel stripes to create dimensional form throughout the 1970s, so it is not surprising that she relied on this device as the focal point of the first tapestry in the series. The irregularities of the stripe edges convey the coarse fabric of the garments. The stripes have character,

Daughters of Auschwitz

60" x 54", 1979

Color plate 6a

with subtle shifts in an appealing color palette of greens, blues, and purples highlighted with pink. The drape of the fabric, and the variety of postures and personalities, are masterfully portrayed. Indeed, the figures are captivating.

The sense of light shining down upon these women conveys a quality of grace as it warms their faces and falls in a pink glow on their crude garments. The radiance is, however, not enough comfort to relieve the stark bleakness of the camp implied by the pale mauve background.

This tapestry has received some criticism from survivors because the women are depicted with hair, whereas inmates would have had their heads shaved. However, the image came from a photograph taken by a Russian soldier who liberated them. It has been suggested

these may have been women kept by the Germans as prostitutes and thus allowed to keep their hair. Nezhnie was very conscious of maintaining accuracy in details during the design stage. She was concerned that if she misused a photo, or mixed images and documents from different incidents or camps, it would discredit the authenticity of the event and detract from the impact of the tapestries.

Daughters of Earth, *81" x 53", 1981*

Daughters of Earth is also composed of five females documented in harsh reality. One is a child who appears to be trying to hide and deny that reality. The group was photographed in Lijepaja, Latvia, in 1941.

The two tapestries complement each other. The most striking parallel is how physically connected both groups of women are. The women of *Daughters of Earth* have arms linked; they cling together and gain warmth from each other. Both groups of women have come to know the value of support.

There is, however, a major distinction between the two tapestries. The women in *Daughters of Auschwitz* were photographed at their liberation. The photograph of the women in Latvia documents them just before their imminent death. In the lower section of the tapestry, Nezhnie has made a subtle reference to the edge of the grave pit. One woman has wet her undergarment in fear, indicated with a shift in the shadow color. There is a wide range of expressions on the women's faces. Two show their horror, while one young woman faces death with defiance in her direct gaze.

Daughters of Earth reverses the palette used in the Auschwitz tapestry so that the women are woven in warm delicate peach and mauve, with soft brown accents against a predominantly blue patterned background. Despite the appealing color combination, the tapestry depicts exposed women, all their outer garments stripped from them. Three are barefooted. In a telephone interview with Vivian Alpert Thompson, Nezhnie stated that the "shapes in shadowy form in the background represent soldiers, legs of children hiding behind the group, and scattered clothing."

The lighting in this tapestry is flatter than in

Daughters of Earth

81" x 53", 1981

Color plate 6b

the first one. The women do not appear to be comforted by the light, merely exposed. It spreads over them, leaving them with no place to hide. There is a sense that they have been thrust out into the open with only their physical contact for solace. The arched tombstone shape of the tapestry and the muted but unrestfully busy setting in which they stand underscore how vulnerable they are, much as the lack of complexity in the background of *Daughters of Auschwitz* conveys the bleakness of the camp.

The lower section of the tapestry, woven separately by apprentice Christel Maassen, implores in English: "Earth hide not my blood," and in Hebrew, the text from Job 16:18 states: "Let there be no resting place for my cry." The message and the look of unrest on the women's faces make a powerful statement.

The five figures exemplify the pinnacle of Nezhnie's talent as a weaver, especially with portraiture. She had learned how to effectively use a very limited palette in the silk miniatures woven earlier, but the extra demands of similar values and neutral tones for this tapestry proved an even greater challenge. Part of the solution to providing definition was to incorporate a fine accent yarn into both the figure and the background. For instance, a dark brown thread meanders randomly to imply unruly curls in one woman's hair, then briefly solidifies to outline her face, and finally roams off into the gray-blue background behind the figure to provide a textural accent. (See color plate 7d.)

Adam's Daughters, *25" x 21" each, 1981*

A set of five small tapestries was woven of the faces of the women in *Daughters of Earth*. Each portrait is cropped into a rectangle, with a portion of background and garment, and is accented by bold brown bands on two adjacent sides. The face is set in a larger frame of blue and gray marbled with delicate pink highlights.

These faces were woven by Maassen, who was already an experienced weaver when she came to work for Nezhnie. She, too, was interested in portraiture and sought the best weaver she could find for that specialty. Having an assistant who could skillfully follow her instructions allowed Muriel to

Adam's Daughters
25" x 21" each, 1981

complete more of her images than would have been possible by herself. These portraits were woven at the same time as *Daughters of Earth*.

Ghetto Child—Stroop Report, *60" x 48", 1982*

Nezhnie discussed her plans for a piece inspired by images she gleaned from the Nuremberg trials documents.

> One I'm planning to do is the opening page of a document of the Nuremberg trials that has beautiful German calligraphy on it that says, "There are no more Jews in Warsaw." This is a document concerning the destruction of the Warsaw Ghetto that was prepared by General Stroop for Hitler. And this document has some of the most famous and most highly publicized pictures of the war [such as] that of the little boy with his hands up who is coming out [of] a house with women and children while German soldiers look on. Underneath it says in beautiful German script: "These were bandits resisting arrest with arms." And there wasn't a gun or a weapon visible except the soldier's — nothing! But the front page of this document has the Nuremberg Trial Tribunal stamped on it, and the date, and "U.S.A." stamped on it; it has the German script. And it has a Nazi stamp on it with the eagle.
>
> I know that I am going to blow this page up. And I know what image I'm going to use. As in the "Charms" this concept allows me to integrate all of my graphic instincts with the visual figurative stuff. (Castro, 26-27)

Apparently, Muriel was originally going to use a different photograph to combine with the front page of the document. Castro asked Nezhnie if she heard news about the Holocaust when she was a child. In response Muriel talked more about the image she intended to combine with the Nuremberg trial documentation.

> Oh, yes, it [information about the Holocaust] was always coming out. People didn't believe what they heard, and we didn't hear facts and details 'til later. I certainly remember when the first pictures came out. In fact, I'm doing a work with one of the earliest: a picture of people being herded, running through the streets of the Warsaw Ghetto. There was a female in the front line of that picture. From my childhood, I remember that picture; I identified with the female. I thought she was a child, but when I recently found the authentic photograph, she's not; she's a grown woman. She did look the way I looked then. She had similar characteristics—straight hair and a high forehead—and she was wearing socks and shoes like some I had. . . . I was rather startled with what I found. (Castro, *River Styx*, 40)

Nezhnie intended to superimpose the image of the people in the streets

onto the large blank section of the trial document. In the end, however, she chose to use the
image of the little boy. Perhaps she perceived the
image of the solitary, confused child to be more
poignant than that of the woman, despite her
personal connection to it.

She used the beautiful script that declares in
German: "The Jewish quarter of Warsaw is no
more," and one of the stamps from the front page
of the *Stroop Report* as she discussed. The lettering is woven in several shades of red to give more
nuance to the script. However, it is the solitary
figure of the young boy that tells the story.

While Nezhnie preferred conceptually complex compositions, she was quite skilled at focusing
on the elemental aspects and discarding unessential
details. Such is the case with *Ghetto Child — Stroop
Report*. Nothing is added to distract the viewer from
the impact of the image. The background has a
very subtle repeat of revealed warp threads but is basically uniform across
its neutral pale mauve surface. The dark side borders provide balance and
emphasize the crisp nature of the tapestry.

*Ghetto Child—
Stroop Report*
60" x 48", 1982
Color plate 7h

Again, the lighting is key. Presenting the image with high-contrast
lighting meant that little blending of tones was necessary for the face and
hands to be convincing. Harsh light defines the edge of the boy's hands
raised in surrender. It hits his hat, lapel, and even the backs of his legs, leaving no doubt that he is trapped.

The Nuremberg Trial Tribunal stamp is masterfully woven to look imprinted on the surface of the cover of the document. The tapestry was woven
entirely by Maassen. Nezhnie checked frequently to see that the weaving was
conveying the desired effect. Only some minor adjustments needed to be made
on the boy's mouth, which seemed to be the area of portraiture where Nezhnie
gave most instruction to her apprentice. One letter in the German script was
rewoven several times, trying to get the best balance of color in the lettering.

The tapestry was sold to a private collector, but Nezhnie could not
accept it being in a private home. She really had not considered the matter
before, but realized that the work needed to be displayed in a public place,
where it could impact many viewers. She convinced the buyer to find an
acceptable home for it, and he was given a seriograph of the design for his
personal collection. *Ghetto Child — Stroop Report* is now on permanent loan
to the Dallas Center for Holocaust Studies.

Liberation
36" x 47", 1987
Color plate 7c

Liberation, *36" x 47", 1987*

Liberation presents two weary-looking men propping up a third, who, though weak, looks out with a hint of optimism on his face. Like many of the other images in the series, it accentuates the reliance on physical contact. As in *Ghetto Child*, the tapestry is reduced to its most elemental message. Only a single line of German text, woven in subtly varied brown tones, interrupts the uniform background. It states: "We salute our liberators." The inscription was from a banner fashioned by survivors of the German concentration camp, Dachau, where these men were photographed.

The color combination is similar to *Daughters of Auschwitz*, with bits of stronger color used sparingly, such as the muted ochre collar and cuffs of the central figure and the reddish hair peaking out from under the hat of the man to his left. The garments are strikingly detailed. Bold folds in the striped uniforms and ribbing on the cuffs complement the interesting variations in the men's features and styles of hat. It is this identifiable connection with clothing, and the individuality of the men, that brings the viewer to look again and again at the tapestry.

Deportation, *54" x 53", 1988*

Deportation is based on a photograph taken by Mendel Grossman, one of a series he took during the September 1942 deportation of over 1500 Jews from the Lodz Ghetto. Many of the Jews deported in that weeklong action were children, and Nezhnie chose to focus on a child for this weaving. The composition of Grossman's photograph is remarkable. Nezhnie did nothing to alter the design except to give more definition to the apparently damaged lower right edge.

The tapestry is bold and visually complex. Chain-link fencing expands over most of the tapestry, except for the border. The young girl is positioned to the right of center, gripping the fence with one hand and supporting her face with the other. Her face is woven in absolutely minimal color shifts of oyster white and soft neutral pink with light gray for the mouth and eyes. A muted brown, used in the hair, provides subtle accents in the face and hands.

The pale face portrays a look of complete forlornness. Equally telling is the girl's hand grasping the fence while clutching a handkerchief.

Although the face is pale, in this tapestry there is a slight overall shift towards stronger colors, with more purples and a brighter blue than in the earlier ones. The weaving is superb in conveying details as well as in leaving some areas vague. A mottled sweater appears under the coat, which has large buttons at the cuff. The effective details keep the viewer looking, despite the extreme sadness reflected in her face.

Deportation
54" x 53", 1988
Color plate 7g

In the upper left corner, a hand is thrust out, which parallels the diagonal of the fence wires. It serves to balance the composition, which otherwise would be too heavy on the right side. The child is passively grieving, while the hand juts out menacingly in reaction to confinement.

Deportation is the first tapestry of the series to be fringed. The muted neutral threads of the fringe serve to anchor the almost square composition held within the dark frame with its precise lettering. Bold lettering is placed around the prominent border. The German translates as "Forced resettlement." The Polish says "Expulsion," and the Hebrew says "Driven out." "Lodz Ghetto 1940 - 1944" is written in the bottom border. In 2000, the tapestry was acquired by the Holocaust Museum and Learning Center of St. Louis, Missouri.

Parting Lodz, *48" x 96", 1987*

Nezhnie decided to abandon tapestry momentarily and present the narrative as a painting. It depicts two men in a farewell kiss. It is masterfully painted with exquisite details, such as the highlights in the hair and the pattern details of the hat. The hatless man looks emaciated and lifeless. Yet, as in the weavings of the women, love and tenderness are communicated. The composition is striking. Although painted before *Deportation*, it makes use of many of the same elements. The chain-link fencing becomes a uniquely shaped border, much wider on the sides than on the top or bottom. In this painting, the wire mesh is far more loosely interpreted, less uniformly conveyed. Most of the background

Parting Lodz
48" x 96", 1987
Color plate 7e

in the body of the painting is filled with bold lettering that surrounds the two figures. Text from Samuel I 20:3, "The Lord liveth and as I so liveth there is but a step between me and death," is written in Hebrew across the top with "Lodz Ghetto, 1940-1944," in the lower portion.

Parting Lodz was displayed without a frame or stretcher bars. Muriel had purchased large iron nails that looked handcrafted and put dark grommets into the canvas to tack it to the wall. However, the idea was an impractical method for temporary mounting and never used. Thus, it was presented in much the same manner as the tapestries, mounted on the wall with no apparent hanging device. The paintings she typically made while designing were small — less than two feet in length— and painted with gouache. However, *Parting Lodz* was as large as the tapestries and painted in acrylics. Although the painting was never intended to be woven, it is easy to see how it could translate into tapestry. She was very proud of this painting and attracted to the image.

These six tapestries and the painting discussed above were the basis of the exhibit "Images of the Holocaust," first mounted in July 1988 at the

Documentation of "Images of the Holocaust."

Sazama-Brauer Gallery, in Chicago, Illinois. The exhibit was in conjunction with the Handweavers Guild of America's international convention, the 1988 Convergence. The exhibit traveled to the Center for Tapestry Arts in New York City in 1989 and the Mendocino Arts Center in Mendocino, California, in 1990. Only the cartoon of the tapestry *Liberation*, was displayed in the Sazama-Brauer Gallery so that the weaving could be part of the juried American Tapestry Alliance exhibit, "World Tapestry Today," which was also on display in Chicago at the time of Convergence.

Along with the centralized theme of the exhibit, there was a striking cohesiveness displayed in the controlled, subdued color palette used by Nezhnie. The color tonality gave the tapestries a quality of old photographs and faded newspaper clippings resurfacing to put a human touch on an inhumane chapter of recent history. Most important, the appealing colors had a magnetic power to draw viewers to the images.

Displaying supplemental paintings, drawings, prints, and other related documentation heightened the impact of the tapestries. Several cartoons were displayed, such as the partially painted one for *Daughters of Auschwitz*, as well as early versions of designs showing photo clips of the other components that went into the final image. This repetition of the images, at various stages of development, served to imprint the exhibit's content more deeply upon the viewer's mind. It also revealed how ingenious Nezhnie was in combining text and imagery.

In order to give herself more range of expression, Nezhnie had taken classes in printmaking during 1979. She designed a folio called *Remnants of Despair: An Homage to Nelly Sachs*, produced in 1983 in a limited edition of twenty. Selected poems from the 1966 Nobel Prize winner's collection of poems, *O the Chimneys*, were accompanied by six manipulated intaglio prints of the face of one of the women depicted in *Daughters of Auschwitz*. The fact that Sachs incorporated biblical quotations in her poems correlates with Nezhnie's juxtaposition of biblical text with the scenes portrayed in the tapestries.

Nezhnie working on "Remnants of Despair." Courtesy of Rick Stankoven.

Nezhnie derived her image from a color photocopy of the woven face. She tore the print into strips and reconstructed the face, weaving and stitching the images back together. One assemblage incorporated a second print of the face. The not-always-subtle shifts in alignment reflect the disintegration of humanity, as expressed in the woman's despair. Each assemblage was framed with a companion poem for the exhibit, rather than presented in folio form.

The cohesiveness of tone, the myriad of detail to remind observers of the scope of the Holocaust, and the impact created by the commanding presence of the tapestries made the exhibit unforgettable. It is interesting that the tapestries might be considered as medium-sized work in comparison with much of Nezhnie's mid-career and commission work. Yet, because of their impact, viewers anecdotally remember them as being quite large.

Pogrom, *64" x 48", 1989*

Nezhnie was able to weave one more Holocaust tapestry before her health failed. *Pogrom* depicts an obviously frightened woman whose clothes are in

Pogrom
64" x 48", 1989
Color plate 6f

shreds, undergarments and breast exposed as she runs. She is pursued by soldiers who are very young boys. Her face is coarsened with fear; their's are totally focused on malice. It is a masterful portrayal of action and truly hard to look at. The boys look like animals circling in for the kill.

However, the composition, as a whole, draws the viewer to it. The treatment of a swastika above the action is ingenious, even visually attractive, despite its negative connotation. The lower third of the swastika appears as a bright red triangle, with two black lines delineating its angled lower stems. The upper two thirds are in the tapestry's top border of brown. The part of the swastika in the border is a slightly lighter shade of brown than its background. The black lines continue throughout the brown part to define the swastika's shape. Superimposed over the portion that is in the border are the words from Lamentations 3:52: "They hunted me like a bird / They are my enemies without cause." The text, written in Hebrew, is in a contrasting gold color.

Because the top of the tapestry arches, it trims off the upper extremities of the swastika, creating an interesting chevron pattern in the border. Cropping the top border, creating an abrupt color change from red to brown, and placing the lettering over a portion of the swastika all allow the symbol to be revealed, but not as a confrontation that might turn a viewer away. One soldier's head is framed with a diamond of light background color within the lower, red angles of the swastika. His face is quite close and level with the woman's eyes. This juxtaposition heightens the feeling of aggression.

As with the other tapestries in the series, a collection of preliminary drawings for the design and photographs accompanied this tapestry at exhibits. Again, an examination of the material underscores Nezhnie's remarkable ability to get to the essence of the situation she was depicting, in this case shown in the evolution of the swastika in the composition.

The tapestry makes use of an even wider range of colors, with more intensity than is seen in the previous ones. The background, however, is still the neutral, pale mauve used earlier. It has horizontal lines of faint orange, created by weaving in the same shed for two or three rows, in order to expose orange warp threads, as in *Ghetto Child*. The device is used here to suggest movement, with many of these lines originating at the feet of the runners, not necessarily stretching all the way across to the borders. The narrow side borders, the weighty lower border with its documentation of the incident, and the short fringe at the bottom provide a visually pleasing frame to contain the frightening action.

Fortunately Nezhnie was able to weave long enough to create this disturbing tapestry. Although it may not have quite the level of perfection as the others, with slightly less controlled edges, it is powerful. Several examinations are required to come to terms with the piece. Once really seen, its masterful depiction of brutality serves as the culmination of what Nezhnie was trying to accomplish: tapestries that are hard to dismiss.

She was not finished with her series when she was forced to quit weaving. In fact, she still had copious amounts of the mauve background yarn waiting for other projects. It had been specially dyed for the series. Her daughter, Ilisha, has vivid memories of images waiting to be woven. One was of a rabbi lying on his back and praying. He is cradled in his tallith, the traditional Jewish prayer shawl that is striped with bands of black or dark blue. The concept alludes to the irony that both the garments the inmates were forced to wear and the sacred shawl were similarly striped. Another image was of a group of Jews sitting in a circle on a covered well, facing out. The photograph reveals the large star on one of the men's back. What especially interested Nezhnie about the scene was that she spotted an accidental star that emerged from the background area between the heads of two other men. One of the aspects of tapestry weaving that appealed to her most was that in the weaving process, both figure and ground assumed equal importance. She planned to create a net above the group, as if they were trapped, formed of "lazy lines," a Navaho technique for breaking up large areas of a single color into small diamond shapes that are more convenient to weave. The result is subtle diagonal breaks in the uniformity of the surface that can make a net-like pattern.

Ilisha recalls:

> The figures were in a sense alone, all facing away from each other, not like other tapestries where figures were holding on for comfort. Both this and *Pogrom* are bleaker visions. . . . Both are less about the triumph of the spirit than they are about the loss of hope.

Although these pieces were never made, given the already apparent signs of confusion and loss of memory, she was fortunate to have accomplished what she did. In a very insightful book, *A Mission in Art: Recent Holocaust Works in America*, Vivian Alpert Thompson analyzed Nezhnie's artwork and the factors driving her determination to confront the Holocaust, Thompson asserts: "The empathy of the artists who are not survivors is at times so deep that some of them have taken on characteristics normally attributable to survivors."[16]

The common traits she refers to are a need to portray the narrative with complete accuracy, an awareness in the artist that the drive to work with the issue increases instead of fading with mounting publicity or details of the atrocities, and a conviction that the artwork must be received by an audience. Thompson poses:

> Finally the creation of these works is not cathartic for the artist — perhaps because not enough people have seen their works, or more likely because the conditions of evil that their art warns against still exist. (Thompson, 47)

The interpretation explains why Muriel was not able to take the advice of her well-meaning friend, why she could not ignore her uncomfortable but persistent interest in the Holocaust. From her husband's account, it is unlikely that Muriel ever saw the book. Thompson had first compiled the information in 1982, while working on her thesis at Emory University.

The Holocaust series represents more than the synthesis of a historical narrative art form with a contemporary issue. It signifies more than the meshing of Nezhnie's tapestry exploration with her special talents in graphics and portraiture. The work expresses the union of the mature woman's vision with the emotional responses to genocide and cruelty, imprinted on the child she had been during the war. She pushed herself to deal with the subject she feared would be too emotionally demanding in order to contribute to the fight for human rights.

---

16 Vivian Alpert Thompson, *A Mission in Art: Recent Holocaust Works in America* (Macon: Mercer University Press, 1988), 67.

A Melding of Media

In looking at the body of work that Nezhnie created, it is amazing to realize that she accomplished such versatility with only two brief encounters with any instruction in weaving techniques. She had the casual introduction to the process while making blanket squares as a schoolgirl and the four months' observation of artists weaving in Germany.

Another interesting phenomenon is that despite how articulate Muriel was, her records provide little commentary about failures. As mentioned in a previous chapter, *Stella* is a rare example of a completed piece that is not successful. Even when a weakness is apparent in a tapestry, as in a few of the faces in *Prairie Journey*, the overall impact of the work is commanding enough to carry the flaw. Given the experimental nature of her pieces and the evidence that she often sought advice from her husband, it is plausible that she struggled her fair share of the time. On the other hand, it is also probable that she didn't dwell on the issue of failure. From the initial assembly and warping of the loom that the Helfmans brought back from Germany, a lot of guesswork went into the creation of her artwork. Having to rip out or discard an attempt might not have been interpreted as a failure, but as a step tried. Such an attitude complements an inventive mind.

What motivated her to experiment independently in her studio rather than seek out classes or an experienced weaver to emulate? She had gone to great lengths as a teenager and college student to learn from professionals. Why was the situation different with weaving?

Her lack of interest in more technical training could, perhaps, be understood by looking at the consequences of what had happened to her at The Cooper Union. Being told that she would have to leave if she continued to specialize in portraiture might easily have made her wary of relying on authorities for personal validation. As it was, the bias for abstraction and censure against realistic imagery existing in the art world, and her assessment that no other weavers were working figuratively, inhibited her throughout the 1960s.

> I'm very interested in people imagery in one sort or another. It started off with tremendous fear initially, again because no contemporary was weaving anything with images. (Castro, 10)

However, the answer more likely relates to her ability to stay challenged and directed by her own discoveries. Whatever perception convinced her, so decidedly, that she could do better than the first examples she saw, and to almost immediately learn the basics of tapestry weaving, must have been very profound. The receptivity that she displayed for weaving as a child is relevant, too. She had a natural affinity with the medium. Many of her solutions remain fresh and distinctive today.

By analyzing specific works over the various stages of her career a pattern to her experimental journey can be discerned. In her early work, she started to determine what was essential to the process and to examine to what extent the structure of weaving could be altered. This led to the conclusion that neither the rectangular format nor a uniform weft-faced weave need limit her visual expression. In fact, the exploration quickly led her to the understanding that the more the structural features were revealed, the more lively and effective the image became.

Then Nezhnie shifted her focus to the elemental ingredients needed for creating form and imagery. In weaving, imagery is created with lines of yarn and the horizontal layering of color. At this stage in her exploration, her background in graphic design began to gain weight equal to her painting skills. Controlling line to produce color and definition in weaving is similar to working with the dots in printing. Her skillful solutions for manipulating line are a significant contribution to the tapestry community.

It was essential for Nezhnie's self-esteem that her response to any task be innovative. As her friend Maria stated with conviction and awe, Muriel put creative energy into whatever she did. Thus it is understandable that she did not look to past traditions for answers when it came to her artwork.

She was caught in a delicate balancing act between her inner conviction about what style of art she wanted to create and her need to receive support for her endeavors from the art community. While she was very self-reliant, it still was important that her innovative work be well received.

Therefore, during the early years when she felt the sanctions against portraiture, her solution was to create the abstracted free-form little people and the large, totemic female forms. It was a way to stay within the prevailing trends without denying her own interests in working with human forms.

In the process, Nezhnie made free-form shaping look easy. She was at the cusp of the movement to break away from rectangular boundaries. The majority of weavers demonstrated little inclination to alter the grid-like nature of weaving at the time. It takes a lot of confidence to trust that a shaped image that requires a customized support system will remain stable and attractive. Also, the procedure would add another time-consuming element into a process more suitable to the rectangle.

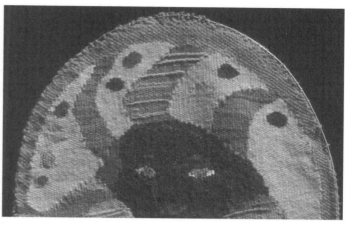

Anyone who has cut into a piece of fabric, or has had the edge of a Persian rug wear away, can understand what happens to weaving that is not firmly anchored at its edges. It ravels or comes undone. The stability of the entire fabric is dependent on all of its edges being secured. The sides of the weaving are held in place, as the weft yarn turns and lies in the alternate shed, and are further stabilized when subsequent rows are beaten in place. When the edge is stepped, leaving uncovered warp beyond where the shape ends, there is nothing to compact the weft below. The typically uniform appearance looks distorted or crudely woven because the turns are not compressed and therefore appear thicker than the rest of the weaving. Knotting the stepped portion of warp threads after the tapestry is off the loom must be carefully done to ensure that the irregular edge still looks firmly woven. Distortion can be minimized by securing the tapestry to a support or backing material. Nezhnie became very skillful at knotting warp ends. If the shaped figures were not fringed, the knots were either hidden behind the weaving or used as a decorative element, just tacking the ends behind the surface and leaving the knots to show as a finishing detail. It looks vaguely like a beaded edging. *Navahope* is an example of the beading effect, but it also shows the result of weft not being compressed in some areas.

Doll Baby
(detail, showing
wire support)

Navahope
(with milagros
and washers)
20" x 10", 1968

Having someone who was willing to experiment with constructing armatures helped give Muriel greater freedom in the shaping process. The frames supported the forms without being intrusive. Sometimes a band of braiding or a wrapped edging might be added to disguise the wire frames. In general, though, the supports were not really hidden. The weaving was matter-of-factly knotted to the wire frames and the warp ends allowed to become fringe where useful as decoration.

In the early 1970s, within five years of when Nezhnie began shaping these forms, many more weavers became inspired to manipulate the traditionally rectangular nature of weaving. The trend resulted from a growing interest in exploring more varied methods of constructing fiber art. Free-form wall

hangings came into vogue. It also became an era when armatures, frames, and found objects used as supports were commanding the attention of fiber artists. Muriel showed little interest in expanding on the idea of elaborate armatures. By then, she was ready to explore new concepts. However, the skills acquired through manipulating shapes during the 1960s continued to aid her throughout her career.

Nezhnie was equally effective in solving the other issue she dealt with in her figurative work of the 1960s. Her choice to expose warp required that she find ways to keep the structure stable, while shifting from completely weft-faced areas to segments where warp was allowed to show through. Not only was stability an issue, but the general consensus existing within the tapestry community, as she knew it, placed high value on a uniformly woven surface.

Two different tapestry traditions were present in 20th century European tapestry weaving. Scandinavian countries have sustained a well-established tradition that includes pictorial imagery woven in pattern threadings that do not completely cover the warp. This was the tradition in which Helena Hernmarck developed her unique style. The tapestries are also woven in a wider range of fibers than wool, cotton, or silk. Less pliable yarns, such as linen or sisal, do not pack down as densely as wool does. Traditionally, weavers using this style have not been troubled by the inevitably looser packing of yarns or the wavy drape that can result from this approach. Polish tapestries exhibited in North America in the 1970s and early 1980s often were woven in this style, too. The tapestries used sisal predominantly, as did the more sculptural style of Polish weaving, and buckled frequently. Most were monumental in scale and boldly expressive in a narrative manner.

The second European tapestry tradition, closely associated with French weavers, prized a surface in which the warp is completely hidden and the structure is firm and essentially uniform in appearance. Well-defined rules for creating specific effects have been passed down from generation to generation. As documented in the first chapter, there have been many exhibits in the United States of French tapestries, contemporary and centuries old.

In the later part of the 20th century, the majority of contemporary American tapestry weavers were more in sympathy with the French consensus than with the Scandinavian style. A third tradition, reflecting the geometric Moorish Kilim flat weaves, was established in America by the early Spaniards and adopted by the native weavers who contributed their own dynamic aesthetic to that of the Spanish. This style shared a strong tradition with the French for producing a finely packed, uniform surface. It was the predominant form of tapestry in American decor and thus was present in the consciousness of American fiber artists in general. Often it was the first style of tapestry weaving they learned. It likely influenced North American weavers to prefer a firmly packed weft-faced weave. Late in the 20th century American art shifted from abstract to more representational subject matter. Since the French style delineated more procedures for creating realistic imagery, tapestry weavers sought to emulate its techniques.

Obviously, Nezhnie was not interested in limiting herself exclusively to producing weft-faced weaving. However, she was aware that in order for her work to gain recognition from her peers, it had to appear competently woven. Any exposure of warp would have to show evidence that it was there by design.

Several options proved successful for her. Sometimes she chose to reveal warp only in shapes of a specific color. In *Embrace*, which includes at least eight colors, the bright red/green warp shows through only in a dark lavender shape. In *Mother 1*, brown areas reveal the same red/green warp. Since all the other shapes are solidly packed, it is evident that the flecks are intentional. In both pieces, the colors definitely look livelier by occasionally revealing the contrasting warps. The effect looks controlled, not haphazard.

The subtle introduction of warp colors into the body of a tapestry also served to balance their presence as fringe. Several of the little people were woven on the same orange-red and vibrant apple green warp. It is quite different, in character, from the main colors in the various figures. Without including hints of these strident colors, their use as fringe would appear illogical to the overall color impact.

Little Egypt and *Large Embrace* both have areas where the warp is left entirely unwoven. The segments of warp that were allowed to float freely tend to be triangular in shape with one straight edge along the warp. If *Large Embrace* is turned on its side, it is easy to see that the band between the two sets of warp floats keeps the spacing intact. The unit does not sag when rotated to its proper orientation.

Ploys such as incorporating a noticeable support for hanging the free-form objects, or allowing the warp to contribute to the color scheme in the weaving, were quite consistent with Muriel's approach to tapestry. In fact, they were at the basis of her belief that revealing the relationship between the structure and the simultaneously created image was essential for tapestry to be effective as an art medium.

Large Embrace
(detail, on its side
as woven)

She also employed some pattern weaves and floating warp segments in her commissions, again judiciously limiting the patterns to defined areas. The two sections with textural surfaces in *Odyssey* are narrow. They have minimal curves and are woven in thick weft yarns that dominate the thinner warp threads.

Muriel had successfully created at least six of the little people before attempting one of the larger free-form females. Although hints of warp floats still elaborated the tapestries, in general, the series of totemic figures was more about texture and yarn drape than the interplay of warp and weft. Fringe became an integral part of the shaping and character of the image, particularly where it implied hands. The boldly curved figures were an expression of her confidence in pushing her skills to create highly imaginative images.

By the end of the decade, Nezhnie was a very proficient weaver. She could control shape and texture to create formally composed pictorial imagery, as in her commission work, or imaginative free-form representations. Both her conservative and innovative pieces displayed technical skill, in keeping with the best standards of contemporary American tapestry weaving.

Given Nezhnie's goal-oriented approach to life, it is remarkable that she was able to leave the field of painting, a pursuit she was committed to from a very early age. Still, while there is plenty of evidence that she did not dismiss a goal easily, she was also pragmatic and resourceful. Her path as a painter was seemingly blocked a second time by her personal circumstances. Her future was shaped by the perception that her marriage would suffer if she chose a career in painting. It is quite possible that she would have decided to give up painting even if she had been allowed to continue in portraiture. A student with a less defined selection of subject matter might have succumbed to the prevailing trends and worked in whatever style of painting would have been acceptable, while remaining at The Cooper Union.

It was fortuitous that Nezhnie chose to switch to graphic design. Perhaps it was more an example of a savvy awareness of her talents, rather than luck, operating in her decision to pursue an alternate course. In either case, forced to put aside her choice in subject matter, she acquired the means to later interpret imagery in tapestry so successfully. Intensive classes in graphic design gave her a broader scope of options for interpreting imagery than she would have had if she only specialized in painting. Methods of combining colors in printing are actually more compatible with weaving than the means most often used by painters in blending colors.

It was a fortunate choice in many ways. Certainly, she used her knowledge of calligraphy and poster design throughout her career to convey her message. The benefits of her graphic background are most apparent in her mature work, the Holocaust series. However there were other subtle insights that she acquired from a thorough understanding of the printing process that allowed her to interpret imagery effectively throughout her career.

In the printing business, a photograph is considered "continuous-tone copy." That means that an original photograph produced from a negative, even more than a conventional painting, is made up of a variety of tones or colors that flow into one another. A black and white photograph has gray areas created in the developing, the result of how light and chemicals affect the exposed paper. On the other hand, ink is opaque and singular in color and therefore can only print in solid units. The methods by which a printer or graphic designer reproduces tonality have many of the same limitations that a weaver finds in working with yarns. Once constructed, the yarn color is set and can only be changed in combination with other equally specific yarns or by some application of color onto the surface after the fact. A newer generation of graphic designer would use the analogy of pixels or dots per inch on a digital image.

Nezhnie's graphic training was fresh in her mind as she observed the weavers in Germany. It is no wonder she understood the importance of yarn selection early in the design process. The translation of an image into weaving might be quite different if ten yarns were available for combining rather than if the quantity of shades were in the hundreds, as in some circumstances.

She trusted her eye and her inner voice. Consider that while in Germany she must have had immense confidence in her powers of observation in order to make it worthwhile to take classes without verbal instruction. Besides serving her well in analyzing the steps needed to weave tapestry, she most likely was employing the same acute attention to visual detail while viewing the items at the calligraphy museum.

The *Imprints* commission, completed fifteen years later in 1971, allowed her to look at tapestry through the eyes of a graphic designer. The commission is a virtual catalog of graphic devices, including references to stenciling and halftones. Used in combination with various textures and weaves, they produced the kind of complexity Muriel enjoyed. It afforded her the freedom to create details meant to represent objects literally. She was even able to convincingly embed portraits into the composition. The success of the commission, and finding a fellow weaver willing to address contemporary culture, had her primed to work out her own style.

Wild Cherry Charms was the expression of her new sense of freedom and confidence. For subject matter, she intuitively selected the theme of visual manipulation. It was not only a topic of interest to the avant-garde, but one that went to the core of her personal experience. Her visual acuity, honed as a young child to assuage boredom, became her most highly developed skill. Her keen sense of observation, visually and intellectually, was at the heart of her self-confidence. She relied on her own judgment. The process seemed to consist of muddling through trial-and-error attempts to arrive at a clarity that could express her intent. However, at the core of her talent was the ability to conceptualize the options to try.

Nader and *Shining Knight* are the best design solutions to the challenge Nezhnie defined for herself in response to Hernmarck's work. They create images that appear realistic at a distance but at close viewing break away from recognizable details into fibrous textural fields. As the focus changed, she wanted the abstraction to be as attractive as the representational image.

Shining Knight is not a large piece. The face, approximately 17" x 17", is larger than life-size, but still on a human scale. The cartoon, however, was magnified greatly from the small picture found in a pamphlet. A slide was taken of the printed photographic image and projected onto a wall. The image would not have been continuous-tone, but a dot matrix that degenerated further as she expanded it. Her ploy for creating a novel interpretation of the photograph was to eliminate all but the most essential lines needed to convey the features. Eliot's face was striking for the straightness of his aquiline nose and thin, unwavering mouth. Photographs of both the young and old man, found in the archives of Washington University, reveal few curves or contours to his features. There is a surprising consistency of expression. The minimalist approach was in keeping with the linear nature of the features.

The process of creating the cartoon was time consuming and exacting. Using it for three tapestries was expedient. Of the three versions, the close-up view of *Shining Knight* appears the least recognizable as a face. The break-up of features, so enticing to Nezhnie, occurs because the soft brown cotton roving tends to blur the information the lines provide as cues, needed for an observer's mind to interpret at close range. The compelling impact of viewing the image from three feet away is the visceral novelty of uneven, seemingly disconnected, blue and brown lines deeply embedded in the soft fiber. In contrast to the other two tapestries, the viewer does not interpret the sparse information of the lines into a face until further away. The same intense combination of yarns is used to hold the shiny Mylar in place. It is the contrasting elements, and the surprising shift in focus, that provide the excitement in the otherwise minimal design.

With *Nader*, neither enlarging the scale nor eliminating extraneous details was enough to get the dual effect of offering unique views close up and at a greater vantage point. The added complication of having to fill such a huge expanse was challenging. A treatment needed to be found to provide interest in the area between features and to unify the long surface. Besides creating the background out of very textural yarns, her solution was to insert parallel vertical stripes throughout the piece. No doubt, when lines were drawn on the image during the process of copying it to scale, she could see the exciting effect of abstract forms collecting around the stripes in the areas of detail.

She also decided to use a wide variety of colors to weave these abstract shapes. However, varying the colors to the extent she did created another challenge for her. She needed to control the disintegration in a way that would still produce the proper value shifts needed to convey dimension so the eyes would look realistic at a distance. The resulting abstraction of repetitive rust stripes and splatters of vivid color, collected in a seemingly random manner around the orderly progression, is very enticing. It required a well-developed awareness of color value to control the shading and shaping for the eyes to look convincing.

Nezhnie clearly manifested a highly refined sensitivity in controlling values and the corollary degree of contrast. It was a critical asset in allowing her to work with large numbers of colors together. Her success with color is especially noticeable in commission work, where each solution is contingent on unique external requirements. Her first woven commission, *Grotto*, created in 1963, was designed as a backdrop for a statue. The Madonna was placed on a long, low cabinet in a busy hall of a children's hospital near the chapel entrance. The tapestry extended the length of the attractive blond wood cabinet. It depicts a small cave entrance placed directly behind the statue in a long expanse of quartz-like rock formations. Photographed by itself, it is of minimal interest. The deep blue cave entrance, graded from a deep center to lighter shades, seems too heavy when removed from the context of the statue. However, the irregular shapes of varying off-white and warm pastel tints of the rock formations come to life in the setting because the colors perfectly complement the wood tones of the cabinet. The dark entrance is seen only in passing and effectively brings the viewer's attention to the statue.

The way *Grotto* enhances its surroundings seems coincidental, since none of its colors are specifically present in its environment. Yet, the perception of an effective match between elements is characteristic of her commissioned work. There are many examples, such as both woven versions of *Jacob's Dream*.

Other works show her sensitivity to color and light. It is unlikely that the choice to combine muted prismatic colors with the highly reflective silver Mylar for *Prisma* was accidental. Muriel surely noted how the Mylar caught every nuance of color and light in the environment, just as she was trying to capture the dusty atmosphere of a circus tent when she chose to break up the imagery in *Circus*. Also, she frequently used black, or a dark color, and white elements to unify divergent areas of a design, relying on the contrasting combination to highlight transitional segments.

People respond to color more emphatically than any other element in a composition. Therefore, its skillful use gives an artist more freedom for innovation

Nezhnie receiving award for window decoration.

in other, more contentious, areas. As Nezhnie understood in selecting the color palette for the Holocaust images, a beautiful color scheme would hold her audience's attention in a positive way despite the painful subject matter. In *Pogrom* dividing the swastika into two very divergent colors was a truly inspired decision. It allowed her to portray a negative symbol in a visually exciting manner that enables the viewer to engage with the symbol and face up to its horrific associations.

There is no record of the specific art classes Muriel took as a teenager on her Saturday ventures into the city. Certainly, she had extensive drawing experience. What is also apparent, from her award-winning window decoration from that period, is that she was already quite a skillful artist. The dancing skeletons are fluid and merry.

The most fascinating aspect of the painting is her use of decorative symbols at the side of the composition. Nezhnie already reinforced the content of her imagery by presenting a graphic code to complement the action. The musical notes set the stage along with checkmarks, a quintessential symbol for communication. Her visual vocabulary and a deepening urge to communicate with the world at large were developing at a very early age.

The seeds of her need to be an artist were germinating even further back, when she was left to fend for herself during the day as a very young girl. How could a child remember all the comments and observations she wanted to share with her sister or mother when they would finally be home? A few pictures or clever constructions would get their attention and maybe provide the impetus for more extended conversations. The more resourceful she was, the better chance of garnering attention from family members who were most likely hoping for some peace and quiet upon returning home, not more interaction.

The frustration she felt during her early career about the negation of content in artwork can be understood in the context of this role that artistic expression had in her life. It explains why she was less concerned about the specific technique, or even the medium used, than the clarity of concept contained in the works of art she produced.

Perhaps the reason Nezhnie did not seek any further training in weaving was simply because she was able to use the myriad skills she had already developed so effectively that she did not feel limited in expressing her ideas as woven art. Her understanding of the unique style of imagery that could emerge most potently in tapestry was remarkable.

> There is more to be gained than texture when one translates an idea from a painted study into a tapestry. First of all the weaving process itself alters the design; smooth lines become stepped and crude. Yet as the image becomes degraded it also gains character because it is intrinsically real. (Crump, 2)

What might have no logic in painting can be the very thing that makes an image believable in tapestry. That is because the usage is consistent with the process of weaving. Therefore, however tempting it may be, relying on painting conventions is not always the most effective means to capture an expression or detail in tapestry. This assessment is not meant to diminish the importance of painting in Nezhnie's development artistically. Painting had helped to cultivate more than her sophisticated color sensitivity. She perceived that painting would be the primary focus for the lifestyle she chose, that of an artist. It was exceptionally courageous of Muriel to set such an essential part of her identity aside. Only her far greater need to communicate and her emerging affinity with woven images enabled her to make the transition.

Not only was she willing to change media, she exerted voluminous amounts of energy towards altering her environment, increasing the exposure she desired. Her efforts at the Craft Alliance gallery helped secure a place for crafts in the regional art community.

However, it was only late in her career, during the 1980s, when opportunities to begin interacting specifically with other tapestry weavers came Nezhnie's way. A dramatic change occurred within the tapestry community between 1985 and 2000. Exhibits designed exclusively to showcase tapestry emerged at a fairly predictable frequency, often in conjunction with related conferences. While these exhibits did not significantly impact the art community as a whole, they allowed an increasing interchange between the weavers. Finally, Nezhnie's work received notice from her peers.

Because of her dynamic personality and independent style of working, she left a memorable impression on the weavers who came in contact with her. However, because of her encroaching illness she did not have a sustained opportunity to impact the field collectively. In reality, what was transmitted to most other weavers regarding her philosophy about the medium, can be credited to the efforts of her former apprentice, Deann Rubin, rather than Nezhnie's own interaction. Rubin was an influential part of the tapestry community in the early 1990s, through teaching and briefly editing the International Tapestry Network's journal. Still, many of the tapestries described within the pages of this book are revealed to the tapestry community, as well as the art world, for the first time. They comprise a fascinating collection of options for interpreting imagery. Nezhnie took a fresh and very insightful look at what tapestry weaving had to offer the world of art.

Epilogue

Muriel Nezhnie Helfman died on April 9, 2002, the 27th day of Nisan in the Jewish calender. That day, called Yom HaShoah, had been designated by the international Jewish community as the day to mourn the decimation of six million Jews during the holocaust of World War II. It is also referred to as the "Devastation and Heroism Day," which suggests its general function. Being a relatively new holiday, established in 1950, it is not observed in a set of formalized rituals. Some Jews see it as a time for sanctioned anger at a deity that could allow such a fate; others emphasize the subsequent rebirth of faith. In Israel, the day is a national holiday. Sirens blare at 10:00 a.m., and all activities are stopped. Cars are parked, and everyone stands to observe two minutes of silent remembrance. In the rest of the world, it is a time for candle lighting, speeches, and gathering at memorials.

Whatever significance this coincidence may have, it is worth noting. For one observer, the significance of the date lies in a different Jewish tradition. A person's death is honored each year as an anniversary, or Yahrzeit, on the coinciding date in the Jewish calender. The primary ritual is to light a twenty-four-hour candle. Muriel's Yahrzeit will always be on the Yom HaShoah, thus eternally linked to it. I personally believe that in some inexplicable way, Nezhnie felt the force of the collective energy of Jews around the world, despite her lack of conscious, coherent functioning. It seems as if an energy so concentrated in its intent gave her the impetus to release her hold on life. She joined with them in spirit, though it was not an easy death. Muriel died of a massive seizure.

When I first met Nezhnie, she had been ill with Alzheimer's disease for over ten years. I had minimal expectations of what I would find as I accompanied her husband to the nursing home to visit her. He planned his visits, two or three times weekly at lunchtime, so that he could feed her. He explained that she still had a good appetite and it was the most interactive and rewarding way to spend his time with her. The staff appreciated the timing of his visits as well, since Muriel was incapable of feeding herself.

Muriel was deep in sleep when we arrived. She looked older than I expected of a sixty-eight-year-old woman, with straight gray hair cropped to her ear in a casual cut. Shelly shook her gently on the shoulder, and she woke with a beaming smile for him, for both of us really. I was surprised at how delighted she appeared. Her face went from stark vacancy to pleasure within a moment. We pulled up chairs, and Shelly got one of the generously large bibs of colorful pastel stripes for her. The common room, where lunch was served, was cheerful. She held his hand or he rubbed her shoulder and back while we waited for the lunch cart to arrive. She looked at me frequently and would lean just slightly forward and point a finger up as if trying to say something. When I extended my hand, she took my fingers briefly. Mostly she would smile. At times, she would turn directly to face Shelly and smile broadly at him.

Once the food tray came, I had an excellent opportunity to watch her mobile face flit through a myriad of expressions. The main dish was a stew with relatively large chunks of beef. Muriel would sometimes show discomfort at the unexpected size and then devote several moments to chewing the piece thoroughly. Each bite was responded to, pondered, and digested. When a new texture was brought to her mouth, it elicited an even more contemplative look on her face. Muriel slowly ate everything. Gradually, her attention was directed less and less to either of us or to the food brought to her mouth, and she looked more tired by the dessert course. Shelly went to her room to get a toothbrush and proceeded to clean her teeth. Although she showed she was not pleased with the invasion of the brush in her mouth, he persisted. Several years earlier, her teeth had deteriorated before anyone realized she needed more dental attention.

Within minutes of finishing lunch, she drifted back into sleep. While feeding her, he explained that early on she had experienced several seizures and was subject to falling. She had a large, though discreet, "starburst" scar on her high curving forehead and had also broken her nose as the result of a fall. Her once aquiline nose now had a distinct curve to the right. She was no longer allowed to walk on her own. Her medication needed constant monitoring, and she continued to have small twitches and seizures.

Her smile and the overall expressiveness of her face was so much more than I had anticipated. I was surprised that she still had the capacity to give back something to those in her presence. I realized, however, how much easier it was for me to observe Nezhnie than it would have been for anyone who had a memory of the vital, gregarious woman she had been. Because she had been so articulate, it was extremely difficult for others to observe the change.

A few months after my first introduction to her, the seizures started occurring more frequently. Still, it was a surprise to everyone, staff included, when she suffered the massive seizure that caused her death.

At her funeral, one mourner expressed how difficult it had been to grieve over Nezhnie's loss during the decade that she was incapacitated. It was a sentiment shared by many. The service was a much-needed farewell for many artists, friends, and family members.

In retrospect, weavers who worked either as apprentices or under contract for her in the mid-1980s see many peculiar instances of the incremental deterioration caused by the disease. At the time, they considered her unpredictable or temperamental. Because she was still relatively young, turning fifty in 1984, they may have attributed her inconsistencies to a hormonal imbalance. Nezhnie required one experienced local weaver to redo several Torah covers. Finally, the weaver simply said she would not redo one because there was nothing the matter with it. By then, she was feeling cross and resentful that her skill was not being appreciated. Muriel accepted her answer and the cover. Despite the increasing difficulties in working with Nezhnie, all who wove for her during this phase report learning innumerable aspects of the process, making the experience worthwhile.

The transition and end of her career was not an easy process for the family to accept, either. At first, they were hesitant to label her condition openly. They were afraid she would be very upset about hearing the diagnosis. Her mother had suffered from what had been called "hardening of the arteries," but was really Alzheimer's. Over the years Muriel had openly shared her distress about the deterioration of her mother with anyone on intimate terms with her. Thus, there was a genuine reluctance to compare her condition with that of her mother, and in order to protect her, they did not reveal the extent of her problems to friends or clients.

Yet, Nezhnie knew she was not functioning at her previous level of coherence and that she was experiencing the same types of malfunctions as her mother had. Her closest friend states that Muriel clearly was the first to know how much her memory was failing. Commissions became extremely hard for her to accomplish. In the last years of her career Shelly tried to simplify her designs, hoping to make the weaving easier. However, on days when she was not functioning at normal capacity, she could make no more connection to simple manipulations than to complex ones.

Ilisha had observed that her mother lost the ability to edit her designs. She explained that Muriel became less able to simplify an idea. She was not able to conceptualize the whole process ahead, and therefore wasn't able to modify design aspects pragmatically. As early as 1984, during the weaving of *Cascade*, a private commission, the discrepancy between her natural attraction for complicated compositions and her capacity to actually execute such feats became apparent. *Cascade* was intricately detailed, depicting rocks and vegetation at the edge of a waterfall, with reflections in the water. It was a literal interpretation of the photograph provided by the client. The weaving was triangular, 18" x 36", with a long cascade of fringe. Despite the small weaving area, the project proved to be an immense ordeal for her to complete, and for family members to watch her struggling through. Luckily, the tapestry gives no indication of the effort it took to complete it. It is delicate and charming.

Nevertheless, Nezhnie accomplished several of her major Holocaust tapestries after that time. Besides the intricacies of the scenic design, she had no personal drive or fascination with landscapes. The subject matter was not something she chose to work with at any stage in her career, although one other naturalistic landscape had been designed for an apprentice to weave.

By 1988, she had started a log of what she did each day and maintained it for at least several months. Only a brief five-month section of the log remains. It recorded who called or what errands she did. Sometimes it recorded things she had forgotten to do, other times what she hoped to do. Some days it would list how she felt, with several references to being stressed. She was under pressure to finish *Deportation* for the Chicago exhibit of the Holocaust tapestries. She was also working on the design layout for the brochure that accompanied the exhibit. The brochure was a very attractive red four-fold sheet with black and white photos of all the pieces, along with the painting of the then unfinished tapestry. It also included her resumé and artist's statement. The task of layout seemed to eat up hours, and she was feeling the need to clean up her studio to improve her environment and attitude. It was a time when the couple was involved in many social obligations, thus taking many evenings away from work. She was having trouble sleeping and would get up early to start on the day's weaving.

Fortunately, she continued functioning well enough to accept the honor of being one of the featured speakers and also to conduct a workshop at the "Tapestry Forum" held at Oregon School of Arts and Crafts in 1990. It was a tremendous struggle to prepare for the event. She would select a slide to use in the talk and then completely forget what its relevance was. Shelly helped and actually wrote the speech for her. She read it at the conference, rather than delivering it spontaneously, which was her usual style. Her workshop assistant, Linda Hutchins, quickly understood that Nezhnie was not as sharp as at the earlier workshop she had conducted there. Hutchins assumed more responsibility than she had planned, prompting Muriel back on track when necessary. In that manner, Nezhnie was able to communicate most of the concepts she wanted to share with the workshop participants.

Nevertheless, it was an ironic moment. All of her contemplation while weaving, and the subsequent writing and revising she did over the years, had been a preparation for just such a moment. It had been her aspiration to stand in the spotlight and share her deep understanding of the tapestry medium as art. She was the one most upset about her performance during the gathering, according to Hutchins, although her former apprentice, Deann Rubin, also witnessed the event as heartbreaking.

At least Nezhnie knew that her efforts had been recognized. She was there, and people were interested in her work and what she had to say. The participants at the symposium included the majority of well-known American tapestry artists. It was the largest of such meetings in the United States in many years, and Nezhnie was the keynote speaker. Some of the organizers had attended a 1988 symposium in Melbourne, Australia, which brought the international community of weavers together for a major gathering that focused exclusively on tapestry. The success of the event infused new energy into the field, exemplified by the enthusiastic attendance at the Portland symposium. In the end, it was the artwork, the tapestries Nezhnie exhibited and presented through slides, that left a mark on the symposium attendees, the legacy of an artist that speaks for itself.

Two years later, Nezhnie accepted an honorary doctorate from the University of Missouri – St. Louis for her contributions to art. It was her last public appearance. Again, she was fortunate enough to be able to attend the ceremony and know, on some level, that she had been recognized. Her communication skills enabled her to make it through the award ceremony and the dinner that followed. Many special guests had been invited to share the moment with her. She had always had the ability to get others to talk about themselves, thus deflecting attention away from herself.

In the words of her sister-in-law, who knew her as a young girl, and as an associate from her Craft Alliance days confirmed, "She had a way of making people love her." Judging from the magnetism of her smile on good days, even a decade later when her capacity for speech was gone, it seems likely she made all the guests feel honored, too.

The words of journalist Richard Rubin, sent to Shelly after Muriel's death, reiterate my impression of her during the last months and capture her essence well.

> In the nursing home, even during a short visit, Muriel exhibited the full range of emotions that infused her work: joy, fear, sorrow, and delight in companionship. She could not speak. It was not clear what she thought or whom she thought was there, but it was obvious that her emotional life was not over.
>
> Now that it is over, let the fullness of her life resonate, not just her times of public accomplishment and moments of high living or great affection, but her obstinacies and confusions and the slow playing out of her human existence.
>
> A weaver sees or dreams an image. Then day after day she

works on it, having faith that in spite of the intricacies and moment-to-moment problems of her task, it will emerge with even greater force than it had when she first perceived its strength.

In looking at the last major tapestry that Nezhnie was able to create, *Pogrom*, it is not hard to appreciate why, out of all the images she was interested in using, her final expression depicts a woman in fear for her life. Hurtling forward, exposed, there is no ground to anchor her. Even her assailants are floating, feet propelling in undefined space. A heavy threat, "enemy without cause," hangs above her. Still, the gift of her magnetism and her art remains.

Appendix A: Production Chronology

D99-02 indicates site visit or confirmation of status
Unless specified, all items are rectangular wall hangings.

1960   **The Elements**
B'nai Amoona Congregation, St. Louis, MO.
Appliqué, 45" radius each. Free-form hangings. Silk. D99-02.
Given as gift in 1972. Circular. Four Torah mantles. No longer in use because of wear, but still in existence as of June 2002. May eventually be framed.

1961   **Burning Bush**
Private collection, Yellow Springs, OH.
Tapestry, 39" x 30". Wool on jute warp. D99-02.
Tapestry destroyed by moths.

Tiger Rag
Private collection, Ft. Lee, NJ.
soumak, 49" x 32". Jute warp.

1962   **Arethousa**
Private collection, Bloomington, IN.
Tapestry, 39" x 33". Wool and cotton.

Blue Ground
Artist's estate, St. Louis, MO.
Tapestry, 40" x 37". Wool and cotton.
Orange warp deliberately revealed. Pictured in review of "Young Americans '62," *Craft Horizon*, 1962. In exhibit at St. Louis Art Museum, 1974.

Chameleon
Private collection, St. Louis, MO.
Tapestry, 40" x 36". Wool and cotton.
D99-02. Also titled "Uki-Yoe." In exhibit at St. Louis Art Museum, 1974.

Evangelismos
Private collection, St. Louis, MO.
Appliqué, 57" x 16". Wool and cotton. D99-02.
Pictured in review of "Craftsmen of the Central States," *Craft Horizon* 1962.

I Set the Lord Before Me Always
Private collection, Stockbridge, MA.
Tapestry, 51" x 35". Wool and cotton. D99-02.
Prototype for later hooked versions. Mother-of-pearl inserts top and bottom borders.

Oracles
Private collection, St. Louis, MO.
Tapestry, 31" x 34". Jute warp.
Surface loop accents. In exhibit at St. Louis Art Museum, 1974.

Vesperal
Our Lady of the Snows Shrine, Belleville, IL.
Appliqué, 36" x 114". Commission. Table cover. Wool and cotton.
First commission.

1963   **Grotto**
Cardinal Glennon Memorial Hospital, St. Louis, MO
Tapestry, 36" x 48". Commission. Wool and cotton. D99-02.

Roman Holiday
Private collection, Half Moon Bay, CA
Tapestry, 40" x 15". Wool and cotton.

Veronica's Veil
Private collection, location unknown.
Tapestry, 40" x 32". Wool and rayon.

Xylem
Private collection, Newark, DE.
Tapestry, 35" x 35". Wool and cotton.

1964   **Vestment Stoles**
St. Marks Episcopal Church, St. Louis, MO.
Tapestry, Commission. Stoles. Wool and rayon. Set of four vestment stoles.

1965   **Burning Bush**
Edward Fields, Inc., New York, NY.
Hooked, 78" x 54". Commission. Wool and cotton.
Fabrication by Edward Fields, Inc.

Genesis
Private collection, Stockbridge, MA.
Tapestry, 81" x 84". Wool and cotton. D99-02.
Designed by Sheldon Helfman and woven by MNH.

1966   **A Super Egg for Henry Liu**
Private collection, Beverly Hills, CA.
Tapestry, 60" x 12". Commission. Wool and cotton.

Blackfoot
Private collection, Portland, OR.
Tapestry, 26" x 12". Free-form hanging. Wool and cotton.

Embrace
Private collection, Portland, OR.
Tapestry, 21" x 10". Free-form hanging. Wool and cotton.
Pictured in book *Creative Handweaving* by Xenia Ley Parker.

Little Egypt
Private collection, St. Louis, MO.
Tapestry, 22" x 10". Free-form hanging. Wool and cotton. D99-02.
In exhibit at St. Louis Art Museum, 1974.

Mother I
Private collection, Stockbridge, MA.
Tapestry, 21" x 14". Free-form hanging, Wool and cotton. D99-02.
In exhibit at St. Louis Art Museum, 1974.

Mother II
Private collection, St. Louis, MO.
Tapestry, 21" x 14". Free-form hanging. Wool and cotton. D99-02.

1967   **Bedouin**
Private collection, location unknown.
Tapestry, 8" x 4". Free-form hanging. Wool and cotton.

Bursting in Air
Private collection, St. Louis, MO.
Tapestry, 17" x 45". Wool and cotton. D99-02.
Three pillows cut down from original tapestry, most likely originally called
"For One Brief Shining Moment." Collection includes the original framed painting.

Foursome
Private collection, St. Louis, MO.
Tapestry, 27" x 25". Wool and cotton. D99-02.
Originally hung in the Dept. of Ophthalmology, Washington University, St. Louis, MO.

Genesis
First Plymouth Congregational Church, Lincoln, NE.
Tapestry, 132" x 84". Commission. Wool and cotton.
Merit Award, Guild for Religious Architecture, AIA, 1969, Davis & Wilson, Arch.

No Excuse for Being
Private collection, St. Louis, MO.
Tapestry, 24" x 8". Free-form hanging. Wool and cotton. D99-02.
Turquoise beads. So named because of a comment by a juror that the piece had
"No excuse for being!"

Odyssey
Private collection, St. Louis, MO.
Tapestry, 60" x 60". Commission. Wool and cotton. D99-02.

Odyssey '67
Private collection, St. Louis, MO.
Tapestry, 48" x 96". Commission. Wool and cotton. D99-02.
In exhibit at St. Louis Art Museum, 1974.

Strata
Private collection, location unknown.
Tapestry, 75" x 30". Wool and cotton.

Venus
Private collection. St. Louis, MO.
Tapestry, 57" x 24". Free-form hanging. Wool, cotton, and rayon.
In exhibit at St. Louis Art Museum, 1974.

1968   **In Thy Light We See Light**
Private collection, Annapolis, MD.
Tapestry, 41" x 30". Wool and cotton.

Large Embrace
University City High School, St. Louis, MO.
Tapestry, 41" x 29". Free-form hanging. Wool and cotton. D99-02.

Magdelania
Private collection, St. Louis, MO.
Tapestry, 20" x 11". Free-form hanging. Wool and rayon.
Silver ornaments. In exhibit at St. Louis Art Museum, 1974.

Navahope
Private collection, St. Louis, MO.
Tapestry, 20" x 10. Free-form hanging. Wool and rayon. D99-02.
Silver ornaments. In exhibit at St. Louis Art Museum, 1974.

Somebody
Private collection, Stockbridge, MA.
Tapestry, 78" x 36". Free-form hanging. Wool and cotton.
Pictured in book *Creative Handweaving* by Xenia Ley Parker.

Tablets of the Law
United Hebrew Congregation, St. Louis, MO.
Tapestry, 144" x 66", Commission. Ark curtain. Wool and cotton. D99-02.
Edward Mutrux, Arch. Whereabouts of tapestry unknown, 2002.

The Door
Private collection, St. Louis, MO.
Tapestry, 59" x 58". Wool and cotton. D99-02.
Acquired in trade for architectural help in remodeling basement for studio.
In exhibit at St. Louis Art Museum, 1974.

1969 **Gypsy Moth**
Private collection, St. Louis, MO.
Tapestry, 90" x 40". Free-form hanging. Wool on rayon and silk warp. D99-02.
In exhibit at St. Louis Art Museum, 1974.

Loreli
Private collection, Stockbridge, MA.
Tapestry, 58" x 47". Free-form hanging. Rayon and wool on cotton warp.
In exhibit at St. Louis Art Museum, 1974.

Mandrake
Location unknown.
Tapestry, 32" x 20". Free-form hanging. Wool and cotton.
In exhibit at St. Louis Art Museum, 1974.

Peacock Wood
Private collection, Needham, MA.
Tapestry, 22" x 66". Wool and cotton.
Based on wood grain pattern.

Punchinello
Private collection, Bloomfield Hills, MI.
Tapestry, 16" x 16". Free-form hanging. Wool and cotton.
"I took some classes at Cranbrook and worked with Walter Nottingham."
In exhibit at St. Louis Art Museum, 1974.

Shady Braidy
Private collection, St. Louis, MO.
Tapestry, 58" x 47". Free-form hanging. Rayon and wool on cotton warp.

Simeon
Private collection, St. Louis, MO.
Tapestry, 36" x 8" x 5". Free-form hanging. Linen and fur. D99-02.
Three-dimensional, tubular. Gift of the artist.

1970 **Big Egypt**
Private collection, Stockbridge, MA.
Tapestry, 36" x 15". Free-form hanging. Wool and cotton. D99-02.

Flaggedy Ann
St. Louis Art Museum, St. Louis, MO.
Tapestry, 126" x 60". Free-form hanging. Wool and cotton. D99-02.
Gift of Mr. Thomas Alexander, 1978.

1971 **Imprints**
University City Public Library, St. Louis, MO.
Tapestry, 80" x 192" each. Commission. Wool and cotton. D99-02.
Two curved and reversible panels. 213 sq. ft. total. Smith & Entzeroth, Arch.

Jacob's Dream
Temple Israel, St. Louis, MO.
Tapestry, 216" x 96". Commission. Ark curtain. Wool, linen, and cotton. D99-02.
Honorable Mention, Guild for Religious Architecture, AIA. Interior lined with tapestry.
Twelve ropes 18' long.

The Knocker
Private collection, Washington, DC.
Tapestry, Pillow. Wool and cotton.

1972 **Exodus**
Congregation Anshei-Sphard-Beth El Emeth,Memphis, TN.
Hooked, 415 sq. ft. Commission. Ark curtain. Wool and cotton.
Walk Joans & Francis Mah, Arch., fabricated by Edward Fields, Inc.

Mt. Sinai
Adas (Adat) Shalom Synagogue, Farmington, MI.
Tapestry, 168" x 48". Commission. Ark curtain. Wool, cotton, and Mylar. D99-02.

Tree of Life
Congregation Anshei-Sphard-Beth El Emeth, Memphis, TN.
Tapestry, 15 sq. ft. Commission. Table cover. Wool and cotton. D99-02.
No longer in use due to wear from placing Torahs on the fabric. Woven of fine wool.

Wild Cherry Charms
Private collection, W. Cornwall, CT.
Tapestry, 60" x 138". Wool and cotton. D99-02.
In exhibit at St. Louis Art Museum, 1974.

1973   **Eye**
Private collection, St. Louis, MO.
Tapestry, 27" x 14". Wool and cotton.
Like eye in *Imprints*, also called "Large Eye." In exhibit at St. Louis Art Museum, 1974.

Jacob's Dream
Adas (Adat) Shalom Synagogue, Farmington, MI.
Tapestry, 276" x 120". Commission. Ark curtain. Wool, cotton and Mylar. D99-02.

1974   **Springfield Genesis**
Private collection, Springfield, IL.
Tapestry, 66" x 39". Commission. Free-form hanging. Wool and cotton.
Soumak accents. Discrepancy in date, listed as 1976 on original production record.
In exhibit at St. Louis Art Museum, 1974.
Pictured on cover of *Creative Handweaving* by Xenia Ley Parker.

Breath of Life
Congregation B'nai Israel, Charleston WV.
Tapestry, 84" x 324". Commission. Wool and cotton. D99-02.
Gift of Howard and Isabel Baer. At the St. Louis Art Museum,
1974, displayed in central Sculpture Hall.

Library Echo I
Private collection, St. Louis, MO.
Tapestry, 80" x 21". Wool and cotton.
Detail of *Imprints*.

Library Echo II
Private collection, St. Louis, MO.
Tapestry, 80" x 31". Wool and cotton.
Detail of *Imprints*.

Praise and Study
Temple of Aaron, St. Paul, MN.
Tapestry, 16 sq. ft. Commission. Torah mantles. Wool and cotton.

1975   **Cherry Cartoon**
Artist's estate.
Tapestry, 40" x 37". Wool and cotton.
An outline detail of *Wild Cherry Charms*.

Circus
Private collection. St. Louis, MO.
Tapestry 126" x 60". Commission. Free-form hanging. Wool and cotton. D99-02.

Constellation
Private collection, St. Louis, MO.
Tapestry 84" x 84". Commission. Free-form hanging. Wool and cotton. D99-02.
Star-shaped. One of Muriel's favorite tapestries.

Covenant of the Rainbow
Private collection, Montague, MA.
Tapestry, 23" x 38". Free-form hanging. Wool and cotton.
Wavy edges.

Duet
Private collection, New Brunswick, NJ.
Tapestry, 27" x 40". Commission. Free-form hanging. Wool and cotton.
B & W portraits.

Eternal Light
Temple Beth El, Hammond, IN.
Tapestry, 28 sq. ft. Commission. Wool and cotton.
First tapestry with a Holocaust theme.

High Holiday Ark Curtain & Bemah Cover
B'nai Amoona Congregation, St. Louis, MO.
Appliqué, 148" x 98". Commission. Ark curtain. Silk. D99-02.
No longer in use because of wear. Table cover, 30 sq. ft.

Jacob's Dream
Temple Israel, Boston, MA.
Hooked, 126" x 132". Commission. Free-form hanging. Wool and cotton.
Triangular shape, fabricated by Edward Fields, Inc.

Landmarks
First National Bank of Springfield, Springfield, IL.
Hooked, 248 sq. ft. Commission. Free form hanging.
Wall relief, five quadrants. Graham, O'Shea & Wisnosky Arch.

Prisma
Private collection, St. Louis, MO.
Tapestry, 29" x 29". Free-form hanging. Wool, cotton and mylar. D99-02.

Sinai
Sons of Israel, Woodmere, Long Island, NY.
Hooked, 50 sq. ft. Commission. Ark curtain. Wool and cotton.
Fabricated by Edward Fields, Inc. Perhaps originally called "Exodus."

Stella
Private collection, St. Louis, MO.
Tapestry, 29" x 29". Free-form hanging.
Star-shaped.

1976   **Acrobats**
Private collection, St. Louis, MO.
Tapestry, 42" x 252". Commission. Wool and cotton. D99-02.

Covenant of the Rainbow
Smith College, Northampton, MA.
Tapestry, 39" x 60". Wool and cotton.
Gift of the artist to Smith College Chapel, acquired 1985.
Possibly woven by Jan Jungkuntz.

Eliot
First Unitarian Church, St. Louis, MO.
Tapestry and pile weave, 64" x 60". Commission. Wool and cotton. D99-02.
Woven by Hannah Roth.

Four Crowns
B'nai Amoona Congregation, St. Louis MO.
Tapestry, 4" x 48". Commission. Wool and cotton. D99-02.
Ribbon for reading table shelf.

J Rug
Private collection, St. Louis, MO
Hooked, 120" x 156". Commission. Rug. Wool and cotton. D99-02.
Hooked by Vsoske, Inc., Puerto Rico.

Nader
Private collection, St. Louis, MO.
Tapestry, 39" x 188". Wool and cotton. D99-02.
Diptych with *Trio* but separated for sale. Jan Jungkuntz co-weaver.

Rainbow
Private collection, New York, NY.
Tapestry, 36" x 63". Free-form hanging. Wool and cotton. D99-02.
Wavy lower edge. "Watercolor version" woven by Jan Jungkuntz.

Shining Knight
Private collection, St. Louis, MO.
Tapestry, 43" x 36". Wool, cotton and Mylar. D99-02.
Exhibited in "Textiles: Past & Prologue," Greenville County Museum of Art,
Greenville, NC, 1976.

Spearmint Charms
Private collection, Half Moon Bay, CA.
Tapestry, 60" x 138". Wool and cotton. D99-02.
Male counterpart to *Wild Cherry Charms*.

Tablets of the Law
Beth Israel Hospital, Boston, MA.
Hooked, 84' x 60". Commission. Ark curtain. Wool and cotton.
Merit award, Guild for Religious Architecture, AIA, 1969.
Limited Edition, Edward Fields, Inc.

Trio
Artist's estate.
Tapestry, 39" x 47". Wool and cotton. D99-02.
Part of diptych with *Nader*.

U. S. Court of Appeals (8th Circuit, St. Louis)
8th Circuit Court of Appeals, St. Louis, MO.
Hooked, 48" radius. Commission. Free-form hanging. Wool and Cotton.
New design for the 8th Circuit. Fabricated by Edward Fields, Inc.

Women
Tapestry, 60" x 23". Wool and cotton.
Lost in fire 4/11/89, at the Sazama Brauer Gallery, Chicago, IL.

1977   Burning Bush
Temple Beth El, Spring Valley, NY.
Hooked, 78" x 54". Commission. Ark curtain.
Fabricated by Edward Fields, Inc.

Doll Baby
Private collection, St. Louis, MO.
Tapestry, 19" x 16". Free-form hanging. Wool and cotton.

Exodus
Temple Emanuel, St. Louis, MO.
Hooked, 60 sq. ft. Commission. Free-form hanging, Wool and cotton. D99-02.
Diamonds extend out from rectangle. Fabricated by Edward Fields, Inc.

Illustration 96
Artist's estate.
Tapestry, 62" x 39". Wool and cotton.
Woven by Jan Jungkuntz.

Portrait of the Artist as Young Woman
Artist's estate.
Tapestry, 60" x 43". Wool and cotton.

Saying of the Fathers
Sons of Israel, Woodmere, Long Island, NY.
Tapestry. Commission. Torah mantles. Mixed materials D99-02.
Four tapestry covers by Jan Jungkuntz and seven appliqué covers by Eva Wilson.
See *Sinai* 1975.

Sea Quence
Private collection, Half Moon Bay, CA.
Tapestry, 30" x 35". Free-form hanging. Wool, cotton, and rayon.
A woven flexigon. Woven by Jan Jungkuntz.

Tablets of the Law
Congregation Brith Shalom, Springfield, IL.
Hooked, 74" x 51". Commission. Ark curtain. Wool and cotton. D99-02.
Fabricated by Edward Fields, Inc.

Tree of Life
Shaare Zedek Synagogue, St. Louis, MO.
Hooked, 65 sq. ft. Commission. Ark curtain. Wool and cotton. D99-02.
Red version, seven unit spread limited edition, Edward Fields, Inc.

Valentine I
Private collection, St. Louis, MO.
Tapestry, 20" x 28". Wool and rayon. D99-02.

Valentine II
Private collection. St. Louis, MO.
Tapestry, 36" x 44". Wool on rayon. D99-02.

Zelda
Private collection, W. Cornwall, CT.
Tapestry, 10" x 9" plus fringe. Silk. D99-02.

1978   **Eliot Again**
Private collection, St. Louis, MO.
Tapestry, 8" x 10" plus fringe. Silk. D99-02.

Phil Ochs
Private collection, St. Louis, MO.
Tapestry, 9" x 11". Wool and silk. D99-02.

Portrait of Dr. Ferry
Private collection, St. Louis, MO.
Tapestry, 24" x 26". Commission. Wool and cotton.

Prairie Journey
Isasora Pottle Fund, Public Library, Macomb, IL.
Tapestry, 45 sq. ft. Commission. Wool and cotton. D99-02.

Search
Monsanto Environmental Health Laboratory, St. Louis, MO.
Hooked, 60 sq. ft. Commission.
Design based on actual graphic material used in research. Unknown fabricator.

Seed of Science
University of Missouri – Rolla. Rolla, MO.
Tapestry, 31 sq. ft. Commission. Wool and cotton. D99-02.
Five square units, joined by metal rods.

Young Artist
Tapestry, 36" x 80". Hanging. Wool and cotton.
Destroyed in fire 4/11/89 at the Sazama Brauer Gallery, Chicago, IL.

Young Wife
Artist's estate.
Tapestry, 64" x 38". Wool and cotton.
Apprentice work.

1979   **Daughters of Auschwitz**
Artist's estate.
Tapestry, 60" x 54". Free-form hanging. Wool and cotton. D99-02.
Holocaust series.

Library Echo III
Artist's estate.
Tapestry. 35" x 51". Wool and cotton.

Library Echo IV
Tapestry, 80" x 21". Wool and cotton.
Destroyed in fire 4/11/89 at the Sazama Brauer Gallery, Chicago, IL.

Pillar of Fire & Pillar of Cloud
Congregation Beth Israel, Hammond, IN.
Hooked, 88 sq. ft. each. Commission. Free-form hanging. Wool and cotton.
Two triangular wall hangings, fabricated by Edward Fields, Inc.

Tree of Life
Temple Solomon, Centralia, IL.
Hooked, 78" x 84". Commission. Ark curtain. Wool and cotton.
Limited edition, ark curtain, fabricated by Edward Fields, Inc.

Young Husband
Artist's estate.
Tapestry, 40" x 58". Wool and cotton.
Woven by Deann Rubin.

1980   **Constance**
Private collection, New York, NY.
Tapestry, 6" x 8". Silk. D99-02.
Portrait of poet Constance Urdang of St. Louis. Silk warp and weft.

Evangelos
Private collection, St. Louis, MO.
Tapestry, 11" x 10". Silk. D99-02.

1981   **Adam's Daughters**
Artist's estate.
Tapestry, 25" x 21" each. Wool and cotton.
Holocaust series. Set of five faces from the *Daughters of Earth*, woven by Christel Maassen.

Daughters of Earth
Artist's estate.
Tapestry, 81" x 53". Free-form hanging. Wool and cotton. D99-02.
Holocaust Series.

Mr. Lincoln's Hometown
Convention and Visitors Bureau, Springfield, IL.
Hooked, 50 sq. ft. Commission. Free-form hanging. Acrylic and cotton.
Based on earlier design for the First National Bank of Springfield (1975). Landmarks
six quadrants, 39" radius each. Fabricated by Paul Wieland, Grand Rapids, MI.

1982   **Covenant**
Congregation Gomely Chesed, Portsmouth, VA.
Hooked, 54" x 50". Commission. Free-form hanging. Wool and cotton.
Fabricated by Edward Fields, Inc.

Cruciform
Maryville College Chapel, St. Louis, MO.
Hooked, 60" x 32". Commission. Hanging. Acrylic and cotton. D99-02.
The Cruciform has a reliquary at the center of the cross concerning five nuns martyred
by the Huns. 2" relief carving of pile. Fabricated by Paul Weiland, Grand Rapids, MI.

Ghetto Child—Stroop Report
Holocaust Museum of Dallas, Dallas, TX.
Tapestry, 60" x 48". Wool and cotton.
Holocaust series. Given on permanent loan to the Dallas Center for Holocaust Studies.

Revelation Ark Curtain
Children of Israel Congregation, Youngstown, OH.
Tapestry, 105" x 50". Commission. Ark curtain. Wool and rayon.
Woven by Christel Maassen.

1983   **Bamboo Garden**
Private collection, St. Louis, MO.
Tapestry, 12" x 81". Commission. Wool and cotton.
Landscape woven by Christel Maassen.

Psalm
Temple Brith Shalom, Springfield, IL.
Tapestry, 24 sq. ft. Commission. Free-form hanging. Wool and cotton. D99-02.
Pyramidal shape woven by Christel Maassen.

1984   **Cascade**
Private collection, St. Louis, MO.
Tapestry, 18" x 36". Commission. Free-form hanging. Wool and cotton.
Triangular shape. Plus long warp fringe, making a waterfall.

Double Portrait
Private collection, St. Louis, MO.
Tapestry, 4 sq. ft. Commission. Free-form hanging. Wool and cotton.

Harvest Home
Agra Bank, St. Paul, MN.
Tapestry, 34 sq. ft. Commission. Wool and cotton.
Farm Credits Bank of St. Louis, original owners, but went to Agra Bank headquarters
through a merger.

In Memory of Stephen
Jewish Community of Amherst, MA.
Tapestry, 46" x 41". Commission. Ark curtain. Wool and cotton.
Gift of Mrs. J Greenberg.

1985   **Redemption**
Shaare Emeth Temple. St. Louis, MO
Tapestry. Commission. Torah mantles. Wool and cotton. D99-02.
Set of seven Torah mantles incorporating *Pillar of Fire and Pillar of Cloud* theme.
Some completed in 1981.

1986   **Aleph**
Congregation B'nai Juhudah, Kansas City, MO.
Tapestry, 56 sq. in. Commission. Torah mantle. Wool and cotton.

Shalom
Jewish Geriatric & Convalescent Center, Kansas City, MO.
Hooked, 32" x 131". Commission. Ark curtain. Wool and cotton.
Fabricated by Edward Fields, Inc.

1987   **Ethics of the Fathers**
Jewish Reconstructionist Society of North Shore, Roslyn Heights, NY.
Tapestry, 56" x 42". Commission. Wool and cotton.
Commissioned by May Soll.

Liberation
Artist's estate.
Tapestry, 36" x 47". Wool and cotton. D99-02.
Holocaust series.

Parting Lodz: The Kiss
Artist's estate.
Painting, 48" x 96". Acrylic on canvas. D99-02.
Holocaust series.

Portrait of Shawn
Private collection, St. Louis, MO.
Tapestry, 31" x 19". Commission. Wool and cotton.

1988   **Deportation**
Holocaust Museum & Learning Center, St. Louis, MO.
Tapestry, 54" x 53". Wool and cotton. D99-02.
Holocaust series, purchased in 2000.

Portrait of Katie
Private collection, St. Louis, MO.
Tapestry, 12" x 12". Silk. D99-02.
Elizabeth Clayton, original owner.

1989   **Pogrom**
Artist's estate.
Tapestry, 64" x 48". Wool and cotton. D99-02.
Holocaust series.

1990   **Confluence**
Washington University Medical School Library, St. Louis, MO.
Hooked, 144" x 144". Commission. Rug.
Medical School seal and reference to research. Fabricated in the Philippines.

1991   **Tree of Life**
United Hebrew, St. Louis, MO.
Tapestry, 122" x 58". Commission. Ark curtain. Wool and cotton. D99-02.
Lower portion of curtain is retractable blue ropes. Woven surface 48" x 57".

Torah Covers
Temple Israel, St. Louis, MO.
Tapestry. Commission. Torah mantles. Wool and cotton. D99-02.
Completed by Sheldon Helfman.

Appendix B: Lists by Theme or Style

Portraits

Constance 1980
Constellation 1975
Double Portrait 1984
Duet 1975
Eliot 1976
Eliot Again 1978
Evangelos 1980
Foursome 1967
Nader 1976
Phil Ochs 1978
Portrait of the Artist 1977
Portrait of Dr. Ferry 1978
Portrait of Katie 1988
Portrait of Shawn 1987
Prisma 1975
Shining Knight 1976
Stella 1975
Trio 1976
Valentine I 1977
Valentine II 1977
Young Artist 1978
Young Husband 1979
Young Wife 1978
Zelda 1977

Ark Curtains

Burning Bush 1977
Exodus, Long Island 1977
Exodus, Memphis 1972
High Holiday Ark
    Curtain 1975
I Set the Lord
    Before Me Always 1976
In Memory of Stephen 1984
Jacob's Dream,
    Boston 1975
Jacob's Dream,
    Farmington 1971
Jacob's Dream,
    St. Louis 1971
Mt. Sinai 1972
Revelation Ark Curtain .. 1982
Shalom 1986
Tablets of the Law,
    St. Louis 1968
Tablets of the Law,
    Boston 1976
Tablets of the Law,
    Springfield. 1977
Tree of Life, St. Louis 1977
Tree of Life, Centralia 1979
Tree of Life, St. Louis 1991

Commissions

Acrobats 1976
Aleph 1986
Bamboo Garden 1983
Breath of Life 1974
Burning Bush,
    New York 1965
Burning Bush,
    Spring Valley 1977
Cascade 1984
Circus 1975
Confluence 1990-91
Constellation 1975
Covenant 1982
Covenant of the
    Rainbow, Montague 1975
Covenant of the
    Rainbow, St. Louis 1976
Cruciform 1982
Double Portrait 1984
Duet 1975
Eliot 1976
Eternal Light 1975
Ethics of the Fathers 1987
Exodus,
    Long Island 1975-77
Exodus, Memphis 1971-72
Exodus, St. Louis 1977
Genesis 1967
Grotto 1963
Harvest Home 1984
High Holiday Ark
    Curtain & Bemah
    Cover 1975
Imprints 1970-71
In Memory of
    Stephen 1984
Jacob's Dream,
    Boston 1975
Jacob's Dream,
    Farmington Hills 1972
Jacob's Dream,
    St. Louis 1971
Landmarks 1975
Mr. Lincoln's
    Hometown 1981
Mt. Sinai 1972
Odyssey 1967
Odyssey '67 1967
Peacock Wood 1969
Portrait of the Artist 1977
Portrait of Shawn 1987
Praise and Study 1974
Psalm 1982-3

Redemption .... 1981 & 1985
Revelation Ark
    Curtain 1982
Shalom 1986
Springfield Genesis 1976
A Super Egg for
    Henry Liu 1966
Tablets of the Law,
    Boston 1976
Tablets of the Law,
    St. Louis 1968
Tablets of the Law,
    Springfield 1977
Torah Covers 1991
Tree of Life, Memphis 1972
Tree of Life,
    St. Louis 1990-91
Vesperal 1962
Vestment Stoles 1964

Free-Form Hangings

Flaggedy Ann 1970
Gypsy Moth 1969
Landmarks 1975
Large Embrace 1968
Little Egypt 1966
Loreli 1969
Magdelania 1968
Mandrake 1969
Mother I 1966
Mother II 1966
Mr. Lincoln's
    Hometown 1981
Navahope 1968
No Excuse for Being 1967
Pillar of Cloud 1979
Pillar of Fire 1979
Prisma 1975
Psalm 1983
Punchinello 1969
Rainbow 1976
Sea Quence 1977
Shady Braidy 1969
Simeon 1969
Somebody 1968
Springfield Genesis 1973
Stella 1975
Venus 1967

Appendix C: Honors, Exhibitions and Publicity

Honors:

1992 Honorary degree: "Doctor of Fine Arts," University of Missouri – St. Louis, St. Louis, MO.

1986 Artist representing the United States in the American Tapestry Alliance exhibition
"Panorama of Tapestry," featured work: *Daughters of Earth*, Toronto, Ontario, Canada.

1976 National Endowment for the Arts, Master Craftsmen Apprenticeship Grant.

1972 Honorable mention, "Guild for Religious Architecture Conference Exhibition,"
Atlanta, GA, *Jacob's Dream*, handwoven tapestry ark curtain, Morton J. May
Memorial Chapel, Temple Israel, St. Louis, MO.

1971 Honorable mention, "Guild for Religious Architecture Conference Exhibition,"
Los Angeles, CA, *Tablets of the Law*, handwoven tapestry ark curtain, United Hebrew
Congregation, St. Louis, MO.

1969 Merit award, "Guild for Religious Architecture Conference Exhibition," St. Louis, MO,
Genesis, handwoven tapestry, First Plymouth Congregational Church, Lincoln NE.

1964 Louis Comfort Tiffany Grant for investigation of pattern weave in tapestry.

One-person exhibitions

1990 "Images of the Holocaust: tapestries, drawings, and prints,"
Mendocino Arts Center, Mendocino, CA.

1989 "Muriel Nezhnie, Images of the Holocaust: tapestries, paintings, prints and drawings,"
The Center for Tapestry Arts, New York, NY.

1988 "Elegies: tapestries, painting, drawings and prints," SXC Gallery, St. Xavier College,
Chicago, IL.

    "Images of the Holocaust," Sazama-Brauer Gallery, Chicago, IL.

1987 "Past and Present Works on Holocaust Themes," Meramec Library Art Gallery,
St. Louis, MO.

1983 "Elegies," Bixby Gallery, Washington University School of Fine Arts, St. Louis, MO.

1982 "Works on Judaic and Holocaust Themes," Temple Beth Shalom, Miami Beach, FL.

Two person exhibitions

1983 "Muriel Nezhnie: Artist-Designer-Weaver and Sheldon Helfman: Artist,"
Private Stock Gallery, Kansas City, MO.

1976-77 "Nezhnie and Helfman: tapestries, watercolors and paintings,"
Mark Twain Gallery, St. Louis, MO.

1974-75 "Third St. Louis Artists Exhibition: Muriel Nezhnie and Heikki Seppa,"
St. Louis Art Museum, St. Louis, MO, November 1974 - January 1975.

1963 "Patricia Degner and Muriel Nezhnie Helfman," Martin Schweig Gallery, St. Louis, MO.

Group exhibitions

1990   "Tapestry Exhibition 1990," Contemporary Crafts Gallery, Portland, OR.

"Tapestry: Point of View," Hoffman Gallery,
Oregon School of Arts and Crafts, Portland, OR.

1989   "American Tapestry Weaving Since the 1930s and Its European Roots,"
Art Gallery, University of Maryland, College Park, MD.

1987   "Inaugural Exhibition", Sazama-Brauer Gallery, Chicago, IL.

1986   "Panorama of Tapestry," University of Toronto, Toronto, Ontario, Canada.
Sponsored by American Tapestry Alliance.

1985   "Vestments and Visions: Judaic Textiles," B'nai B'rith Klutznick Museum,
Washington, DC.

1981-82 "Traditions and Fantasy in Jewish Needlework," Yeshiva University Museum,
New York, NY.

1978   "Fiber Forms '78," Cincinnati Art Museum, Cincinnati, OH.

1977   "Guild for Religious Architecture Conference Exhibition," Milwaukee, WI.

"The Artist-Craftsman," St. Louis Art Museum, St. Louis, MO.
Sponsored by Craft Alliance.

"Hip Pocket Weaving," University of Illinois, Normal, IL.

1976   "Textiles: Past and Prologue," Greenville County Museum of Art, Greenville, SC.
National Handweavers Invitational Exhibition.

1972   "Eight Illinois-Missouri Craftsman." Invitational exhibition circulated by the
Illinois Arts Council and the Missouri Arts Council in cooperation with the National
Endowment for the Arts .

1969   "Discovery 1969: The Midwest," Halls Exhibition Gallery, Kansas City, MO.
Sponsored by the American Institute of Interior Designers.

1964   "The Crafts and Worship," Dallas Museum of Fine Arts, Dallas, TX. Invitational exhibition.

1962   "Craftmen of the Central States," Museum of Contemporary Crafts, New York, NY.
Circulated by the American Federation of the Arts.

"Young Americans '62," Museum of Contemporary Crafts, New York, NY. Circulated by
the American Federation of the Arts.

1961-62 "Contemporary Jewish Ceremonial Art," Jewish Museum, New York, NY.
Circulated by the American Federation of the Arts.

Film, Video

1988   "Art in Perspective," one segment of a video series featuring St. Louis artists and their
works, sponsored by the St. Louis Artists' Coalition, produced by Double Helix and
Vocal Point Productions, St. Louis, MO.

1987   "Art of the Holocaust," one segment of the video series "The Holocaust, Why Remember?"
TV Educational Programming, Harry Cargas producer, RTV Creative Services, St. Louis, MO.

"See-Hear," video interview with Muriel Nezhnie, American Cable Vision, St. Louis, MO.

1984   "Supple Epitaphs," Emmy award–winning video documentary feature of Muriel Nezhnie's Holocaust work, St. Louis Skyline, Jill Petzall producer, Public Television, St. Louis, MO.

1983   "Turnabout," news magazine video interview, American Broadcasting Company, St. Louis, MO.

1977   "Nezhnie," 16mm film, Carol Quintachino Greenfield producer and filmmaker, Astoria, NY.

1971   "Images and Things: Everybody Makes Things," color telecast, National Instructional Television Center, Bloomington, IN.

Publications

Duffy, Robert W. "Threads of Life: Weaver Honored with Degree for Tapestries on Holocaust." *St. Louis Post Dispatch* (August 9, 1992).

Rubin, Deann. "Muriel Nezhnie Receives Honorary Doctorate Degree," *ITNET Journal* (Fall, 1992): 18-19.

Shaw, Courtney Ann. *The Rise of the Artist/Weaver: Tapestry Weaving in the United States from 1930-1990*, Ph.D. diss., University of Maryland, 1992.

Nowak, Lynn. "Artist Weaves Holocaust Tapestry into Fiber Art." *The Port Townsend Jefferson County Leader* (March 14, 1990).

Family of Woman: Portrait of the Artists," *St. Louis Business Journal* (September-October, 1989).

Exhibition catalog. "American Tapestry Weaving Since the 1930s and Its European Roots," with comments by Courtney Ann Shaw, University of Maryland, College Park, MD, 1989.

Exhibition catalog. "World Tapestry Today," American Tapestry Alliance, Chiloquin, OR, 1988.

Jimenez, Gilbert. "Art Sensitively Depicts Horror of the Holocaust," *Chicago Sun Times* (June 17, 1988).

Thompson, Vivian Alpert. *A Mission in Art: Recent Holocaust Works in America*. Macon, GA: Mercer University Press, 1988.

Goldman, Betsy S. "Artists and Their Families," *American Artist Magazine* (October, 1987).

Nezhnie, Muriel. *Tapestry Topics*, American Tapestry Alliance, Chiloquin, OR, August, 1987.

Exhibition catalog. "Panorama of Tapestry." American Tapestry Alliance, Chiloquin, OR, 1986.

Adams, C. B. "Weaver Muriel Nezhnie Preserves Images of Holocaust," *St. Louis Globe Democrat* (September 27-28, 1986).

Greenberg, Sue. "Nezhnie Transforms Holocaust Images into Artistic Statements," *West End Word*, St. Louis, MO (March 20, 1986).

Townsend, W. D. "Weaving the Horror of the Holocaust," *Shuttle, Spindle and Dyepot*, Handweavers Guild of America (Summer, 1984.).

Helfman, M. N. *Remnants of Despair: An Homage to Nelly Sacks*, A suite of six intaglio monoprints accompanied by six Nelly Sachs poems , St. Louis: Little Aegis Editions, 1983 (completed later by Sheldon Helfman).

Townsend, W. D. "A Powerful Weaving of Art and the Holocaust," *St. Louis Globe Democrat* (October 31, 1983).

Castro, Jan. "The Holocaust Tapestries: A Talk with Muriel Nezhnie, Artist Weaver," *River Styx* 9: "The Elements" Big River Association, St. Louis, MO (1981): 36-44.

Harris, James R. "Muriel Nezhnie: Portraits," *Chicago Art Examiner* (February, 1980).

Ziemke, Dene. "Eclesiastical Weaving Part IV," *Shuttle, Spindle and Dyepot*, Handweavers Guild of America (Spring, 1979). With three photographs of Nezhnie tapestries.

Crump, Nancy. *Interweave*, Interweave Press Vol. 4 No. 2 (Spring, 1979).

"At the Museums, and More News," Photograph of *Breath of Life* and artist. *Jewish Art: A Quarterly Review* (Summer, 1977).

Rubin, Richard M. "Interview with the Helfmans," THE SEEN Newspaper of the Art Coordinating Council for the Area, St. Louis, MO (January 1977).

Parker, Xenia Ley. *Creative Handweaving*. New York, Dial Press, 1976. With photographs of several of Nezhnie's tapestries.

Exhibition catalog. "Textiles: Past and Prologue," National Handweavers Invitational Exhibition, Greenville County Museum of Art, Greenville, SC, 1976.

Griffith, Ann. "'Breath of Life' Tapestry Represents Natural Human State," *Charleston Daily Mail*, Charleston, WV (January 29, 1975).

McCue, George. "Seppa, Nezhnie Craft Objects as Fine Arts on Display at Museum," *St. Louis Post Dispatch* (December 10, 1974).

Peters, John Brod. "Helfman, Seppa Works Displayed," *St. Louis Globe Democrat* (November 30 - December 1, 1974).

Helfman, Muriel Nezhnie. "Tapestry for a Midwest Chapel," *Handwearer & Craftsman* 2, No. 2 (1970): 8.

Haggie, Helen. "First Plymouth Dedicates New Project," *Lincoln Sunday Journal & Star* (September 22, 1968).

Art Scene, Chicago, IL. (September, 1968).

Swanson, Peggy. "Trial Looms Large in Technique," *St. Louis Post Dispatch* (November 2, 1967).

"Craftsmen of the Central States," *Craft Horizon* (November-December, 1962).

"Young Americans '62," *Craft Horizon* (July-August, 1962).

index

A

A Mission in Art: Recent Holocaust Works in America 127
Abakanowicz, Magdalena 95
Abstract art 8, 39, 108-109, 133
Acrobats 82-83, 93
Adams, Mark 108
Adam's Daughters 119-120
Adas Shalom Synagogue 60, 64, 111
Albers, Anni 16
Albers, Josef 15, 16
Alzheimer's disease 2, 107, 141, 143
American Abstract Artists 14
American Crafts Council 32
American Tapestry Alliance 1, 124
Annunciation of the Virgin Mary, Pontormo's 79
anti-Semitism 4, 112-114
apprentices 22-24, 26, 28, 31-33, 84, 104, 139, 143-144
Arabic 56
ark curtains 53
armatures 43, 44, 55, 67, 131-132
Army, U.S. 3, 7, 8, 13, 16, 115, 116
Arthur U. Newton Gallery 10
artist, as husband, partner 8, 15-18, 20, 77
artistic process 23-25
Associated American Artists Gallery 10
Association des Cartooniers-Peintres 10
ATA newsletter 9
Aubusson 10, 108

B

Bauhaus 9, 16
Bayeux tapestry 112
Bell Laboratories 106
Beyond Craft 95

Biblical quotations 125
  Genesis 28:12 59
  Genesis 28:16 62
  Job 16:18 119
  Lamentations 3:52 126
  Psalm 126 113
  Samuel I 20:3 124
Biennale Internationale de la Tapisserie 74, 95, 111. *See* Lausanne biennial
Black Mountain 9
blocking tapestries
B'nai Brith Girls Club 6
bookmaking 8
Bounty Land 68
Braque 40
Breath of Life 28, 65-66
Brennan, Archie 57
Burde, Sharon 107
Burning Bush 36-37, 54, 58, 117

C

Calder, Alexander 39
calligraphy 8, 21, 56, 77, 120, 134
calligraphy museum, 9, 56, 135 *see Klingsphor, The*
career
  goals 2, 8, 13-14, 48, 66, 97, 107, 134
  painting 1, 7-8, 106, 108-9, 111, 134, 139
  weaving 2, 10-11, 35, 97, 106, 108-115, 130, 134-135
cartoon 22-23, 33, 79, 80, 89, 125, 136
Cascade 143, 144
Castro, Jan Garden 4
Castro Interview
  second segment 4,
  typed transcript 8, 21, 40, 48, 73, 76, 77, 98, 111, 113, 115, 120, 130
  River Styx 112, 115-116, 120
Center for Tapestry Arts 124
Central West End, St. Louis 98
Charms 75, 96, 120. *See Wild Cherry Charms*
Charms tapestries 78, 96.

See Wild Cherry Charms
Chicago Art Institute 9
Chinese 56, 82
Christ 115
Christian 50, 53
Church of Santa Felicita, Florence, Italy 79
Circus 81, 90, 137
color, skillful use of 24, 36-40, 44-45, 57, 70, 82, 93, 117, 122, 124, 133-134, 137-139
commission work, 33-34, 44, 64-65, 95, 116
  philosophy about 33, 49-51, 70
  private 44, 69
  religious 50-51
Communist Party 6, 71
Congregation Anshei-Sphard-Beth El Emeth 63
Constellation 19, 79-81
Contemporary Art Association 10
content 51, 75, 112, 125
contracts 30
Convergence, 1988 1, 27, 124. See Handweavers Guild of America
Cooper Union, The 6, 8, 9, 10, 16, 36, 71, 129, 134
Craft Alliance 16, 33-34, 70, 98-100, 105, 139, 145
Craft Horizon 95
craftsmen, French 23
Creative Handweaving 39, 95
Creativity 71
Croft, Charlotte 113
Crump, (Nancy) question-naire 69, 109, 130
Cubism 39-40
Cummings, Richard 98

D

Dallas Center for Holocaust Studies 121
Daughters of Auschwitz 96, 114, 116-119, 122, 125

Daughters of Earth 1, 17, 91, 118-120
David, Madeleine 10
decorative art 109-110
Deportation 122-123, 144
design fees 69
diptych 84
Doll Baby 88-89
Dora Mar Seated 48. See also Picasso.
dual role 15
dying yarns 21
dyslexic 38

E

edges 37, 39, 41, 131
Edinburgh Tapestry Workshop 10
Edward Fields Inc., 34, 50, 54, 63
Egypt 4, 58
Egyptian hieroglyph 56
Eliot 85-86, 136
Eliot Again 91-92
Eliot, William Greenleaf 85
Embrace 40, 133
Emerson 68
Encyclopedia of New York City 6
European Jews, 5, 60
European trip, 1973 65, 111
Evangelos 92
Exodus 63
experimentation 2, 40, 45, 48, 75, 80-81, 93, 95, 128-130, 135-136

F

family relationship 8, 100-101, 106-107
family tragedy 5, 107, 113
Fields, Jon 50
First Unitarian Church of St. Louis 85
Florida, trip to 32
food preparation 103-104
Fornasetti plates 87
Foursome 38-39
Frankenthaler, Helen 15
French Cultural Center 10
fringe 41-43, 64, 87-88, 90, 133, 134

G

Gateway Theater 98
Gelfand, Alfred 6
Genesis, S. Helfman design 36,
Genesis, Nezhnie 48, 51, 72

Genesis 28:12 59
Genesis 28:16 62
German-American BUND 113
Germany 7-9, 21, 35, 56, 135
Ghetto Child — Stroop Report 120-122, 126
Gobelins 10
graphic design 7-8, 43, 71, 112,128, 130, 134-135
Greek, interest in things 45, 104
Greenberg, Clement 15
Grossman, Mendel 122
Grotto 137
Guild for Religious Architecture AIA 48, 52
Gypsy Moth 43, 48

H

Halloween 6, 72, 75
Handweavers Guild of America Convergence 1, 27, 124 *See Convergence*
Harrison, George 84
Harvard University 106
Hebrew 18, 53-54, 59-60, 62-64 66, 117, 119, 124, 126
Helfman family *See Helfmans*
Helfmans 13, 16, 18-20, 25, 29, 32, 45-46, 82, 101, 103-104, 107, 129
Helfman, Ilisha 5, 32, 42, 88, 101-106, 127
Helfman, Jonathan 7, 19, 104-107
Helfman, Muriel Nezhnie 1, 12, 141. *See Nezhnie.*
　as mother 16
　awards 13, 51-53, 70
　childhood 2-6, 72, 138
　death of 141
　last major public appearance 12, 145
　mid-career 110
　mother's death 114
　self-esteem 130
　Shelly's influence upon 20
Helfman, Sheldon 7. *See Shelly.*
Henry Snyder High School 6
Hernmarck, Helena 77-78, 132, 136
Hicks, Sheila 95
Hinduism 52

Hitler 120
Holocaust 114, 120, 125, 127-128
Holocaust images 138
Holocaust Museum and Learning Center St. Louis 116, 123
Holocaust series / tapestries 2, 75-76, 96, 100, 102, 113, 116,128, 134, 144
Holocaust survivors, 113, 128
Holocaust texts 18
Human rights 105, 128
Hutchins, Linda 57, 144-145

I

Illinois River 68
Images of the Holocaust 1, 115, 124
Imprints 2, 17, 54-58, 71-72, 75, 78, 135
International Tapestry Network 140
Islamic faith 53

J

Jacob's Dream 58-63, 137
　Boston version 62-63
　Farmington version 60-62, 65
　St. Louis version 18, 29, 58-59,
Jacob's Ladder 62
Jean Lurçat: Designing Tapestry 49
Jefferson School of Social Science 6
Jewish 4-7, 19, 50. 53, 105, 113, 121, 127, 141
Jews 5, 111-113, 141
Job 16:18 119
Johannsen, Rudolf 4
Judaism 5, 53
Jungkuntz, Jan 24, 26, 28-32, 84, 90

K

King, Harry 62
King, Martin Luther, Jr. 105
Klingsphor, The 9, 56, 135
knotting 18, 27, 56, 59, 131
Krasner, Lee 14-15

L

La Corde 95
La Demeure 10
Lamentations 3:52 126
Lamentations 3:52 126
Landau, Ellen G. 14-15

Lane, Mary 33-34
Large Embrace 41-42, 47, 133
Larochette, Jean Pierre 11
Larson, Jack Lenor 95
Latvia, Lijepaja 118
Lausanne Biennial, 1973 74, 95, 111. see Biennale Internationale de la Tapisserie
Leclerc, Nilas 25
Liberation 122
Library of Congress 115
letterforms 56 *See symbols*
Liftman, Dorothy 3
Liftman, Jean Shiezer 2. *See* mother, Muriel's
Liftman, Robert 2, 5, 8
lighting 47, 82, 117-119, 121, 135, 137
line 44, 46, 48, 66,78, 82-87, 89-92, 130, 136
Little Egypt 133
Little Richard 77
Lodz Ghetto 122, 124
loom 21, 25
    German 25
    Nilas Leclerc 25, 38
    Shannock 25
Loreli 42-43
Louis Comfort Tiffany Grant 38
Lurçat, Jean 10, 49, 70

M

Maassen, Christel 24, 28, 29, 31-33, 104, 119, 121
Macomb Public Library 68
Majorel, Denise 10
Mary Institute 85
Maryland Institute 32
masks 39, 73
Mason, Alice Trumbull 14
Matisse 40
May, Morton 76
Mavor, Ann 15
McQueen, John 57
Mendocino Arts Center 124
Metropolitan Museum of Art 10
Michaelides, Maria 103, 112, 130
Mission in Art 128
Mississippi River 68
Moorish Kilim 132
Mother I 133
Mother II 43
mother, Muriel's 2-5, 100-101, 143 *See* Jean

Shizer Liftman
Mt. Sinai 64-65
Museum of Contemporary Crafts 10
Mylar 86-87, 90, 136-137

N

Nader 29, 31, 83-84, 86, 89, 136
Nader, Ralph 83
Nader/Trio 83
National Archives 115
Navahos 56, 127
Nazi persecution 1, 111-113
Nevelson, Louise 14-15
New Deal 14
New Library of Alexandria, Egypt 58
Nezhdotnie 5
Nezhnie 1-2, 4-13, 15-17, 20-21, 23-40, 43-45, 47-58, 60, 62-67, 69-71, 73-84, 86, 88, 90-91, 93-100, 102, 105-146. *See also* Helfman, Muriel Nezhnie.
    artist's statement 49
    relationships with clients 50
    author's meeting with 141-142
Nezhnie, Isadore 2-3, 5, 113
Nezhnie, Nathan 2, 5
Nezhnie, Sarah 2,4-5, 107, 113
Nezhnie, Tanya 2
Nierendorf, Karl 15
Nobel Prize 114, 125
Nuremberg trials 120

O

O the Chimneys 125
occupational therapy 8
Odysseus 45
Odyssey 44-46, 48, 134
Odyssey '67 46-48, 79
Offenbach Werkkunstschule 9
Old Testament 66
Oregon School of Arts and Crafts 12, 33, 144

P

pattern weave 37-40, 44-46, 57, 66, 82, 84, 93-94, 134
Parker, Xenia Ley 39, 95
Parting Lodz 123-124
Penelope 45

Pentagon 115
Pereira, I. Rice 14
Phil Ochs 90, 93
photography/photographs 48, 68, 71, 74-75, 77-78, 83, 85, 89, 95, 115-116, 125-126, 135-136, 144
Picasso 39, 40, 48
pick and pick 59
Plymouth First Congregational Church 51
Pogrom 38, 125-127, 138, 146
Polish weaving 88, 132
Pollack, Jackson 15
pop culture 71, 82, 112, 121, 128, 135
Portland State College 33, 102
Portrait of Dr. Richard Ferry 81, 93, 95
Portrait of the Artist as Young Woman 89-90
portraiture 8, 28, 71, 96, 119, 121, 128
    bias against 71
Prairie Journey 68-69, 129
Prisma 80, 86-87, 137
Protestant 53
Psalm 126 113

Q

Que magazine 14

R

recognition 15, 47, 95, 106, 130, 133, 139, 144-145
religious expression 4-5, 7, 52-53, 116
religious instruction 4
Reigel, David 29
Remnants of Despair: An Homage to Nelly Sachs 125
Rhode Island School of Design 33
Righting the Balance 14
River Styx 112, 116, 120 *See* Castro interview
role-playing 73, 76-77
Rubin, Richard Marc 77, 145 *See* THE SEEN
Rubin, Deann 28, 29-30, 32-33, 45, 89, 139, 145
Roth, Hannah 29, 85
Russia 3
Russian War Relief 4
Rya 85

S

Sachs, Nelly 125
Samuel I 20:3 124
San Francisco Tapestry
    Workshop 11
Sazama-Brauer Gallery 1,
    31, 124
fire in 31
Schumacher, Ann 62
Scientific American 103
*Seated Woman (Marie-
    Therese)* 48. *See also*
    Picasso.
Seed of Science 66, 67, 68
self-portraits 89
Shaw, Courtney Ann 11
Shelly (Helfman) 7-10,
    13, 16-20, 24-25, 27, 31,
    35-37, 43, 46, 50, 59,
    75, 77, 97-98, 101-103,
    106, 142-145. *See*
    Helfman, Sheldon.
Shining Knight 86-87, 96,
    136
Smith College 106
soumak technique 38, 46,
    52
Spearmint Charms 76-77.
    See also Charms.
Spoering, Kathy 58
Springfield Genesis 95
St. Louis Art Museum 13,
    28, 66
Stella 80, 129
Steuer, Ulrick B. 113
*Strong Hearts, Inspired
    Minds* 15
Stroop Report 120-121
studio 25-27, 144
    in home 30,
swastika 126, 138
symbols 51-52, 54, 56-58,
    66, 67, 80, 138

T

Tablets of the Law 48, 53-
    54
tapestry,
    contemporary 9-12, 23,
        134
    impacting surroundings
        49-51, 70, 125
    nature of 22, 130-131, 133
    traditions 132
        European 90, 132
        French 10, 23, 132-133
        Polish 132
        Scandinavian 132

    Moorish, kilim 132
    Native American
        132-133
Tapestry Forum 12
Temple Beth-El,
    Hammond, IN 113
Temple Israel
    Boston, MA 62
    St. Louis, MO 58
Tewel, Georgia 29, 90
text 51,74, 125
    English 66, 73, 119
    German 117, 121-123
    Hebrew 18, 53, 59,
        62-64, 66, 117, 119,
        124, 126
    Polish 123-124, 126
The CRAFTSMAN 98
The Door 88
*The Preferred Wife
    Occupies Her Nights* 95
THE SEEN 10, 17, 56, 74,
    76, 77
Theodora Pottle Memorial
    Collection of
    Contemporary Art 69
Thompson, Vivian Alpert
    102, 118, 127-128
Tomkins, Calvin 14
Torah mantles 53
Tree of Life 64
Trio 84
Tworkov, Jack 15

U

Ulmer, Robin 29
University City 99
University City Public
    Library 2, 54
University of Missouri –
    St. Louis 2, 145
University of Missouri –
    Rolla 66
Urdang, Constance 84

V

Valentine I 87
Valentine II 87
Venus 40-41, 43
Vesperal 51
Virginia Commonwealth
    University 33
Visual vocabulary 20, 138

W

Warhol, Andy 71
War of 1812 68
warp,
    exposed 37-38, 41, 46,

    52, 57,68, 94, 121, 126,
        133-134
    preparation 37
Warsaw Ghetto 120
Washington University, 7,
    17, 85, 105, 106, 136
    School of Architecture 17
weavers,
    Algerian 9
    French 132
    German 10
Weavers Guild of St.
    Louis 31
weaving, training in 4, 9,
    21-22, 129-130
Weeping Woman 48. *See*
    Picasso.
weft faced plain weave 37
Wiesel, Elie, letter to 114
Wild Cherry Charms 72-
    74, 80, 95, 109, 135. *See*
    Charms.
Woman 31
Women's Movement 7,
    15, 100
Works Progress
    Administration 14
World Tapestry Today 124
World War II 6, 10, 14,
    90, 112, 141.

Y

Yad Vashem archives,
    Israel 116
Yale University 7, 13, 15,
    16, 106
yarn 55, 57, 83, 86, 90-92
    character of 22, 132
    selection 22, 24, 35, 65,
        78, 135
    floats 39, 133 See warp,
        exposed
Yivo Institute 114
Yom HaShoah 141
Young Artist 89
Young Husband 89
Young Wife 89

Z

Zapf, Hermann 9
Zelda 90-91, 96